Sources Of American Spirituality

Félix Varela
LETTERS TO ELPIDIO

Edited by Felipe J. Estévez, S.T.D.

PAULIST PRESS
New York ◆ Mahwah

Library of Congress Cataloging-in-Publication Data

Varela, Félix, 1788–1853.
  [Cartas a Elpidio sobre la impiedad, la superstición y el fanatismo en sus relaciones con la sociedad. England]
  Letters to Elpidio / Félix Varela ; edited by Felipe J. Estévez.
    p. cm.—(Sources of American spirituality)
  Translation of: Cartas a Elpidio sobre la impiedad, las superstición y el fanatismo en sus relaciones con la sociedad.
  Bibliography: p.
  Includes index.
  ISBN 0-8091-0422-9 : $24.95
  1. Irreligion. 2. Superstition. I. Estévez, Felipe J., 1946–
II. Title. III. Series.
B1029.V29C313 1989
261.2′1—dc19   88-38883
                                                           CIP

Published by Paulist Press
997 Macarthur Boulevard
Mahwah, N.J. 07430

Printed and bound in the United States of America

CONTENTS

vi   *Contents*

To the entire Community of
St. Vincent de Paul Regional Seminary
Boynton Beach, Florida

ACKNOWLEDGMENTS

This critical translation has come about from the living solidarity of a group of volunteers who have cooperated with the editor in the different stages of its production.

The Reverend C. Rozas, of Fort Wayne, Indiana, stands out among others for the valuable help he gave in translating all the letters on Superstition.

The following persons produced an initial English draft on the letters on Irreligiosity: the Most Reverend Augustín A. Roman (fourth letter); Dr. and Mrs. Jimenez (second letter); Professor P. Aurensanz (sixth letter). Others did their translations in group work: the Cuban American students at St. Vincent de Paul Regional Seminary under the leadership of Rev. Marcellus Fernandez (first letter); the members of the Nazareth Fraternity, New Orleans, Louisiana, in cooperation with Dr. and Mrs. C. Estévez (third letter); and a number of parishioners of St. Joan of Arc, Boca Raton, Florida, in cooperation with Dr. and Mrs. V. Rangel (fifth letter).

The involvement of such a large number of persons required then the patient work of careful revision of the English style. The members of the faculty of St. Vincent de Paul Regional Seminary were most generous in providing constructive criticism and professional advice. A special gratitude is acknowledged to the Reverends T. Foudy, M. Fernández, C. Schreck, J. Cunningham, E. San Pedro, Dr. E. Wrapp and Br. Mazsick. Our friends Dr. Demmers and Judge W. Stuart were very helpful at this stage also.

The suggestions and criticisms of Msgr. Raul del Valle,

Drs. M. Garcia-Tudurí, J. I. Lasaga, H. Piñera, S. García and
E. García have certainly improved the final draft of the section
introducing the *Letters* and qualifying footnotes. The personal
interviews with Drs. Levi-Marrero and L. Cabrera were most
stimulating in conveying the *Letters'* rich potential for the aca-
demic community.

The administrative assistance of Rev. Michael M. Rhodes,
Mrs. P. Green, A. Neumann, K. Fischer, Miss I. Cuervo, Mr.
P. Corces and Mr. E. Aponte enabled the completion of a
presentable manuscript for publication.

As editor, I join them in thanking Dr. John Farina and the
Paulist Press for having chosen our work as a sample of a multi-
cultural experience of God in our great American continent.

The object of our interest, *Letters to Elpidio,* was composed and written according to the Spanish grammatical and
literary conventions known to their author in the early years of
the nineteenth century. Therefore, I would like to explain
some editorial procedures we have applied to the material.

First of all, it was my strong desire to avoid sexist language,
but forced by the grammatical limitations of our language I was
unable to avoid using, in most instances, the third personal singular masculine pronoun. But let it be clear that I have used it out
of grammatical necessity and not because of lack of sensitivity
for what the use of inclusive language represents.

The original text is composed of lengthy paragraphs, some
of which even span a few pages. In order to assist the reader to
perceive the author's sequence of thought, or to locate particular themes, I decided to create and add brief subtitles to the
text of my translation. I also made a deliberate effort to recognize new paragraphs when required for the sake of clarity. To
make a point or to express humor, Varela was in the habit of
underlining key words. Our English text is meticulously faithful
to his practice. His way of making reference to other sources
was, for the most part, incomplete according to present stan-
dards. I chose not to improve his own method. To stress the
conversational, intimate tone of the *Letters,* Varela frequently
repeats the name "Elpidio." This practice would create monot-
ony for the modern readers. Therefore, sometimes I simply
omitted translating "You see, Elpidio," and so on.

GENERAL INTRODUCTION

Calle Ocho! One-hundred-nineteen thousand people danc-
ing the Conga down the streets of Miami's Little Havana into
the *Guinness Book of Records* on a warm March day in 1988. A
bank of heavy duty speakers blaring out the Latin beats of
Miami Sound Machine. The smell of pork sandwiches mixing
with the smoke of countless long, smooth Cuban cigars. Gold
chains adorning the olive skins of the sun-drenched revelers
bouncing with the happy, brassy vibrations. And on every
tongue and every store sign, Spanish.

On another end of Eighth Avenue at the Koubek Center of the University of Miami, a more subdued though no
less passionate celebration had taken place the night before
the annual Calle Ocho festival. It drew a sophisticated crowd
made up of people like the auxiliary bishop of Miami,
Agustin Roman, recently brought to national prominence by
his role in negotiating a peaceful ending to the Cuban prisoner uprising in Atlanta, and José Ignacio Rasco, founder of
the Christian Democratic Movement of Cuba suppressed by
the Castro regime during their consolidation of power in the
early 1960s. Along with the people in their sixties, whose
memory of leaving Havana with one suitcase and $5.00 is as
vivid as it was some twenty-eight years ago, there was also a
younger set whose adult lives have been lived in the U.S. but
whose hearts have not forgotten their Cuban roots—men like
Javier Souto, a meticulously dressed Florida State Senator
from the 40th district, and Jorge Sosa, a young, energetic
Miami Beach attorney.

On the podium is the fiery Felix Alvarez Cruz, an instructor of Philosophy and Logic at Miami Dade Community College. He is a serious, impassioned man in his fifties, whose jagged, thin features match the sharpness of his words. He is denouncing the Castro regime as an oppressive, suffocating presence in his home land. "Cuba will someday be free," he declares as he challenges his fellow expatriates to work vigorously to advance the coming of that day. In place of Castro and his Marxist dictatorship, he presents an alternative vision. It is one of a liberal democratic Cuba, in the best tradition of the French Enlightenment *philosophes* like Condillac, the Englishman Locke, and the Spanish Benedictine Benito-Geronimo Feijoo. But his main inspiration is none of those but a Cuban born two centuries ago, Felix Varela.

Varela (1788–1853) was a Catholic priest who began his career as a professor of philosophy at Havana's San Carlos College. Between 1812 and 1822 he distinguished himself as one of the brightest lights in the nineteenth-century Latin American philosophical world, publishing his *Lecciones de filosofia,* and his *Miscelanea filosofica.* His love of Enlightenment philosophy was the basis for an active political career. During his tenure Cuba, along with Puerto Rico, were the only two of the original Spanish colonies still loyal to Spain. Yet talk of independence was in the air, and Varela was among its most articulate advocates. In 1821 he was elected a delegate to the Spanish Cortes in Madrid. There he presented two landmark pieces of legislation. The first was a call for greater Cuban independence from Spain, which was expanded in his *Project for Colonial Autonomous Government.* The *Project* was, in effect, a constitution for an autonomous Cuba. It argued for the establishment of a system of self-governing Spanish dominions similar to the one that the British were putting into place. The second initiative was a plan to systematically abolish slavery in Cuba. In his *Memoria* of 1822–23, Varela argued: "Constitution, liberty, equality are synonymous; and their very names repudiate slavery and inequality of rights."

But it was another action in the Cortes of 1823 that determined the strange twist of fate that made Varela the *"primer exiliado Cubano.*" King Ferdinand VII of Spain, though outwardly cooperative with the Cortes, was secretly appealing to members of the Holy Alliance to help extirpate the threat to his country from the democratic liberals. Early in 1823 a force of Russian, Prussian, Austrian, and French troops began an invasion that resulted in the hasty disbanding of the Cortes. Ferdinand, restored to his despotic throne, took vengeance on his opponents, and the only recourse left to those like Varela who had escaped the armies was to flee the Spanish dominion.

Varela arrived in New York City in 1823 and there began a remarkable career that combined his work for Cuban independence with an active role as a journalist and pastor. His zeal for freedom was not lessened by his arrival in a new land. In 1824, during a brief residence in Philadelphia, Varela began publication of a magazine, *El Habanero, papel politico, cientifico y literario.* Among the Cuban exiles in the U.S. there were divergent voices at this time. Some, like Cristobal Madan, sought annexation of the island by the United States—an option that was particularly appealing to President Madison. Others favored a Colombian invasion to liberate their homeland from Spanish rule. That failing, they looked to the new government of Mexico for military assistance in establishing an independent state. Still others, like José Antonio Saco, hoped for the restoration of constitutional government in Spain and in Cuba.

In *El Habanero* Varela tried to create a middle ground on which all patriots could meet. He staunchly maintained that Cuba must be an independent republic, free from any foreign control. However long and slow the process of self-liberation, it was to be preferred if Cuba were to take its place as a sovereign nation in the Americas. He counseled against political hysteria, blind nationalism and ambition, basing his arguments on his belief in the noble destiny of the person as created in the image of God. He was a lover of liberal democracy, of what he called the "American principle," that assured the dignity of the individual and the rule of reason. He translated into Spanish Thomas Jefferson's *Manual of Parliamentary Procedure* as a model of orderly procedures for his countrymen to follow on the road to freedom. Varela's magazine became the center of the independence movement and the focus of the Spanish government's attempts to oppose such a movement. *El Habanero* was banned in Cuba and all Spanish dominions. That suppression was followed by an unsuccessful effort by the governor of Cuba to assassinate Varela in Philadelphia, which failed after Varela talked down his would-be assailant.

Varela's message attained its most developed form in his 1835–38 two-volume work, which is presented here for the first time in English, *Cartas a Elpidio* (*Letters to Elpidio*). The *Letters* were written to Varela's young friends and disciples in Cuba and were a blend of philosophical speculation and personal commentary on the times. Their title is a key to their message. "Elpidio" is derived from *elpis,* which is the Greek word for hope. The letters are, in fact, a message of hope in the midst of a society threatened by irreligiosity, superstition, and fanaticism. To the liberal democrats among the Cuban intelligentsia who had come to view religion as part of the unenlightened world view that stood in the way of human progress. Varela presented a warning. A rejection of the knowledge and experience of God, in the lives of individuals or of nations, leads to unhappiness, a lack of hope, and ultimately to despotism. By attacking religion, secular governments undermine the very basis of virtue on which they must depend for success. With the moral foundations corrupted by lack of belief, the very fabric of society is torn: "Honor becomes a vain work; patriotism, a political mask; virtue, a fancy; and trust, a charade men are forced to play."

Religion is not the enemy of human freedom, but its greatest guardian. "Where the Spirit of the Lord is, there is liberty," and that liberty assured free scientific and intellectual speculation and the extension of civil liberties to all classes of people. In his advocacy of the compatibility of religion—specifically Catholicism—with liberal democracy, Varela was one with such a progressive voice as France's Robert de Lamennais. His thought preceded by almost a decade the message of North American Catholic "Americanists" Orestes Brownson and Isaac Hecker, and amazingly, though he became vicar general of the Diocese of New York during the late 1830s, his work seems to have been virtually unknown to North Americans.

In the second book of *Letters* Varela took on the threat of superstition. In Cuba as in Spain, the Catholic church was most often aligned with the crown in its opposition to liberal democratic reform. The church's support of democracy during the nineteenth-century was anemic at best, as a perusal of Gregory XVI's *Mirari Vos,* or Pius IX's *Syllabus of Errors* makes clear. Fearing the anti-clerical extremes that were unleashed during the French Revolution, Rome took a skeptical view of the new independence movements of the age. Varela implicitly rejected this and the dualistic spirituality that lay at its base. The church had a responsibility to stand for freedom, and Christians a call to work for a social order in which the gospel values were incarnated. "Superstition" was his word for the misuse of the religious sentiment. It was a perversion that caused individuals to be irrational and blind, all in the name of the God who had created humans to live in the freedom of his love. Superstition enabled people to be manipulated and used for the ambitions of others.

Fanaticism, though not dealt with at length in the *Letters,* is a theme running throughout the first two books. The over-excitement of the mind and passions that blinds persons to receiving the truth was a danger to society. It could manifest itself in religious or political guises and the effects could be equally injurious. Moreover, it led to irreligiosity, in that it elicited a strong overreaction on the part of those inclined to disregard religion.

Varela's problem was a delicate one. On the one hand he had to oppose traditional elements in the Catholic church in Spain who would use religion—including appeals to superstition—to maintain their power through the king. On the other, he had to convince the liberal democrats that they should not discard religion as part and parcel of the old, anti-democratic order. It was a battle that was shared by Christian democrats throughout Europe as democratic revolutions swept the continent.

The U.S. scene was very different. Democrats there had little animus toward religion. The diatribes of Tom Paine had been denatured into the sweet waters of baptism washing the minds of the Protestant establishment that, during the days of frontier revivalism and Charles G. Finney, believed that Christian America could attain millennial perfection. There was virtually no criticism of liberal democracy among American Protestants. It had taken its place, alongside the dogmas of the Christian faith as part of their beliefs.

Among Catholics it was otherwise. Criticism of democracy was present, though in disguised forms. Irish-born Bishop John Hughes of New York was one of several voices that challenged the assumptions of liberal democracy's emphasis on individualism. The breakdown of a sense of the common good and the cruel subjugation of the lower classes to the goals of selfish profit and materialism were castigated by Hughes. He was, nevertheless, careful not to present those faults as shortcomings of democracy as much as the evil effects of Protestantism. By taking up the theological polemic, as controversial as that was, Hughes sheltered himself from a far more ferocious foe that would have all but consumed him and his immigrant Catholic church had he assailed the sacred institution of democracy outright.

Varela spent most of his years of ministry as a priest in the U.S., ministering to Irish immigrants in New York city. He became a master of two cultures. As his *Letters to Elpidio* showed, his experiences in the U.S. encouraged him to dream democratic dreams for his homeland, but he never forgot that American and Cuban democrats spoke different languages.

Today most Cubans would recognize Varela's name, and even his face, which appears in the center of a mural depicting Cuban history on the wall of the stunning new Ermita de la Caridad shrine on Miami's shore. Outside the shrine, looking over the ocean towards his homeland, stands a bust of Varela, beside one of the nationalist leaders who followed in his footsteps, José Marti. Varela—the patriot, the advocate of a free Cuba, the priest—at the right hand of Marti, the man who actually brought about the independence: a fitting symbol of how easily religion and politics blend in the warm Carribean sun.

In the homeland, however, Varela's memory is put to other uses. An annual Felix Varela award in political science is given by the government of Cuba. But he is viewed by Cuban Communists as a proto-Marxist, a brilliant political scientist and patriot who rightly understood the burden of colonialism but whose insights were hampered by his religious beliefs.

These two opposing views of Varela were brought into juxtaposition in April of 1988 during New York's Cardinal John O'Connor's visit to Cuba. O'Connor spoke of Varela often during his four day tour, which included a meeting with Fidel Castro. Repeatedly O'Connor presented Varela not only as a great patriotic figure but as a zealous priest whose faith formed the basis of his social conscience. During his homily at the cathedral in Santiago de Cuba, he hailed Varela and insisted that "all that [he] did was founded in his identity as a Christian and a Catholic."

Yet it was not a confrontational tone that prevailed. O'Connor had gone to Cuba at the invitation of the Archbishop of Havana, Jaime Ortega, on a mission of reconciliation in the hope of affirming a greater respect for human rights, especially those for political prisoners. He was greeted by enthusiastic crowds, who had learned of his coming through Radio Marti. O'Connor spoke of Varela as a bridge between the two nations. The chancellor of the Archdiocese of New York, Monsignor Raul del Valle—a Cuban-born priest and expert in Varela's thought—accompanied the Cardinal as an advisor and delivered a paper on Varela to a group of Cuban academics in Havana on the last night of the visit.

In this volume Rev. Felipe Estevez has used his considerable skills as historian and translator to present Varela's most important work to the English-speaking American audience. The fact that Varela is today such a vibrant, living symbol for political and religious meaning, highlights the power of his ideas. As Estevez emphasizes, "the core of the spirituality articulated in the *Letters* is that a Christian must own the responsiblity to build a free human society in harmony with the Gospel principles. Varela believed that 'Christianity and freedom are inseparable.' His attempts were remarkably balanced and farsighted."

During the last decade the genius of Latin American religious writing has been to draw our attention to the interface of religion and politics. The *Letters to Elpidio* is a clear indication that a concern for the temporal ramifications of religious faith among Latin Americans is not new and, in fact, has been a passion over the last century and a half. But as Varela's own tumultuous career, and the heated debates over the meaning of his legacy that continue today show, the process by which religious ideas take practical effect in the political order is always a tortuous one, in which passion often is more abundant than light. When religion, with its claims to ultimate truth meets the political world of pragmatic compromise, sparks are bound to fly. The hatreds that motivated the Cuban governor to send an assassin to quiet Varela are not unlike those that motivated the killers of Archbishop Romero or the torturers of Reinaldo Arenas. In the light of those realities, we would all do well to hear and understand Varela's counsels to the young Elpidio to guard his soul from the ravages of fanaticism.

John Farina

NOTE TO READERS

Varela's footnotes are indicated throughout the text by **boldface** superscripts—[1]—and are printed at the bottoms of the appropriate pages. The editor's notes are indicated by superscripts enclosed in parentheses—[(1)]—and are gathered at the end of this volume.

INTRODUCTION

A series of eleven essays dealing with the presence and absence of genuine religion at the service or detriment of society were published in New York City in 1835 and 1838. Although the author, Felix Varela, contributed innumerable articles in English to various periodicals and was the founder of Catholicism's first literary magazine in the United States, it is ironic that this founding Father of New York Catholicism, called the pastor of the Irish immigrants, is also recognized as the cultural founder of Cuban nationalism. Varela was recognized by Jose Marti as the "Cuban saint." In spite of these coincidences, throughout the last one hundred and fifty years, the American public has been for the most part unaware of even his existence.

Varela intended to publish his work as three distinct volumes. It took him three years to publish the second volume in which he discussed superstition. Meanwhile, a second edition of the first volume was published in Madrid in 1836. Although it was his habit to enrich new editions of his works with footnotes, the Madrid second edition of his first volume was published without any new additions.

In this translation the first and second volumes of Varela's own edition of the *Letters* are joined in a single book. The reader will find, then, that Varela's frequent references in the second volume to his first volume of letters are superfluous, but those references have been retained in order to preserve the original text as best as possible.

Since no original samples of the volume on Superstition

could be found in the U.S.A. or in the major European museums, the 1945 edition of the University of Havana served as the basis for this translation.

One of the enigmas of the *Letters to Elpidio* that beckons our attention is the identity of Elpidio. The name might be but a symbol for Cuban youth as the hope for the future of the Cuban nation (*elpis* is the Greek word for hope); or, if Elpidio was a real person, perhaps it refers to Luz y Caballero or Jose Maria Casal, two of Varela's most devoted students. Varela himself surrounded the identity of Elpidio with ambiguity.[1] This writer believes that he wrote the *Letters* to his devoted lay students in Havana, but intending them to have the entire Cuban society, or even future Latin American generations, as their wider audience.

Varela completed the first volume of his *Letters* when he was forty-seven years old, including at the end a note anticipating his death. Three years later he published the last of them in New York. The other literary productions of his years as a young adult, which he had composed and published in Spanish, concerned themselves with particular needs, but the *Letters,* reflecting more the fruits of maturity, perceive a more universal scope and articulate a quasi-philosophical view of religion in modern society. They represent his most substantial contribution, conveying as they do his rich and wise insights, the hard-earned product of dedication to search for the meaning of life and live accordingly.

His way of analyzing and perceiving matters was far ahead of his time. He did not presume an objective model of Christian society to which the individual Christian had to conform. Rather, when dealing with the question of religion in society, he analyzed, critically, a particular situation, pointing out demonic forces at work while suggesting that true happiness was possible if Gospel values were upheld. His inductive approach, in the opinion of this writer, is quite similar to the analytic model advocated by the Vatican Council II document, *The Church in the Modern World,* which certainly contrasts with the earlier methodology applied in formal papal statements from Leo XIII to Pius XII.

Varela had addressed the questions related to the existence of God in his *Lecciones de Filosofia*.[2] Following the *Summa,* he treated the vices opposed to the virtue of religion: by deficiency, irreligiosity; by excess, superstition.[3] Varela then added the vice of fanaticism, which, as far as he was concerned, had a devastating effect on the spread of irreligiosity. Finally, he pondered the proper method of presenting religion to youth.

What the young professor was teaching at the *San Carlos Seminary* of Havana became the subject of a mature meditation expressed in a set of *Letters*. As pastor of souls in Transfiguration parish of New York City, Varela sought to communicate his sapient understanding of the Christian involved in the public square of a new society.

THE ECCLESIAL CONTEXT

In the first half of the nineteenth century, the Catholic Church had grown considerably, but it had been beset by trials from within and without. She had faced the challenges of trusteeism and the everwidening responsibilities to care spiritually for many of her members who migrated and encountered ethnic antagonism. At the same time, religious prejudices, the attack of the Nativist movement, and related anti-Catholic crusades militated against her objectives.[4]

The state of New York was under the influence of religious revivalism and turmoil. It was growing so rapidly it became, after 1820, the largest one in the union. The construction of the Erie Canal brought to the region thousands of Irish workers. The Roman Catholic leadership was in a state of transition. Bishop John Connally had died in 1825, and for almost two years an Irish priest, John Power, administered the See until the unexpected appointment of John Dubois, a French ex-Sulpician who was not welcomed by the Irish congregations. It is at this time that Felix Varela began his ministry as pastor of one of the only four parishes of New York City. Yet a significant transition would take place in less than a generation, transforming the Church of New York into the leading center of Roman Catholicism.[5]

Feelings against Roman Catholics were at a peak when Varela was ministering in New York. The arrival of an unending influx of poor Catholic immigrants in New York during the early part of the nineteenth century had sparked a revival of latent nativist feeling and zenophobia, which had falsely identified Catholic migration as certainly incompatible with American interests.[6] Consequently, Catholics had been forced to assume a defensive posture, and this explains what might appear as a lack of ecumenical sensitivity in some of the *Letters*.

Although such was the immediate religious and sociocultural context that was foremost in the mind of Varela, he nevertheless was writing his *Letters* to a small but highly influential class of intellectuals who were in close contact with emerging European ideas, deeply rooted in the French Revolution's defense of the inalienable right of personal freedom. His position, therefore, was highly complex. He was a member of an institution that had been perceived as being deeply associated with the political status quo of an old economic, social and cultural model, and the ideals of the French Revolution called for new systems of government, democracies and constitutional monarchies. As the cultural revolution grew in opposition to the institutional Church, the Church was called upon to find a new mode of presence in a new situation, and Varela found himself in the midst of these drastic transformations.

When at the beginning of the nineteenth century a significant advancement of ideas and scientific discoveries was shaking and transforming secular society, Catholic theology was entrenched in defending itself against rationalism and modernism. But the effort was largely unsuccessful; "it failed for the most part to enter into a frank dialogue with the modern era, as the age of transcendental philosophy and the beginnings of the 'exact' sciences."[7] The new progressive trends continued to develop outside the Church, and as the the gap widened between scientific thinking and the ecclesiastical world, a number of European Catholic intellectuals became insulated from the issues that were affecting their soceity.[8]

Obviously, the Church began to experience very threatening challenges. Was it possible for her to maintain a dialogue with the ever expanding culture of liberalism? Did she have to accomodate herself to the ideology of the French Revolution, and if so, how? Was it legitimate for her to take advantage of those unavoidable and radically new forms of thinking about the freedom of the press, of worship, and of conscience and suit them to her own mission to foster supernatural goals, or were those new ideas to be forcefully opposed as true threats to the spiritual welfare of the faithful?

Catholic leadership split and veered in two opposite directions. On the one hand, the majority of the clergy and the laity began to perceive the Church as the best equipped social and political force (preferably officially allied to a Catholic state) to halt social changes and to shelter them from a threatening world. On the other hand, a minority (later called *liberal Catholics*) sought to reconcile the Church and liberalism, opposed any accommodational associations between the Church and the state, and feared that if Theology were not to enter into dialogue with the new scientific world, the latter was going to move further away from the world of faith and theological discourse.[9]

At the same time, liberal Catholics did not hesitate to criticize the extremes of radical liberalism: the rejection of proper authority, the unwillingness to acknowledge the sovereignty of God over society, the spurning of and the restricted role assigned to supernatural revelation, and the Church's magisterium in regards to the intellectual life.[10]

Spain may be singled out among western European nations for having suffered the most devastating consequences of those social upheavals. Absolutists sponsored radical patriotic values and upheld the monarchy and the nation as defenders of the faith, but liberals became increasingly anticlerical because of the close association and collaboration that existed between Church leaders and the crown.[11]

The turmoil of the *Cortes* of 1823—the one in which Varela participated as delegate from Cuba—was but a religious confrontation pitting two conflicting parties:

. . . those which were in favor of religion's renewal under the protection of the Constitution and those who defended that same religion on account of the conservative principles of the union between the throne and the altar. Religion was used as a pretext for fighting and as an integral dimension of the parties' program.[12]

Immediately afterward, when King Ferdinand VII was restored to power, until the year 1833, the absolutists managed to prevail. Religion became an instrument in the hands of civil authorities, yet the Church was unable to mediate between the two conflicting forces to exercise a ministry of reconciliation because she herself was too closely associated with the interests of the king. But years of violence and anticlericalism continued the extremism of unrestrained absolutism:

> Things were made worse by the dynastic war between Carlists and liberals, who in 1835 renewed the measures against monasteries, further restricted ecclesiastical liberties, and issued laws of amortization confiscating much church property; it was the final act of a campaign by the state that had gone on for centuries and had been especially hard in the 1700s. Convents were burned and religious were murdered in Madrid (1834), Saragossa, Murcia, Barcelona, and elsewhere (1835), and several bishops were exiled in the bloody persecution of the Church.[13]

Except for the last decade of the nineteenth century, according to Revuelta Gonzalez, the Church "looked old and destroyed. It did not enrich herself from her dynamic past, it did not give any answers to the new questions."[14]

Spanish religious thinking entered a period of decadence. Jaime Luciano Balmes (1810–48) was the only Catholic intellectual figure worthy of mention, but he did not write anything until the last ten years of his life, when Varela's literary career had already come to an end. This lack of creativity in Spanish Catholic culture explains in part why J. M. de la Guardia, a philosophy professor at the Sorbonne, affirmed that Felix Varela and Jose de la Luz were the greatest philosophers of that time in the Hispanic world.[15]

Cuban scholars have proposed that Benito Feijoo's *Teatro*

Crítico (nine volumes) and *Cartas Eruditas* (five volumes) were the dominant literary inspiration for the *Letters to Elpidio.* Feijoo did indeed distinguish sharply between faith and superstition, dogma and sciences. Furthermore, he believed that science was not objecting to Church dogmas, but only to specific interpretations of dogma presented by certain schools of theology. Feijoo further explained that it was the superstitious practices of some groups in the Church, not authentic Catholic doctrine as such, that was deemed offensive by the scientists.[16] Similar ideas are echoed in Varela's admonitions to Elpidio.

But it is doubtful that the *Letters* were deeply influenced by *Teatro Crítico* and the *Cartas Eruditas.* Whereas Feijoo used a free and spontaneous style to treat a variety of subjects selected from diverse contexts, Varela wrote systematically on a carefully chosen theme. Nor did they agree on their ultimate objectives. Feijoo's was to free Spain from its isolation by promoting discussions on a variety of subjects; Varela's was to caution the Cuban people lest they could possibly become involved in establishing a new society based on irreligious principles.

The opinion of this author is that Varela was more influenced by French thinking than by Feijoo's writings. The *Letters*' themes, for example, are quite similar to Lamennais's successful *Essai sur l'Indifference en Matière de Religion,* published in 1817 and intended to be a confrontation with atheism. Lamennais's second volume, published in 1820, attempted to provide philosophic bases for Christianity. Even its title, *De la Religion Considerée dans ses Rapports avec l'Ordre Politique,* is similar to the *Letters,* which aimed to study "irreligiosity, superstition and fanaticism in its relation to society."

The *Letters to Elpidio* are, certainly, an example of liberal Catholic literature from a distinctively Latin American context. Their originality is especially remarkable in view of the fact that Varela was already discussing various ways for the Church to be present in the midst of a new society as early as the 1830s, when most European Catholic thinkers still had not publicly unveiled their opinions about the same issue.

The *Letters* significance lies precisely in the fact that Varela was a remarkably well-educated priest who was clearly identified with the institutional Church but who, at the same time, sought to understand contemporary secular changes. His fundamental idea was that society could not attain full progress without the benefit of religion. Like other Catholic authors of his time, the form of his writings was apologetic. Most of this kind of literature had lacked scientific bases and promoted plain sentimentality and excessive eloquence; in contrast Varela's style is brief, concise, logical. Moreover, consistent with his philosophical formation, he analyzed the presuppositions and coherence of his own thought critically. In short, he found himself at ease in the secular thinking of his time.

Since Varela addressed the *Letters* to Cubans, it is pertinent to summarize briefly what was then the situation of the Church in Cuba. Cuba remained in a state of political instability during the nineteenth century. Between 1800 and 1825 every Ibero-American country was involved in the struggle to gain independence from Spain. But Cuba proceeded with great difficulty to fight for its own national independence throughout the entire nineteenth century. Varela has been recognized as the first important person to call for the political liberation of Cuba.

Three distinctive features characterize the state of religion in colonial Cuba during the early part of the nineteenth century. First, the liberal ideals that had their roots in the experience of the French revolution had won over the educated and affluent classes who had become not simply liberal but openly atheist. Secondly, the Church had failed to evangelize the black slaves that had been brought from Africa. Thirdly, the majority of the clergy were clearly identified with the aims of the Spanish government, but the intellectuals and the working classes believed in independence from Spain; consequently, the Church was perceived as being against the quest for national freedom that was feelingly supported by the majority of the population.[17]

The alliance between Church and state was one of the most grave problems then affecting the Church in Cuba. As in Spain, the mother country, most clergymen serving in Cuba clung to the principles of absolutism; they identified liberty and democracy with the horrors of the French Revolution. Their attitudes and their support of the Spanish absolute monarchy did not earn them the esteem of the people, who deeply distrusted them (the problem was compounded because at that time the government paid the salary of the clergy). Instead, the people vented their negative feelings against their religious shepherds by searching and spreading rationalist and atheistic literature, chiefly among the younger and the educated segments of society. Joseph McCadden succinctly summarizes this condition, which was to become the specific setting of the *Letters to Elpidio*:

> Many young liberals were so enamoured of the new freedom that they kicked over the traces altogether, discarding religion in favor of the French Revolution's goddess of reason. On the other hand, some highly placed Churchmen, fearing for the established order, were allying themselves with the despotic conservatism of entrenched interests.[18]

That lively eighteenth-century Cuban Church which had counted Hechevarría, Morrell, Espada and Caballeros among its distinguished leaders (also acknowledged as persons who had contributed to and positively influenced the public affairs of their society) became, from 1820 on, an increasingly irrelevant institution in Cuban society. The situation became worse when the Spanish extremists suppressed the religious Orders in Cuba in 1820, which eventually had catastrophic results as far as the Church ministries of education and social services in the island were concerned. The morale of the Church was not helped when the important sees of Havana and Santiago de Cuba remained vacant for several years, the former for fourteen (1832–46) years and the latter for fifteen (1836–51).

All of these conflicting events and ways of thinking partly explain Varela's gloomy assessment of an irreligious society. He often stated that reality needed to be examined with "Christian charity and good logic," but that did not prevent him from decrying what he perceived was awry. He claimed that if he were to be despised for telling the truth, then this would be an added incentive for him to keep repeating it.

Abstract logical speculation was not beyond Varela, the experienced professor of philosophy at Havana. But his devotion to strict methodological reasoning was exceeded only by his desire to learn from personal experience. Consequently, he encouraged his students to learn from personal reflections on events rather than from speculations on abstractions.[19] His approach was eminently practical, for he did not believe in abstract thinking for its own sake but judged it to be an element, indeed essential, in a process in which the primary goal was to create a personal art of living that would foster personal happiness. It is not surprising, therefore, that he encouraged Elpidio to have a good regard for anecdotes, a device he employs frequently in the *Letters*.[20]

Varela's position on experience as a means of learning was rooted in his knowledge of European philosophical trends of the previous centuries, for he was well acquainted with the writings of Galileo, Francis Bacon, Antonio Gomez Pereira, and, in particular, he had read carefully Isaac Newton's argumentations on physics.[21] He knew the empirical sciences and had been the first one to introduce them in Cuba.[22] He sought to integrate the new experimental methods with traditional conceptions of a perennial philosophy, an effort he referred to as "ecclectic philosophy."[23] His vision is reflected in the *Letters*, which were not meant to be either a manual or a technical exposition of philosophy but a means to articulate a synthesis of his own philosophical and theological reflections.[24]

No less important was the influence that Descartes had on Varela's concern to discriminate the true elements of human thinking from those that vitiate it. As a surgeon of the spirit he had committed himself to identify and eliminate the subtle corruptions of the human heart and the erroneous processes of the mind. Thus, he constantly advises Elpidio to live with integrity of heart and devotion to truth.

The *Letters* convey some melancholy when Varela often reflects on his past years in Havana and his self-imposed exile. But realizing that his students remained devoted to him and remembered him affectionately, brought him comfort, even to the point of moving him to describe his condition as "an enjoyable torment." The *Letters* truly portray "his ideas, his character and all his soul." They do depict Varela, the patriot, passionately in love with his country, the minister fully dedicated to the cause of religion, the educator concerned with the Christian formation of the new generations.[25]

The mysterious interruptions of the trilogy of the *Letters* after the publication of the second volume points to the secret sufferings they brought to Varela. The letters were meant to be a source of personal consolation, and his goal was not to "exasperate but to warn," yet from the very beginning he had felt apprehensive about the reception that the public would accord to his new literary composition. In the prologue he warned that, on account of his usual frankness, some might be offended by his analysis of human behavior. Furthermore, he anticipated that the other two volumes of the trilogy might not even be published if the first volume were not well received.[26]

His fears were well founded. He wrote a letter to Jose de la Luz openly expressing his frustration at the lack of interest Cubans had shown in the second volume of his "luckless" *Letters,* and he asked de la Luz to send the unsold copies back to New York to see if he could sell them himself to ease his serious financial difficulties.[27] Varela then decided not to publish the third volume, the one on fanaticism, and so the trilogy remained incomplete. Varela also did not write the "polemical treatment" he had intended to publish on the same subject after this work.

In yet another letter to de la Luz, Varela expressed hurt and resentment. This important document reveals that he interpreted the rejection of his *Letters* as an indication that Cubans did not need his services any longer and that he therefore felt free to put himself at the service of others:

> I beg that you tell me frankly why my Letters to Elpidio have been ill-received. Is it because of the doctrines that they contain? Is it because of the way that they are presented? Is it due to sheer hatred of their author? In this last case, I should like to know the cause of such an unexpected hatred in lieu of the

esteem with which my fellow countrymen honored me. An ecclesiastical judge has approved the work, the Government has permitted it, since otherwise Suarez would not dare sell it and, nonetheless, its sale is not announced in the papers, and, although it is well publicized by other means, it does not manage to come out except in a scarce number of copies. I do not know what to think of this business, and I would be grateful if you would bother to explain it to me.

Finally, the disdain in which my letters to Elpidio have been held, which contain my ideas, my character and, I can say, my whole soul is an exponent of the same contempt with which I am regarded . . .

My observation turns, therefore, to a quite different purpose, and that is demonstrating the great benefit that accrued to me through this event. In first place, I have acquired the great treasure of disillusionment; and in second place, a complement of freedom that I was lacking.[28]

The unhappy fate of the *Letters* and how it had affected their author was kept secret by both Varela himself and his contemporaries. If Rodriguez knew about Varela's true feelings, he chose not to comment on them. A rather unknown source, however, later claimed to have had direct information on the topic from Varela.

Alejandro Angulo Guridi, a Dominican lawyer, claimed that he had two personal interviews with Varela in Savannah, Georgia, in 1851. Aware of the importance of those meetings, Guridi took careful notes of both conversations. Fifty-three years later he used them to write a newspaper article. The long passage of time could have diminished the authenticity of the content of the article, but his descriptions of Varela's words and inner dispostion are consonant with the information provided by other reliable sources.

According to the article, Guridi asked Varela to explain the reasons why he had not finished the *Letters*. After a prolonged silence Varela gave Guridi an explanation but requested that his words not be revealed until after his death. Varela's opinion was that Cuban intellectuals had rejected his *Letters* because he had criticized the lack of religious tolerance in the United States, a nation upheld as a model of freedom vis-à-vis Spain. Varela's own words are poignant:

> See, therefore, whether or not it is true that here there does not exist the tolerance that is over-stated and praised. Thus, because I began to combat that error, my fellow countrymen became displeased, and I found out about it through various channels. They reproved me for that! . . . For what reason, then, should I continue with my *Letters to Elpidio?* They hurt me, sir, my fellow countrymen hurt me when with a very wholesome intention towards them I began that little work.[29]

Because of his abiding concern about the adverse effects of fanaticism, Varela had promised Elpidio that he was going to publish a series of letters addressing it. But Guridi's article and other sources show why Varela had not published—perhaps did not even compose—the third volume containing his views on the subject.

AN INCARNATE AND HISTORICALLY
SENSITIVE SPIRITUALITY

The *Letters to Elpidio* are an important means of calling attention to Varela's insight on spirituality, and as such they contribute to a wholesome vision of spirituality. Two important characteristics of his spirituality are that he flatly rejected an ethereal and dualistic brand of Christianity and that he was thoroughly community minded. He called for a vital life of faith and good morals that was mindful of the needs of society and that expressed itself within the context of a secular society. The world was awaiting for personal Christian involvement to achieve its own completion.

Although from its beginning Christianity was sensitive to human weakness and its vulnerability to the attractions of the world, it did not preach separation from the world out of a negative attitude toward creation or because it presumed a dualistic metaphysical structure of the universe. A healthy retreat from worldly ways was but an authentic expression of Christian vocation to witness attachment to God and freedom from earthly goods.[30]

But after the triumph of Constantine, ending four centuries of persecution and bringing Christianity to a position of power, there arose many occasions for some Christians to become overidentified with the political institutions of the newly created Christian empire. Monks then began to flee into the desert to set an example. But, flight from the world became, and regretfully so, a typical way for Christianity to characterize itself. By necessity most Christians had to remain in the midst of the world, attending to family and professional affairs, but any attempts to fulfill these vital needs and engage in leisure and recreation were frowned upon and even deemed to be threatening to the spiritual welfare of the Christian. The world came to be viewed as corrupt, as the setting of temptation.[31]

Much later, a school of spirituality began to orient the Christian to search into creation and history in order to perceive God's providential activity, and to let the signs of his presence in the world become privileged occasions for contemplative activity. At the same time, the Christian was urged not to miss opportunities to renew the world according to God's design but to become actively involved in an effort against the injustice that had been perpetuated through sin.[32] Varela was influenced by this kind of spirituality. The core of the spirituality articulated in the *Letters* is this: that a Christian must take the responsibility to build a free human society in harmony with the Gospel principles. He believed that "Christianity and freedom are inseparable."

These principles had given him the strength to face social inequity, courageously and critically. He had not been afraid even to point out that America did not represent an entirely admirable model of a society based on democracy, civil freedom, and religious tolerance. The religious persecution of

Catholic citizens in the United States was much too evident for him to leave it unnoticed. In his *Letters* he singles out that kind of social evil while at the same time forcefully opposing the Spanish government's attempt to manipulate Catholic religiosity to its own advantage. He wanted to awaken, in every respect, the conscience of his fellow citizens so that they might be free from illusion and deceit.

He promoted the separation of Church and state in order to emphasize that the Church had within herself the secret forces that made her own effectiveness possible: the treasure of the Gospel, the teachings of the Fathers, and the witness of the martyrs. He wanted the Church to stand on its own, neither confused nor allied with any particular ideology of the times. His attempts to articulate a "social vision" were remarkably balanced and farsighted, particularly for someone writing in the third decade of the nineteenth century and from the painful experience of racial and religious bigotry in the United States, oppression in Cuba and the political-religious split of Catholicism in Spain.

PREVIOUS STUDIES

One wonders if it is possible to evaluate the influence that the *Letters to Elpidio* might have had, because even though much research has been done on Varela's thinking there are but five brief studies of his *Letters*.

On December 23, 1835, Jose de la Luz y Caballero wrote briefly on the *Letters* for the *Diario de la Habana*.[33] Instead of reviewing it, de la Luz urged Cubans to read the *Letters*. Then he proceeded to pay tribute to the author, singling out his vast culture and his extensive experience as a minister of the human heart. All in all, de la Luz did not provide any insights on the *Letters* themselves.

When the *Letters to Elpidio* were reedited in 1944, a project sponsored by the University of Havana, Humberto Pinera, a professor of philosophy, was invited to write an introduction to the *Letters,* and Raimundo Lazo, a literary critic, was asked to write an epilogue. Pinera gave a synthesis of each letter,

then he wrote a two page evaluation of each of them. Character-
izing them as a treaty on theological ethics, or an essay on the
foundations of morality in the light of the Christian revelation,
he added:

> A man of his century, Father Varela attempts in this
> work to achieve a reconciliation of the notions of prog-
> ress, enlightenment, and freedom of conscience. As a
> priest and a man of firm belief, he is decidedly con-
> vinced that it is upon the foundation of his beliefs that
> the edifice of morality can be laid. But simulta-
> neously, as a liberal and a progressive, he feels the
> need to oppose evils that are rooted in religion it-
> self.[34]

Lazo felt that Varela, whom he called "a missionary of
culture," had been the first Cuban moralist and one of the
founding fathers of Cuban literature who had produced in the
Letters a precious work. Commenting from the literary point of
view, he said that although Varela had written the *Letters* in the
decade of the 30s, "a period of growth and transformation,"
they should be assigned to the first two decades, "a period of
beginnings." His study of Varela's style revealed that it had not
evolved during his New York period but had exhibited the
same literary expressions of earlier decades.[35]

In 1977 the Cuban Society of Philosophy organized a cycle
of conferences on Varela's thought which took place in Miami,
Florida. Two of six conferences were dedicated to the *Letters to
Elpidio*. Mercedes Garcia-Tudurí, an internationally recognized poet, professor at St. Thomas University in Miami, and
author of various books on philosophy, singled out the significant quality of the *Letters* as "a most original treatise on morality." Along with Piñera she felt that the letters represented
Varela's desire to conciliate religion and freedom of conscience. In her opinion, he had perceived that "the axis of
human essence was constituted by ethical values which in turn
are rooted in a metaphysical and religious order."

She believes that Varela addressed the *Letters* to the entire

Cuban nation to caution them on their way to freedom. If he chose the letter as a literary form, it was to make it more accessible to the average citizen. Furthermore, she states that the trilogy remained unfinished because his rebuking the United States for religious intolerance had not been well received by Cuban intellectuals. Finally, she believes that the unwritten third volume on fanaticism had been nonetheless planned and its contents conceived by Varela, because his treatment on fanaticism was an intrinsic element contributing to the wholeness of a work that was noted for its logical organization.[36]

Alberto Gutierrez de la Solana, from the faculty of New York University and another participant in the 1977 gathering of the Cuban Society of Philosophy, addressed himself to the fourth letter of the first volume in his "Extension of Irreligiosity and the Way of Relating to the Irreligious." He observed that Varela was a pioneer in the area of pedagogy and that he was well endowed with the gift of knowing how to approach the human heart. His psychological insights were progressive and relevant even to the needs of twentieth-century generations, an unusual accomplishment for Varela considering the underdeveloped conditions of psychological sciences in his own era.[37]

According to Angulo Guridi, Varela wrote in his notebook a personal dedication at the end of his second interview. I dare to suggest that this text, which expresses Varela's deep religious convictions, may also be taken as the best and shortest synthesis of the *Letters'* fundamental theme:

> Just as one lone star guides the navigator who would otherwise be led astray by the other stars, so also one sole religion guides the believer who could likewise be led astray by various misguided sects. There is but one disgrace, and that is to be separated from God by whom all the just are happy and the wicked unhappy.
>
> Freedom without virtue is the greatest punishment for pride, which will eventually be brought low and to repentance because of its errors.

Superstition, fanaticism and irreligiosity are the three
great torments of the soul.[38]

REFLECTIONS ON FANATICISM

Varela, it is true, never published his promised third volume on fanaticism, but he intended to write on the three themes,
irreligiosity, superstition and fanaticism, as a unit. This writer
does not find it difficult to summarize briefly Varela's basic
thinking on fanaticism, a topic which, as far as it can be ascer-
tained at the moment, no other scholar has considered.[39]

Varela felt very concerned about the negative effects of
fanaticism. He referred to it as an attitude of the mind effectively preventing persons from attaining truth, as the over-
excitement of the mind which blinds and renders it incapable of
perceiving its proper object along with an imprudent zeal to
propagate it. Writing a critical essay on the philosophy of Kant,
Varela defined it in this manner:

> Fanaticism is a state of excitement of the human intel-
> lect, which renders it incapable of perceiving the ob-
> ject but on one side, and leads him to *overvalue* the
> things or the means to obtain them, and to defend
> them with an imprudent zeal, that is frequently found
> on religious subjects; therefore, the name is taken
> from false inspiration, which the worshipper of Fan
> pretends to receive in his temple or Fanus; in conse-
> quence of which they used to come out in a state of
> derangement and even fury.[40]

Although he had strong feelings against fanaticism, he referred to it but a few times in his writings. Once, for instance,
he identified religious fanaticism in his *Lecciones de Filosofia*
as a cause of irreligiosity inasmuch as the religious practices of
the fanatic encourage mockery on the part of the irreligious.[41]
Mormons, in his opinion, illustrated "modern fanaticism,"[42]
and those who favored temperance were guilty of many fanatic

excesses, going as far "as to condemn as *sinful* any use of intoxicating liquor."[43]

One of the reasons why Varela was so adamantly opposed to fanaticism could have been that it interfered with right thinking and its exact expression, and, as we have seen, he was particularly sensitive to "good logic at the service of true Christian charity."

Letters to Elpidio

PROLOGUE

The *Letters to Elpidio* do not contain a defense of religion, although, by chance, in them are proven some of the dogmas of religion. My only objective has been, as the title makes clear, to consider irreligiosity, superstition, and fanaticism in their relation to the well-being of mankind, while reserving for another time the introduction of a polemical tract dealing with this important matter. I do not believe that I have offended any person in particular, but it has not been possible to avoid packing some punches in certain classes. I would have liked them to have been softer, but I am inclined to go overboard a bit, and so I hit hard.

Even though it could be said that each little tome forms a separate work, I have thought it prudent to present them as parts of one single work because of their relation to one another. Since my object is not to exasperate but to warn, the second and third volumes will remain unedited if by some misfortune the first is not well accepted; and, consequently, this one should be seen as a separate work.

I see that this *turkey* could gain me some enemies, but this is something to which I have become accustomed, since I have long been like the proverbial anvil—always under the hammer. I live very peacefully however; as I wrote to a friend of mine, time and ill luck have battled long in my heart, until, convinced of the uselessness of their efforts, they have left me in peaceful possession of my longstanding and unwavering sentiments.

[F. V.]

21

I. Irreligiosity

IRRELIGIOSITY IS THE SOURCE OF INDIVIDUAL AND SOCIAL UNHAPPINESS

Time passes by, and people along with it, but perennial truth watches the course of their miserable race until they *precipitate* with hesitant steps into the abyss of eternity, leaving behind indelible signs of an existence by no power of their own. Yes . . . No doubt about it.

The unanimous voice issuing from the graves raises to heaven the sorrowful confession of human frailty, and the heavenly vaults send back to mortals a terrifying echo as a warning against daring enterprises and ill-fated ideas. This warning from the Divinity draws our attention to the underworld, where there lie love idols, hate objects, the spoils of war and the ashes of the wise, the victims of wicked power and the powerful themselves. All of them, perpetually calm, warn the fools who walk over them that truth is formed in the highest, that it is one and immutable, holy and powerful, that it is the source of peace and the fountain of consolation, that it is found in the bosom of the Being with no beginning and cause of all beings.

THE EXISTENCE OF EVIL

Those were my thoughts, my dear Elpidio, during some terrible times when my spirit, afflicted with the memories of

25

those who were and now are no more, meditated about the regrettable history of human errors, about the sad consequences of unbridled passions, about the sufferings of virtue, which is always persecuted, and about the victories of vice, which is always in power.[44]

A survey of the annals of peoples throughout the centuries reveals the globe as a large field full of horror and death, where time has left a few monuments as eternal testimony to its power to destroy and to humiliate haughty mortals. But in the middle of such horrible ruins shine several beacons that have never been darkened by the shadows of death. These are, my dear Elpidio, the graves of the just, containing the relics of the temples of their souls, which flew to the center of truth, of the just who made love for truth the norm of their lives, and lived always in unity and peace under its influence.

Over the gravestones that cover up these tabernacles of virtue, imitators solve the great problem of happiness and look with compassion over those who, fascinated by miserable passion, chase after deceitful shadows, and, deceived, become divided; once divided they hate themselves, once hated they destroy themselves.

Why, I have asked myself, why cannot clear ideas and noble examples attract all people to the true object of just love? Why do they not follow the majestic and evident road to happiness? Why is death spread abroad by the trustees of life? Why do those born to love now hate? Why does sorrow fill the faces which should glow with happiness? What are the regrettable causes that change the society of the children of the God of peace into immense hordes of ministers of anger?

These interesting questions soon found an answer. You can see stamped over the ruins of so many precious remains the footprints of three horrible monsters that caused their defeat and still run about sacrificing new victims. Take a look at insensitive irreligiosity, somber superstition and cruel fanaticism, which travel along different paths but all tend to the same end—the destruction of the human race.

These monsters have been the constant object of my observations; I have tried to follow their footsteps, observe their attacks, watch their effects, and discover the means they employ to accomplish many atrocities. It is very clear that these most sorrowful meditations must have filled my soul with bitterness; and since friendship is the balm of affliction and the communication of ideas the relief for sensitive souls, allow me to entrust to you the feelings I have found within me and in a series of letters manifest to you the results of my research. Let us occupy ourselves, for the time being, with irreligiosity.

If experience did not prove that irreligious people do exist, reason could not prove that they *could* exist. When nature inspires love—and love is necessarily attracted to perfections more powerfully than steel to a magnet or celestial bodies are to the center of their circulation—how can a most perfect Being not attract the human will, and by what inexplicable anomaly can that will change the essence of goodness into an object of hate?

TYPES OF IRRELIGIOSITY

But, no, that premise is impossible; a human person never hates the Supreme Being, although, in his fancies, he tries to hide the secret inclination of his soul. Here we have one of the most convincing evidences that irreligiosity is a monster, because its operations go against nature, which may be neglected but never conquered. Among the multitude of irreligious people there are various types, for error is the cause of division; but you shall never find anyone, who, after acknowledging the existence of an Infinite Being and source of all goodness, pretends to hate it. Some people try to cover up for their errors by denying the existence of the very Being in whom they are always occupied, and whose perfections besiege them from all sides and at all times. They pretend to ignore the source in order to carry forward some ideas which will never satisfy them. They are like a madman who out of a strange habit does not want to lift his eyes from the earth and, seeing it well lighted, says, "there is no sun." Others acknowledge the existence of a Supreme Being; but they want Him to obey their commandments, want everything to be according to their way of thinking, everything to satisfy their passions; and they end up by confessing a God that is not God, an unlimited infinite, a Supreme Being subject to the whims of his creatures. There are others who, stubbornly trapped in their vices, confess one God and one law giver but, moved by a horrible desperation, they do not want to obey and they renounce their eternal happiness.

FIRST TYPE—
A DENIAL OF THE CREATOR

Let us start by considering the terrible situation of the human spirit in the three cases we have just considered, and we will see that unbelief is more corruption than ignorance. No matter how often the unbeliever says that he does not know if there is a God, it is easy to find out that he does not know that there is *not* a God; therefore, he remains convinced that his positive statement of the *non-existence* of a Supreme Being is not the outcome of his conviciton. It follows, then, that irreligiosity can be no more than a statement of doubt. Attributing to it the status of a fundamental doctrine and of a behavioral norm in the most important of all issues, irreligiosity cannot be but the effect of unbridled passions.

Let us now consider godlessness a position of mere doubt, and we will see that it is strictly negative, since it is based on the impossibility of perceiving its object and not on repugnance. It is certain that the irreligious person states that a Being with no beginning is repugnant to reason, but we shall notice that the irreligious has to accept an eternal matter, or a world that started to exist before existing, inasmuch as it acted without existing, since it is assumed that the world gave existence to itself, and that is an infinite operation. Could there be something more repugnant than eternal matter? Could there be something more ridiculous than a being acting before existing? Only an erratic thinking can serve as an excuse for such repugnant statements, but never shall a correct thinking nourish such views. All doubts, then, are dispelled. A Being without beginning does not cause repugnance, for the unbeliever who pretends to prove its repugnance admits an eternal matter; and he declares with this affirmation that his own argument does not convince him, and that he is only moved by passion.

Let us then leave human misery to follow its own madness; at any rate may the horrendous cancer which devours the heart of the irreligious spread; let us not pretend to convince him; he is convinced, to his torment.

A veil slips away revealing signs of restlessness, and reflections on the imponderable spark some doubts like unexpected flames of fire surging from an extinct volcano. Imagine an arrogant pilot who having boasted about his skills begins to doubt the accuracy of his own reckoning and to fear an impending danger, which he vainly wishes away because he refuses to acknowledge that he made a mistake. He nourishes an unfounded hope, the fruit of his vanity, and he delivers himself to a fate already clearly suggesting that his ruin is at hand. Observe him pondering in confusion, now gloomy and silent, now enraged and ready to take up the challenge, attempting to disguise his agitation one moment but manifesting it the next. Books do not say what he wants them to, and nature openly contradicts him. Time, the inflexible judge, is ready to pass an irrevocable sentence. Of those who unfortunately have entrusted the precious treasures of their lives to him, some begin to doubt, some to fear, and many to argue openly that he is leading them to their deaths. Fear and remorse seize him and he searches for a way to distance himself, hoping for a happy insight or an unexpected event that could bail him out with honor. Failing to find relief in aloofness he turns once more to his unfortunate partners, whom he tries to dupe with his cleverness. But their questions embarrass him and their gazing pierces his heart like a sharp spear. Fleetingly he feels a desire to open his heart and disclose his pain, but at once he accuses himself of being rashly weak. He redoubles his effort at disdain, which he calls heroism, and determines to pretend he is undisturbed no matter how much it hurts. Is not the image I have just portrayed for you that of the most miserable person on earth? Such is the image of the godless person. Compare it with the original and you will be convinced that it is an exact replica.

See how much he longs for support, for he has no purpose

other than to establish the probability of his ideas through their diffusion. He acknowledges his personal weakness, and then to suppress the ensuing restlessness he tries to convince himself that it is but a suspicion without foundation, since it is not probable that many could perceive the same things without there being solid reasons for such unanimity. Indeed, it is not love for his neighbor that moves him so faithfully. No, he has another goal in mind. Human beings, according to the principles of the irreligious, are but instruments to be used carelessly, and irreligious persons know, as their conscience tells them, that those who are like them cannot be useful. On the other hand, if all ends when we die and if happiness consists in being as fulfilled as possible while on this earth, why must we make so much effort to convince others that their ideas are wrong? Happiness, in that case, is a relative concept, and if the godly person is fulfilled in his piety, why should we take away his piety in order that he may be happy? Is this not an obvious contradiction? Habits become second nature, and the irreligious person knows that it is impossible, or at least very difficult, that religious sentiments nourished from childhood should not produce terrible agitation in the soul of proselytes, and that the pangs of remorse disrupt the momentary serenity that could be obtained through sheer cunning arguments and vain reflections. Is human happiness not, then, the object of so much effort?

You may wonder, why would the irreligious be so interested in pretending that he does not believe? Why must we presume that he is shaken by awful pangs of remorse? It would be more just and fair to acknowledge that, gifted with a *strong spirit,* he has overcome the preoccupations which ignorance introduced and malice confirmed. Ah, dear friend, with similar reflections they have tried to deceive many others after having first deceived themselves. It would be enough to reply that the fanatic, the superstitious, and the hypocrite excuse themselves in the same way. They all affirm, even prove, that their conduct brings them only suffering, but is it not true that sometimes suffering can be advantageous? That same victory over worries, that same title *strong spirit,* that superiority over the rest of mankind, is it not also a notable advantage? Strong spirits and duelists are alike: they enter the contest trying to disguise their trembling, affecting a serenity they lack.

Nobody talks more about religion than those who follow none, and at the same time that they affirm it is a dream they deal with night and day. Those who are always introducing religious questions into conversation are the same who ridicule the believers for caring about them. Is this not a sign that they are interested in the matter? And how can a spirit always occupied with such an important matter be subject to so many doubts; and how can they maintain such an air of calm? It is remarkable that ignorance in relation to natural sciences and other points of interest in society never draws the attention of the incredulous, few of whom try to educate people on these matters, or if they do, do not show the same interest as with religious questions. If religion were, as they claim, an empty image, would it not be ridiculous to give it preference over real objects of obvious usefulness? Neither shall we say that they want to dissipate the shadows of an unfortunate error that causes infinite evils, because it is clear that the idea of eternal punishment, far from inducing crime, will always be a brake that restrains the criminal. Despite the efforts that irreligious persons have made to prove that religion is an abomination, they have only managed to demonstrate that it is of benefit to mankind. A religious and sinful people is like a square circle, that exists only on the lips of those who pronounce these words. This is known and understood by the irreligious, and in vain he tries to close his eyes to the light of truth—its influence penetrates his shaken heart and in removing the cancer that is consuming him necessarily causes the most intense torments.

While the doctrines of a religion regarded as handed down from heaven may be true, happiness does not exist for the irreligious; and when it is probable that a future and terrible misfortune awaits him, we cannot believe him when he says that he is satisfied and at peace. Ignoring the evidence of the arguments brought forth, which he has never been able to counter, his reasoning indicates to him that he does not have nor can he claim infallibility. To do so would be to admit the very religious principle and declare himself a divinity, even as he denies the existence of such a being. If his ideas are not infalli-

ble, their opposites are probable, or at least possible; and here
we have the miserable one convinced by himself; here we have
a confession of his delirium. He finds himself, without knowing
how, playing a very ridiculous role, stating dogma without infallibility, and pretending to prove he fears nothing, when his own
principles prove that he ought to fear, or that he has lost his
power of reasoning.

The pompous declarations of the incredulous have always
seemed to me like the groanings of someone in pain. The
louder they are the more hurt they indicate in the entrails of the
wretched we want to see recovered but whose fortune we have
no wish to share. Far from convincing us of the utility of their
doctrine, then, they preach to us the duty of not admitting it.
They who vainly want to become objects of our applause become objects of our compassion. Nothing is known in religious
matters, we are told by these apostles of ignorance, who surely
we should believe are guided by the same principles they
preach and, at least on this point, have wanted to pay homage
to truth. The clouds of error, having been conducted and con-
densed toward a point by the winds of pride, steal the view of
the sun of justice and leave in darkness these miserable ones
who reach such a degree of obstinate madness that they make
ignorance the arbiter of their fate.

No, my friend, so much degradation is not possible in the
work of the Almighty; the human being never loses his sense of
justice and the happy impulse that leads him toward the truth;
but this results in a terrible and continued clash between reason
and passion, and a mournful anxiety in the soul of the irreligious, who more than anybody else wants to see himself free of
his unbelief. How many have I heard say they want to believe
because, without any doubt, they would be happy! Is not this a
frank confession that happiness is found in belief and that the
unbeliever lives in torment? This irrefutable evidence, which I
have encountered various times, has convinced me that irreligious persons are the first secretly to abhor unbelief. Then why
do they sustain it? Why do they spread it if they detest it so
much? Because these *strong spirits* are very *feeble* when in
combat with their worries, although they boast of having destroyed other people's.

SECOND TYPE—A FORMAL AFFIRMATION
OF THE CREATOR AND A LIFE DENYING HIM

If we look to the second type of irreligious persons, those who admitting the existence of a Supreme Being want to subject Him to their ideas, we will be forced to believe that either they are crazy or they live in constant anxiety. The very idea of supremacy that they confess proves to them that they should receive the doctrine and not invent it. To constitute themselves as oracles of the Divinity, when they pretend to deny that those exist, is nothing more than to reveal a most ridiculous mental disorder, or a most sorrowful condition. Hence the variety of verdicts, of religious debates, and the infinity of sects. Doubting is the bane of life. If once we admitted the possibility of the existence of a Supreme Being we had no proof other than the necessity of some known truths, definite and infallible, the hideous state of someone unstable in these matters would be enough to convince us that these truths exist. Because we could never be persuaded that a Being infinitely wise and just could have destined the human race to live in such agony and just a little reflection on this painful situation will show us that it is not consistent with the divine goodness. Let us turn our eyes away from the horrible image of the godless person who admits that there is a God, and that he has given a law, but does not want to obey that law, considering it irrational and unjust. What nonsense! There is a God, He has given a law, and when He did so He stopped being God, since His law is unjust. Let us not continue our investigation of the condition of such a spirit. He is the prisoner of despair and the victim of ignorance. When alone he despises himself and does not doubt the scorn of his fellow men.

The resistance of the majority of the human race is another reason for the unhappiness of the unbeliever, who loses hope of luring others into following his nonsense, and cannot bear their constant and powerful attacks. He knows that he is a strange being, and the strange is generally companion to the ridiculous. Wanting to take advantage of the people, he cannot enjoy the horror with which they look at him, and his mortified self-love allows him no peace. He seems, it is true, to find advantages and pleasures in this very resistance, but they can never compensate for the terrible feelings caused by lack of esteem.

A state as violent as this nourishes the most regrettable passions. The irreligious person hates, curses and piles up insults upon himself because he knows the origins of his portion. He knows that people are not affected by hearing his insulting phrases, because they do not consider him among the ranks of the human; they place him among the irrational, whose blows should be avoided but never offend. He therefore believes himself surrounded by enemies, considering as such anyone who does not approve his insanity, and society becomes for him a place of torment.

If my ideas may seem inexact, or if perhaps I may seem to give reality to mere suspicions, I appeal to the history of the godless philosophers, and to the pages of the immense volumes in which they have left stamped immense errors as to society. All of these closely examined show not only that they were never pleased with society, but also that they detested it, not by virtue, but rather by despondency. A delirious person who by misfortune has had many imitators insisted on proving to us that the human being is not a social being.

The renowned Grocio, whom I shall not classify among the irreligious, and yet I do not know if I can place him among the Catholics, but who certainly participated in the delirium of those miserable ones; Grocio, otherwise illustrious, states that we have been born for war, and consequently that the state of peace goes against nature. Can there be a greater absurdity? And what could have induced this philosopher, if not discontentment, to leave in his works, in which his talent shines, this evident proof of his misery and of the confusion of his mind. You cannot ignore that prompted by excessive pride a daydreamer established himself as counselor of ignorance, and that by opposing science, he opposed society. Without science, society is reduced to an inorganic mass, and it becomes like a huge mass of stones and other materials, which, heaped up without any order, will never be able to form a building, much less a beautiful city.

Observe the irreligious in their behavior and in the character of their meetings and you will see that they are never happy. The cause of this evil is not their discord with their listeners, since they suffer this and even greater evil, when they are by themselves and proceed entirely according to their principles. Their societies have always ended in scandal, after being the object of ridicule, since even the most ignorant perceive their vehemence. You will not read the life of any of these unfortunates without finding a thousand anecdotes that place them in a ridiculous light, a thousand incidents in which you discover their weaknesses; and, finally, the whole series of their actions will indicate to you that their spirit is in torment and that the farther their ideals deviate from heaven, the farther peace flees from their societies. Enemies of everyone and tyrants over themselves, they live in fear and hate. What else do you want, Elpidio? The picture is very bleak, and nothing more is needed to convince us.

I cannot, on the other hand, allow to pass in silence one of the greatest proofs of the truth which up to now I have exposed. I want, my friend, I want you to observe the irreligious in misfortune, and you will see that they were never happy, since they never possessed the means to be happy. Happiness is the fruit of security, and while we doubt the permanence of good, the more perfect and desirable it appears to us, the greater the anxiety it causes us. When the enervated body denies itself pleasures, or adverse fortune does not provide the means to enjoy them, the irreligious finds himself without any consolation or recourse whatsoever, rather like the unwary sailor who foreseeing a shipwreck did not plan for his salvation, and having been handed over to the enraged waves, finds no object to cling to, while for his greater torment, he sees others floating for having prepared themselves. He then gives in to rage, curses, blasphemes and hates himself as author of his misfortune. Human life presents us, Elpidio, more thrusts of pain than of pleasure, and the number of misfortunate people far exceeds that of those who live in prosperous fortune. How frequent and gloomy, therefore, is this horrible effect of irreligiosity, and how miserable is the life of the irreligious!

Virgil describes to us the fury of the winds which, repressed and chained, finally break free and, casting themselves over the Tirrenean Sea, whip up formidable waves, which toss and destroy the vessels of the Trojan prince. All is confusion and ruin; but a divinity puts an end to so many evils, restores calm, and contentment returns. The soul of the irreligious in misfortune presents to us an image of that agitated sea, and the violent and indomitable passions are more formidable than those unleashed winds; but since the irreligious admits nothing divine, the picture is even more horrible, for consolation is impossible and disaster inevitable.

Meditate, Elpidio, on the destructive doctrines of human liberty, examine their origin, and you will see that they only had as author, and only have as partisans, the irreligious, who, not being able to overcome their passions, have declared themselves slaves to them. Handing themselves over to the waves as ships without pilots after many and repeated efforts to counteract them, and wanting to succumb with dignity, they invented a blind and tyrannical *Hades,* the same ones who did not want to admit a wise and merciful God. Oh vain illusion! Is there not a universal principle, an almighty Being, and is there nonetheless a power to which all yields, and which subjugates even the will of the human person? Destiny operates without submitting to anyone, and without being formed by anyone! This the irreligious admits when he dares to tell us that it is repugnant to accept that there is a God.

THIRD TYPE—A FORMAL AFFIRMATION, A LIFE OF DENIAL AND GENERAL DESPAIR

These desolating doctrines, having been spread through society by the irreligious, produce a fatal discontent that disables people by depriving them of all hope. Such absurdities find many and decided challengers, and in the tremendous fight, peace is interrupted, hate is ignited, vengeance is excited, vice finds dispensation, virtue loses its value, work seems useless and inaction the prudent norm. All is disturbed and, to add to the sorrow, a remedy is considered impossible. Why, then, do they invoke the consoling name of philosophy, those who with their doctrines deprive themselves and their like of all consolation? Do they love wisdom, are they philosophers, those who deny its existence? Those who degrade themselves to the point of rationalizing their weakness by declaring themselves slaves of a blind destiny, how can they persuade us that they possess that holy philosophical freedom that elevates man above material beings, makes him superior to adversity, and keeps him safe amid dangers? They doubt everything and decide about everything. They know nothing and teach everything. They say that misfortune is necessary and urge us to avoid it. They constitute themselves as guides of the human race and confess that they ignore the road of happiness and that in vain have they searched for it all their lives!

These ill-starred people hand themselves over to fate, and with thousands of unwary followers they begin to travel the harsh field of society, wrapped in a dense cloud of error, their eyes blindfolded by the hand of pride. They slide here, trip there. Now they fall, now they rise. Some hurl off a cliff, others drown, several get lost. But being no more prudent than their ancient guides, they unreflectingly enter and become entangled in dense forests, from whence they seek in vain to exit. In the end one sees many miserable ones who fight with the agony born of desperation. But alas! while these dazzled throngs follow their fatal leaders, walking everywhere but seeing nothing, trampling the fragrant flowers which virtue had planted in society, two most beautiful daughters of the Eternal One, blessed religion and kind philosophy, hand in hand and encircled by a rainbow of peace, observe this field of sorrow from the heavens above. Their eyes follow the steps of the horrid monster of irreligiosity, and they pity the miserable luck of those who, for not knowing them, thought they had separated them.

Why has lamentable misfortune attempted to assign different origins to these two emanations of divine wisdom? Hence the overturn of social principles; hence mutual distrust; hence the weakness of laws; hence, in a word, the ruin of society. An irrational religion and an irreligious philosophy are two monsters of the abyss, who try in vain to cloak themselves in alien costumes and take the place of those two daughters of light, those angels of peace who constantly send to the human spirit rays of a different nature, but of the same origin, and fill people with consolation.

IMAGINING THE FUTURE—
HAPPY, HOPEFUL RELIGIOUS SOCIETY

Compare the pitiful picture I have just described with that of a religious society. Imagine that same field traveled not by furious and stubborn people destroying everything, but by a multitude of just ones who, without renouncing the rights of human being, have the sanity to know their origin and respect God. Look at how happily that very philosophy, whose name was profaned by the godless, leads the just, warning them of even the most distant cliff and correcting them in their slightest deviation from the path of knowledge. Observe how religion applauds human activity, rejoicing in the progress of enlightenment, but, at the same time, points heavenward, promising a perfect science and an eternal well-being. Live, she says, live as brothers; investigate as philosophers; worship as believers; and when these beings, who by nature should end, abandon you, an inalterable Being should receive you. With these two pictures in sight, will it be difficult to distinguish the one depicting happiness?

The voice of the people gives even more strength to the arguments of sound philosophy and declares that irreligiosity has always been detested for its pernicious effects, and that social order and peace among people have always been victims of the irreligious, as they have of the superstitious and the fanatic. Considering, then, irreligiosity only in its relation to politics, and without any respect to the eternal good, it is to be avoided as fatal, lest an argument, experienced by so many generations, be left unattended in favor of the theories of a few confused ones. The same arguments by which the godless wants to introduce irreligiosity prove that it must be detested. A visionary poet, as most of them are, asserted that fear was the author of deity; and this sentence, which could have been true with regard to false deities, has been impiously applied to belief in the Supreme Being. But is the invention of new deities not proof of the certainty and experience of people regarding the effects of irreligiosity? The very remedy they sought indicated the cause of the evil they suffered. If one were to say that fear has induced many to want to persuade themselves that there is no God, no doubt one would be right. But let us grant what neither the understanding nor the heart can grant. Yes, let us concede that it is all a human invention. Do those who assume this not say that religiosity was born out of the necessity of governing people. Later in the state of irreligiosity they were not able to govern themselves, and it is clear that without government there is no order, and without order there is no contentment. Let us end such sad reflections, if not the sentiment that causes them. May the people be able to reject irreligiosity, may philosophy be able to discover this monster, whose horrible aspect is enough for it to be detested. May you, religious Elpidio, be happy.

IRRELIGIOSITY DESTROYS HOPE
AND LEADS TO DESPOTISM

The unhappiness that causes irreligiosity is followed, dear Elpidio, by the distrust of nations, a terrible evil which destroys all the plans of the wisest policy and annuls the efforts of the most just government. Once people are persuaded of the need of a guarantee against malice, and cannot find it in laws, which, as an old wise man said, are worthless without good customs, they cry out for a principle that produces and insures them. The life of the irreligious is an irrefutable testimony that they do not seek this coveted principle and that laxity is, almost always, joined by irreligiosity. How can they inspire faith? On their lips the sacred promise is a ridiculous fiction and a most insulting mockery. To swear by a God not believed in, or from whom nothing is expected and nothing feared, is to treat people as children, or as demented, whose ideas are usually heard only to humor and pacify them. Could there be a greater insult? Could one believe that those who begin by betraying a promise have the will to keep it? They present themselves as believers and swear as such, giving the impression that they have the same ideas and the same feelings, while in their minds they contradict each word, with the result that they do not believe each other nor does anyone believe them, no matter how well they play the role of comedian-politician.

THE DESTRUCTION OF SOCIAL VIRTUES

Once irreligiosity is spread throughout the social body, it destroys all links of appreciation, and like poison, it corrupts and kills the body. Honor becomes a vain word; patriotism, a political mask; virtue, a fancy; and trust, a necessity. Do you think that I am exaggerating, Elpidio? Reflect on it and you will see that I am only copying. Yes, in the history of nations you will find the original of this image, you will see the political parties, which like heavy clouds driven by opposing winds clash with fury, but incohesive they dissipate and disappear; or they may mix, forming new clouds which, driven by different winds, clash with distant ones causing the scene to repeat itself; and in this way they observe a dense veil that robs from our sight the luminous rays of the sun of justice. But, you will ask me, is irreligiosity always what forms the political parties? No, but it is always in all of them, without belonging to any, and corrupts them all. The irreligious just thinks of the moment, but the just considers eternity. Societies of the just have consistency, and societies of the perverse are frail. But when, unfortunately, such contrary elements as justice and irreligiosity come together, only a light impulse is enough to separate them; and once the action is interrupted, no matter how solid some of the parts may be, the whole dissolves. Here lies the pernicious effect of irreligiosity!

If the parties had the right of expulsion, and if all that deserved it could be known, then undoubtedly homogeneous political bodies could be formed. But a party is an open house without an owner, which anyone can enter or leave, and where many pretend to have been, whose falsehood cannot be proven. Hence the discredit of many because of a few, who feigned to have left their old friends, which perhaps they never were, because of crimes they saw them commit; hence, the ease of producing great confusion and preventing the ordered operations; hence, finally, the opportunity for political traps. It seems to me, dear Elpidio, that these light observations are enough to explain a phenomenon that some explain as rare, that is to say, how some virtuous and meritorious persons can be found in loathsome parties, and how so many perverse persons are found in the most hallowed parties. These strange beings can sometimes be found at the head of these parties, and that is great proof that the ideas of a group are not always in accordance with the ideas of their leaders.

But to what end, you will say, should one speak so much of parties? In order to make evident that no matter how just their cause, or how sacred their objective, their ruin is inevitable if irreligiosity prevails in them; and since the human race is necessarily composed of parties, the result is that irreligiosity, the enemy of virtue, sows lack of faith in the nations and prevents their happiness. Only an internal link can unite people when they cannot be submitted to external ones. And who does not see that laws and public opinion will never be able to restrain the ravings and perfidies, when a multitude of people disseminated throughout society know how to avoid their blows, and even pretend to be their most faithful observers? Is not trust in a party, then, based on something other than the sense of justice, of good judgment and of honor, which a person of good faith and principles assumes that others have?

Convinced of these truths, and aware of the need of inspiring trust in people if we want to live in peace with them, some have striven to demonstrate that morality does not depend on religion; and even though they are horrified by their own doctrine, they have not dared to deduce the consequences. It is clear that one can infer from this principle that irreligious persons can be virtuous. The two terms, virtue and irreligiosity, having already made contact, their contradiction can, I believe, be felt, and such a great absurdity totally refuted. The subject matter, nevertheless, is of such importance that it is advisable to illustrate it with some reflections.

With respect to eternal life there is but one religion, and one moral derived from it and meritorious for this sacred principle; but with respect to society nominal religions, that is to say, false religious doctrines, can inspire a correct moral, which, like principle, has merit only before people. We see, then, in religious sects, charitable, sober and just people, who for their acts deserve appreciation and excite admiration, without it being said that they are *less worthy* of God. For then we would commit the absurdity of affirming that *all the acts of sinners are sins.*[1] These two lines should be perfectly marked, in order not to incur unfortunate errors concerning the influence of religion in society, confusing it with the production of merit for eternal life. Distinguishing, then, *social* morality from *religious* morality, we can say that the latter is not legitimate and perfect except when it comes from the one and true religion; but the former can be perfect even if its origin is a false religion. As for irreligiosity, it destroys both types of morals, no matter what their apologists say.

An unbeliever lives only to enjoy this world as much as possible, and according to his principles, he is foolish if, able to enjoy himself, he does not because of insignificant voices of virtue and honor; but, according to his own principles and those of a sound moral, even more foolish than he are those who are so naive as to believe what he says. The unbeliever is a beast chained by laws; but if its victim is within reach, or if the chains fail, destruction is certain.

THE GRADUAL DESTRUCTION OF HOPE

Good people, then, fear all parties, and even the irreligious fear when these beasts with human aspect are everywhere and mix with the peaceful people only to devour them. Suspicions arise, inquiries start, restlessness grows, patience and prudence fall short, rage and attacks follow, and once the slaughter has begun, it ends in desolation. Some of the beasts that started it leave satiated; others roar because they have not had their fill; and others, covering themselves with a sheepskin, pretend to be sheep and join the herd in order to prepare a new slaughter. Such is the important lesson that experience has given in all the vicissitudes of the nations, my dear Elpidio, and you know that I have been one of the listeners of this most severe and wise teacher . . .

Oh, how deep are the wounds inflicted on the social body by the venomous claws of the monster of irreligiosity! When

---

1. This was one of Luther's mistakes.

religious sentiments are extinguished or lessened, no consolation can be found; projects are put aside, and it seems that
nations abandon all attempts at prosperity. This past century
gave us in one of the most flourishing nations of Europe an
example of this terrible truth; yes, an example, Elpidio, that
will never be erased from history, but that, unfortunately, has
not been enough of a warning. France was then a fruitful har-
borer of industry and a magnificent palace of science; its abundant crops covered the fields and numerous herds whitened its
hills; its ports were filled with masts and its roads with carriages. But, in the midst of all the splendor, irreligiosity was
making headway, and you already know the fatal results. Let
us not recall all these miseries but only copy from that horrible
picture some light traces that can serve our purpose.

You know that irreligiosity has never before been so widespread and powerful, but do you recall having seen injustice so
widespread? But why am I saying injustice? Was not that wise
and illustrious nation reduced to barbarism? In what person did
faith reside? The murderers themselves were afraid of being
murdered; neither conjugal love nor filial love nor a long and
pure friendship produced any effect since an irreligious public
judged them as foolish. To close one's eyes in order not to
perceive such a clear truth is to augment the disaster with the
torment of having caused it, but how many of these blind people do we not find everywhere? Yes, there is a class, or in other
words, a dispersed multitude of people more perverse than
ignorant, whose pleasure is disagreement, whose science is deceit, and whose object is destruction; in order to justify their
depraved intentions, they invoke with great treachery the re-
spectable names of the most famous patriots, whom they assume to be the authors of the most foolish projects; they speak
against destiny, which has frustrated them, and want to cover
with the veil of heroism that memorable scene of the degradation of the human species. In this matter they foil the healthy
effects of such a terrible experiment and induce nations to
undertake similar ones.

Fortunately popular common sense, that instinct of the
masses to direct themselves to certain goals that favor them and
draw back from others that harm them, is not entirely extin-

guished; and in spite of all the efforts of the irreligious, the naive multitude knows this tendency and can feel the fruits of irreligiosity, which it blames for the blood bath that innundated France; hence the hatred with which nations regard the apostles of extermination. These apostles resort to insults and affronts; they complain about popular ignorance and ponder over the corruption of the people, which renders it incapable of noble undertakings (undertakings which they themselves hinder); and in this way they spend a life of torment, causing grief to others. The people, for their part, irritated from so much insult, hate their slanderers more and more, and distrust grows rapidly when it is seen that irreligiosity grows and that its attacks are treacherous and dreadful. Panic is produced in certain classes and a bellicose furor in others, and when the people become aware of their contrary dispositions, new suspicions arise and new precautions are taken. Everyone sees an enemy in one's neighbor, whom one readily assumes to be irreligious; and since these monsters respect nothing, one tries to live in constant vigilance, the fruit of a just mistrust.

How sad the idea that torments my spirit! What an unfortunate result, even if expected from such elements! I fear, Elpidio, that I will not be successful in portraying with its own colors the monster of irreligiosity exerting its greatest cruelty and its lowest perfidy, that is to say, opening the way so that a no less horrendous and destructive monster can follow: rash despotism. Are you surprised by my assertion? Do you believe that irreligiosity befriends only free people? Do you think that there are no irreligious despots? No, your great soul could not conceive of such degrading ideas of the human species; and your sound judgment will affirm, as that of all good people, that there never was a free individual who was irreligious, nor a despot who was not. Irreligiosity unleashes all the restraints of stable love and lets loose all the stirrings of passion, which quite soon degenerate into furies that exert on the human heart the most unbearable of all despotisms, turning the oppressed into his own oppressor. This cruel oppression is experienced by the despot; his unrestrained passions drag him everywhere and like a mistreated beast he feeds on as many victims as he can find in his forsaken way. The greater the number of his injustices, the greater the uneasiness of his heart, and the greater his obligation to the agents of his cruelties; he is a slave covered with gold in order to make more visible the signs of his slavery. And do you think that holy piety, benevolent by nature, peaceful and loving— do you think, Elpidio, that this gentle and delightful emanation from heaven resides in monsters enslaved by the furies and minister of hell? If he has any faith left, is it not similar to that of the demons? Do we not have good cause to doubt the speculative notions of one who practices irreligiosity?

The two hallowed principles of human happiness, just liberty and sublime religion, are in perfect harmony and inseparable.[45] A political hypocrisy attempts to disjoin them, but such a violent state cannot last long, and time finally lifts the veil and discovers the hypocrite. Hence so many political alterations in both senses; hence so much spilled blood, so many ill-spent riches, so many ruined nations and so many crimes, the memory of which punishes their perpetrators. After so many warnings and such extensive experience, what shall we say of our free people who wish to be irreligious people and our religious people who wish to be enslaved? My sincere answer would be that neither are the former free, nor the latter religious, but rather they are hordes of misguided ones and rogues that under a different attire serve the same master, which is to say, the devil.

THE MONSTER OF DESPOTISM

These masses, apparently so heterogeneous, convene perfectly in attracting crime and repelling virtue; and hence the result is that once the world is flooded by a deluge of evils, good people lose hope of purifying it and become discouraged. Their lack of action cleared the way for the ominous influence of tyranny, to which the perfidious, who pretended to be their enemies when they could not be their allies, soon offered their incense; and fatigued, the people yield to degrading despotism.

Do not think that I speak only of kings amongst whom there have been fathers of the nations and beasts that have devoured them; my observations are directed towards despotism in all its states, and you will see that in all of them it is supported by the monster and irreligiosity. There is, it is true, a popular despotism no less loathsome than the monarchy; and nations have been its victims, obliged, to make matters worse, to vote for this unjust sentence. In the name of nations its riches have been destroyed, its sons killed, its cities destroyed, and, what is more, its laws trampled upon. Only irreligiosity could have taken them to this deplorable state; driving away the virtues from those in whom the people had confided and those who, as faithful keepers of such a valuable deposit, had denied entrance to their enemies, driving away, yes, the tutelar angels of the human species, those genii that Divinity sends to console oppressed mortals, the door is left open to the monster, that soon elects its satellites and begins its devastations.

With the opprobrium of human nature, the need to oppress the nations begins to be preached everywhere instead of the need not to exasperate them. No sophisms of any kind are omitted to deceive the multitudes, whose little-exercised reason yields to the impulses of the imagination, which can be aroused with the terrifying images of so many disasters. The laments of the victims are remembered, but not the blows of their immolators; the causes of so many sacrifices are not remembered, but rather others are invented that are less hideous and cover the effect of perversity with the veil of prudence. In this way nations are chained and imprisoned, and it matters not whether the keys to this horrendous jail be in one or many hands.

No matter how little we reflect on the operations of despotism in all its variations, we will know that this infernal monster can have nothing to do with piety, which is the daughter of heaven; rather, it tries to destroy it in order to reduce people to the state of barbarism and cruelty that is absolutely necessary for its criminal procedures. Only when one is deprived of all fear of God can one reject his divine law, not listen to the dictates of conscience and pounce like a tiger on one's neighbors in order to devour them. Is it not just that what despots do? Neither the tears of the widow nor the moans of the orphan nor the pitiful plaints of the honest head of the family nor the warnings of the wise are enough to keep the despot from his cruelties. Suffering, virtue and science, these three springs of sympathy are insignificant for someone whose barbarous pleasure consists in being feared. Nothing is more analogous to irreligiosity than that which destroys the pleasant link of submission to a supreme and all just Being, who is at the same time, the loving Father of mortals, to whom He has promised a coveted immortality.

THE MEANS DESPOTISM USES TO DISGUISE ITSELF

Allow me to hold your attention still for a few more moments, and let us follow the trail of this viper that has caused and is causing so much harm to nations. Let us investigate, though with great grief, the different means it employs in order to disguise itself and make its active poison palatable.

Despots cry out against the irreligiosity that opened the way for them, and taking their hypocrisy to the limit they lead the nations to believe that the irreligious only aspire to see it destroyed. They invoke the sacred name of religion, but with a semblance that permits their opposite feelings to show, so although not so much that they can be judged irreligious. They count, therefore, on the ignorant and unthinking, who, unfortunately, are many; and they retain their influence, maintaining in both parties a slight hope of total commitment. The religious but heedless person thinks that the remains of irreligiosity that can still be observed in the despot can be destroyed by the abundance of his good qualities, and calls good all those whose malice he does not succeed in perceiving. The irreligious is strengthened when his sentiments are identified with those of the despot and does not doubt that soon they will also agree in what the irreligious call "wise and frank actions," which in reality are bold and fruitless attacks against religion. The despot, meanwhile, profits from both types of deluded people and uses irreligiosity as an instrument that he manipulates in a different way. This is a strange phenomenon: the hatred and fear of irreligiosity subdues the devout and the desire to propagate it restrains the irreligious, leaving both tied by the accursed hand of enlightened despotism, which to insure more victims relies on ignorance which in some takes the name of prudence and in others the name of enlightenment.

Despots tend also to rely on another method even more vile for their incredible perfidy. They assume that irreligiosity is far more widespread than it really is (although the actual extent of it is unfortunate) and describe a fatal and almost inevitable future, and, affecting imagination to its highest degree, they prepare the spirit for suffering of any measure, which they take with affected sorrow and as if by force, when it is but the result of an infernal machinery. The irreligious, for their part, also fall into the trap: believing that they are stronger than they really are, they uncover themselves and attack without reservation; but since they are destroyed in their first attempts, they increase the glories of despotism and establish it with the same means they employed to destroy it, believing it to be related to religion, without heeding that they themselves were the agents used by despotism for common ruin and the building of its bloody and loathsome throne.

The despotism of irreligiosity also serves to void the power of the laws that are its enemies. It wants to destroy them, but their roots are so noble and their influence on pious souls so great that the attempt is risky and it is necessary to prepare for it by dispossessing the human heart of any celestial sentiments that can never be brought to terms with the perversities of despots. These fear losing the battle if they do not find company in their crimes, and unable to be like the just, they must resort to the irreligious, which they can buy off for a small price because they are worth nothing and respect nothing. Since laws are violated by such a large number, the people become accustomed to these infringements and little by little the terrain is being prepared to build another monument to crime. Laws are accused of being unjust or inadequate, the audacity of insolent disobedience presents itself as an effect of popular opinion and beneficial instinct, and the flatterers of the despots begin to make the crowns with which they intend to reward their own perfidy, giving it the name of "superior prudence" and "enlightened devotion," pretending that it is better to disregard the laws which they call inert documents and remove the obstacles to prosperity. Have you not heard this language several times before? And do you think it could come from the lips of religion?

With the laws annulled and passions unleashed people enter into a tragic and inevitable war, having neither their territory defined nor their flag marked in order to be recognized by their enemies. It is a war of perfidies, of vileness and snares, and in this kind of combat despotism knows the superiority of its weapons and how much use it can draw from the irreligious. Triumph is certain, and according to the versatile and loathsome nature of the agents they have used, they find themselves with the strong need to flatter them on the one hand and repress them on the other; in other words, in order to establish themselves, despots at times permit the abuses of irreligiosity and at others restrain its excesses, subjecting it to the same iron sceptre with which they govern the innocent nation. Ancient and modern history present convincing proofs of this truth, and amongst other examples it is sufficient to recall the life of the irreligious Frederick, since there has never been a prince so despotic nor one who has manipulated his irreligious brothers with greater dexterity to make them serve his purposes. The philosopher Verney himself, *the proud God of pleasure,* did not escape from being whipped as a swine at the command of that astute prince, who knew how to promote his pride with extraordinary favors. Irreligiosity was intermittently exalted and repressed, but it always served the purpose of unrestrained despotism; it was not without disgrace to philosophy that this wily tyrant took the title of philosopher.

Irreligiosity succeeds in building monuments to error with similar aborted monsters, establishing them in a blind fame that transmits to posterity, as objects of honor and glory, these iniquitous beings whose names should be erased from the annals of nations and the history of thrones. A brilliant slavery, a disguised misery and an enlightened ignorance are the primary means to fool the gullible and to produce unfortunate and ignorant slaves, proper subjects of infernal despotism. The praises that irreligiosity renders to these famous irreligious persons and the vast arguments it uses to make its terrible memory less loathsome are reefs in which the nations sail and over which tyrants build their thrones. Yes, dear friend, the magnificent fort of tyranny is built amid a sea of passions and human miseries, over the rock of irreligiosity whose foundation is covered by the moving waves, leaving visible only the strong walls. The poorly guided ships direct themselves to this interesting object, believing not only that there is no risk involved but that they will find shelter, but oh! sadly they run into a lamentable shipwreck.

The misfortune is far more lamentable when deceit joins it, and even though an enemy cannot be overpowered, it is consoling to know him. Deceit brings such degradation and ridicule, and human nature never stops resenting this wound, even though time may manage to cover it over. The disgraced person remembers the series of sufferings without feeling new grief, and sometimes even feels satisfaction, regarding them as honorable, but he never remembers without shame his dreams and the deceits to which he has fallen prey. Human pride, therefore, uses all the means possible to hide weakness that causes such dishonor, but since it is impossible to hide the facts it is necessary to distort them. This is the origin of what we may call *political obstinacy,* whereby people attempt to put forth their ideas even though they perceive them as wrong, without caring for the good of the nations, paying attention only to the glory of their own name. I could present to you, Elpidio, infinite examples, but it is hard to give them without making offensive implications, and I find them unnecessary, if you reflect upon the workings of politics.

You will have perceived the direction of my observations, knowing that the cruelest of all despotisms is the one that is exercised behind the mask of liberty; and since the irreligious are rarely despots in any manner other than pretending to be booklovers, their tyranny is the most unbearable, though unfortunately it is the best established. It is very difficult for the nations to know this tyranny; they allow themselves to be swept away by appearances and all attempts to restrain it gives the impression of a defection from the flags of liberty. Once the irreligious see the fear of the good people, they are encouraged to play the role with greater boldness, and to please the despots they pretend to be their enemies. In this manner nations en-

slave themselves, my dear Elpidio; but do not think that I have
finished the sad list of the schemes of irreligiosity to aid despotism; I do not intend to name them all, because I would never
finish; but I must not remain silent on one of the most terrible
ones, invented by a small number of enlightened rogues and
practiced by an infinity of ignorant scoundrels.

THE WRITINGS OF CHURCH FATHERS AGAINST DESPOSTISM

You know how much the irreligious ridicule the works of
the Fathers of the Church and you do not deny that the greater
part of them have not even seen the bookshelves that hold
them. You have noticed many times how bothersome it is to
them when anyone dares to quote from a pious author, and you
are well aware that in this manner they are separating people
from any veneration toward these earlier masters of virtue and
limiting the instruction of their followers to the reading of a few
pamphlets that meet their purpose. Nothing would be more
favorable to the goals of the despots. The irreligious know that
no matter how widespread corruption is, the people always
look suspiciously upon doctrines that come by way of irreligiosity; the irreligious rejoice to see despised the reading of the
works of the Fathers, whose sanctity has great influence on just
hearts; and thus their own statements would be barriers to
irreligious atrocities. All the maxims of free nations, all the
doctrines of civilization have been taught by the Fathers and
can be found in the *bulky bundle of papers* that the irreligious
condemn without having read. Despots would tremble, Elpidio, if people could have at hand the pages in which, openly
and without exception, they are accused and condemned by
those whom the Church has declared saints, and from whom
even the most astute malice has not been able to take away the
merit of their most elevated virtue, by persons who were the
admiration of their century and are now the scorn of fools who
have assumed the title of philosophers.

From various other examples which I am omitting, I will
limit myself to translating a most interesting article written by
Saint Thomas which will surprise you since you certainly would

not expect it to speak in such clear and strong terms. Thus it says:

> Two things must be assured in the establishment of princes in a city or nation. First, that all take part in the princedom; because in this way peace in the nation is maintained, since all will love and support such an institution; secondly, in so far as the type of government or establishment of the princedom, that it is of different varieties; the most notable ones being the *kingdom,* in which one governs *according to virtue;* and the aristocracy, that is, the power of the most favorable in which a few govern *according to virtue.* Therefore, the best institution of princes in a city or kingdom, is when one governs *according to virtue* and under him others govern, also *according to virtue;* and, nevertheless, this princedom *belongs to all,* since all can elect and be elected. Such are all political bodies *mixed* of a *kingdom* insofar as one governs, an *aristocracy* insofar as many govern *according to virtue,* and *democracy,* that is, of the power of the people, insofar as the princes can be elected from individuals of the people, and because *it is the right of the people to elect them.* This was established by divine law: Moses and his successors governed the people as if with one empire over all, and this is a type of *kingdom.* Seventy-two elders were elected *according to virtue,* because it is said: I took from your tribes noble and wise men and I made them princes; and this was *aristocratic.* But it was *democratic* to elect these from all the people because it is said: I chose from the people at large some wise men and appointed them as leaders of the people.[2]

---

2. Respondeo dicendum, quod circa bonam ordinationem principum in aliqua civitate, vel gente duo sunt attendenda. Quirum unum est ut omnes aliquiam partem habeant in principatu: per hoe enim conservatur pax populi, et omnes talem ordinationem amant, et custodium, ut dicitur II Polit (cap. 1). Aliud est quod attenditur secundum speciem regiminis, vel ordinationis principatuum: cujus cum sint diversae species, ut Philosophus tradit in III

In the same article St. Thomas proposes an argument saying that "the kingdom represents the divine government in
which one God governs the world from the beginning. Hence
law should not have left the institution of kings to the people
but rather should have established it itself."[3] The way in which
the saintly Doctor responds to this argument is remarkable.

The kingdom is the best of governments if it does not
become corrupt. But because of the greater power
given to the king it is easy for it to degenerate into
tyranny, unless the individual to whom this great
power is given has perfect virtue. But perfect virtue is
found in few and the Jews were cruel and miserly. For
this reason God did not institute at the beginning a

Polit. (cap.V), praecipuae tamem sunt Regnum in quo unus principatur
secundum virtutem; *et Aristocratia,* id est potestas optimorum in qua aliqui
pauci principantur secundum virtutem. Unde optima ordinatio principum est
in aliqua civtate, vel regno, n que unus praeficitur secundum virtutem, qui
omnibus praesit, et sub ipso sunt aliqui principantes secundum virtutem: et
tamen talis principatus ad omnes pertinet, tum quia ex omnibus eligi possunt;
tum quia etiam ad omnibus eliguntur. Talis vero est omnis politia bene
conmixta ex *Regno,* in quantum unus praeest; et *Aristocratia,* in quantum
multi principantur secundum virtutem; et ex *Democratia,* id est potestate
populi, in quantum ex popularibus possunt eligi principes, et ad populum
pertinet electio principum. Et hoc fuit institutum secundum legem divinam.
Nam Moyses, et ejus successores gubernabant populum, quasi singulariter
omnibus principantes, quod est quaedam species regni. Eligebantur autem
septuaginta duo seniores secundum virtutem: dicitur enim Deut. 1.15. *Tuli de*
vestris tribus viros sapientes et nobiles, et constitui eis principes: et hoc erat
aristocraticum. Sed *democraticum* erat quod isti de omni populo eligebantur,
dicitut enim Exod. 18.21. *Provide de omni plebe viros sapientes,* etc., et etiam
quod populus eos eligebat: unde decitur Deut. 1.13. *Date ex vobis viros*
sapientes, etc. Unde patet quod optima fuit ordinatio principum quam lex
instituit. Thomas, 1.2 ae.q.q. 105 art. 1.
    3. Praeterea. *Optimi est optima adducere,* ut Plato dicit in Timaeo
(aliquant. a princ.) Sed optima ordinatio civitatis, vel populi cuiuscumque est
ut gubernetur per Regem: quia huiusmodi regnum maxime repraesentat
divinum regimen, quo unus Deus mundum gubernat a principio. Igitur lex
debuit Regem populo instituere, et non permittere hoc eorum arbitrio, sicut
permittitur Deuteron. 17.14. *Cum dixeris, Constituam super me Regem . . .*
eum constitues, etc.

king with full power but rather a judge and governor to look over them; but later as if offended by the petition of the people, He granted them a king as it is written: *It was not you they rejected, but me, so that I would not reign over them.* Nevertheless, regarding the establishment of kings, God from the beginning determined, first, the way of electing them, making use of two things: that they wait for divine wisdom in the election and that they not elect foreigners as kings, since such kings usually do not care for the nations they come to govern and therefore do not look over them well. Secondly, in regard to the selected kings, God ordered the way in which they should conduct themselves, that they purposely not multiply their carriages and horses, or have many women, or accumulate immense riches; because greed for these objects makes these princes lean toward tyranny and abandon justice. The Lord also determined the way in which kings should conduct themselves with God, that is, that they read and meditate his law always and always remain obedient and in fear of Him. In regard to their subjects, He ordered them not to scorn and oppress them arrogantly and not to separate themselves from justice.[4]

---

4. Ad secundum dicendum, quod regnem est optimum regimen populi, si non corrumpatur. Sed propter magnam potestatem, quae Regi conceditur, de facili regnum degenerat in tyrannidem, nisi sit perfecta virtus ejus cui tales potestas conceditur, quia *non est nisi virtuosi bene ferre bonas fortunas,* ut Philosophus dicit in X Ethic (cap. 8). Perfecta autem virtus in paucis invenitur: et praecipue Judaei crudeles erant, et ad avaritiam proni: per quae vitia maximae homines in tyrannidem decidunt. Et ideo Dominus a principio eis Regem non instituit cum plena potestate, sed judicem, et gubernatorem in corum custodiam; sed postea Regem ad petitionem populi quasi indignatus concessit, ut patet per hoc quod dixit ad Samuelem I. Reg. 8:7. *Non te abjecerunt, sed me, ne regnem super eos.* Instituit tamen a principio circa Regem instituendum, primo quidem modum eligendi, in quo duo determinavit, ut scilicet in ejus electione expectarent judicium Domini, et ut non facerent Regem alterius gentis: quia tales Reges solent parum affici ad gentem cui praeficintur, et per consequens non curare de ea. Secundo ordinavit circa Reges institutos, qualiter deberent se habere quantum ad

The Saintly Doctor proposes another point in these terms:

> Just as a kingdom is the most perfect government, so
> is tyranny the greatest corruption of a government.
> But the Lord, upon establishing the kings, gave them
> a tyrannical right, since we read: *This will be the right
> of the king who will govern: he will take your sons,* etc.
> So the law did not establish princes in a convenient
> way.[5]

Listen to the answer, Elpidio, and you will be astonished at the
firmness, clarity, and solidity with which the Angel of the
Schools maintains the *angelical doctrine* of the liberty of the
nations:

> One must answer—it says—that said right does not
> correspond to the king by divine institution, but that
> rather the usurpation of the kings, who repeal a
> wicked right, degenerating into tyrants and stealing
> from their subjects, was predicted; which is clear, be-
> cause at the end of the text it is added: *you will be
> slaves,* which properly belongs to tyranny, because
> tyrants govern their subjects as slaves; so one can
> conclude that Samuel only wanted to scare the people
> so that they would not ask for a king, since the text

---

seipsos, ut scilcet non multiplicarent currus, et equos: neque uxores neque
etiam inmensas divitias: quia ex cupiditate horum principes ad tyrannidem
declinant, et justitiam dereliquunt. Instituit etiam qualiter se deberent
habere ad Deum, ut scilicet semper legerem, et cogitarent de lege Dei, et
semper essent in Dei timore, et obedientia. Instituit etiam qualiter se
haberent ad subditos suos, ut scilicet non superbe eos contemnerent, aut
opprimerent, neque etiam a justitia declinarent.

5. Praeterea. Sicut regnum est optimum regimen, ita tyrannis est pes-
sima corruptio regiminis. Sed Dominus Regem instituendo, instituit jus
tryannicum: dicitur enim 1. Reg. 8:2. *Hoc erit jus Regis moderaturus est
vobis: filios vestros tollet,* etc. Ergo inconvenienter fuit provisum per legem
circa principum ordinationem.

continues: *but the people did not wish to hear the voice of Samuel,* etc., etc.[6]

As regards plundering, that Saintly Doctor presents and resolves it with this argument: "Princes take away many things from their subjects through violence, which seems like a kind of pillaging; and it would be a grave thing to say that therefore princes sin, since then almost all princes would be condemned. Then it seems that it is not illicit to take something by pillaging."[7] The answer is tremendous:

If princes—says the Saintly Doctor—demand from their subjects what it takes to *preserve the common good,* though violence is used it is not pillaging; but if princes undeservingly take away something through violence, it is *pillaging* and *thievery.* Because of this Saint Augustine said: *Aside from justice, what are the kingdoms if not great robberies? As for the robberies, what are they if not small kingdoms?* And in Ezechiel it is said: *Its princes in its midst as wolves stealing their prey.* Therefore they are obliged to restitution and are *thieves,* and they sin all the more gravely the more dangerous and commonplace is their action against public justice, for the custody of which they are entrusted.[8]

---

6. At quintum dicendum, quod illud ius non debbatur Regis ex institutione divina, sed magis praenuntiabatur usurpatio Regum, qui sibi iusiniquum constitunt, in tyranndem degenerantes, et subdtos depraedantes, et hoc patet per hoc quod in fine subdit: *Vosque eritis ei servi:* quod proprie pertinet ad tyrannidem: quia tyranni suis subditis principantur ut servis: unde hoc dcebat Samuel ad terremdum eos, ne Regent peterent: sequitur enim: *Noluit autem audire populus vocem Samuelis.*

7. Potest tamem contingere quod bonus Rex absque tyrannide filios tollat, et constituat tribunos, et centuriones, et multa accipiat a subditis suis propter comunne bonum procurandum. Thomas, Segunda 2 ae. q. 66, art. 18.

8. Ad tertium dicendum, quod si Principes a subditis exigant quod eis sucundum justitiam debetur propter bonum commune conservandum, eti-

The text of Saint Augustine quoted by Saint Thomas deserves particular attention and I do not think it will displease you to include it completely. After the quoted words, Saint Augustine continues:

> The same army is of men, governed by the command of princes, subject to the stipulation of society, the prey capriciously divided. If this evil grows by the addition of corrupted people so that it may overpower places, affix its own place, occupy cities and subjugate nations, it will evidently take the name of kingdom, which it is given in public not by agitated greed but by aggregate impunity. A pirate answered great Alexander, who had imprisoned him, truthfully and with elegance when upon the king asking what he thought of his crime of infesting the seas, he said insolently and freely: "the same as you with regard to the globe of the earth; but since I do it with a small ship they call me thief; and because you do it with large armies they call you emperor."[9]

---

amsi violentia adhibeatur, non est rapiña. Si vero aliquid Principes indebite extorqueant per violentiam, rapiña est, sicus et latrocinium. Unde dicit Augustinus in IV de Civ. Dei (cap. IV in princ.): *Remota justitia, quid sunt regna nisi magna latrocinia? quia et latrocinia quid sunt nisi parva regna?* Et Ezechiel (22.27) dicitur: *Principes ejust in medio ejus, quasi lupi rapientes praedam.* Unde ad restitutionem tenentur, sicut et latrones: et tanto gravius peceant quam latrones, quanto periculosius, et communius contra publicam justitiam agunt, cujus custodes sunt positi.

9. Remota itaque justia, quid sunt regna, nisi magna latrocinia? quia et ipsa latrocinia quid sunt, nisi parva regna? Manus et ipsa hominum est. imperio principis regitur, pacto societatis adstringitur, placiti lege praeda dividitur. Hoc malum si in tantum perditorum hominum accesibus crescit, ut et loca teneat, sedes constituat, civitates occuper, populos subjuget, evidentius regni nomen assumit, quod ei jam in manifesto confert non adempa cupiditas, sed addita impunitas. Eleganter enim et veraciter Alexandro illo Magno quidam comprehensus pirata respondit. Nam cum idem rex hominem interrogasset quid ei videretur, ut mate haberet infestum: illi libera contumacia. Quod tibi, inquit, ut orbem terrarum: sed quia id ego exiguo navigio facio, latro vocor; quia tu magna classe, imperator. St. Augustine, *The City of God,* book 4, chapter 4.

Can one talk more firmly and can one attack despotism more harshly? How can it be said that the Church fosters it, when it places upon its altars and reveres the images of these wonders of science, of virtue and of Christian freedom, whose immortal works are the norm of all their theologians? And why then, you will say, does despotism not prohibit these works? They are sure of the effect without running the risk of its being their cause: they have entrusted this responsibility to the irreligious, who by all means will make the reading of such works hateful, and this hate is more powerful than the most severe censorship. The despots manage, therefore, to gull many ignorant ones into believing that their despotism is precisely based on the works of the Fathers, and because of the reverence they have for them do not dare to suspect it is unjust, much less resist it. On the other hand, they scorn the shots from the same irreligiosity that has served them as a tool; since it is so menacing, it is sufficient for them to call irreligious any enlightened person who dares oppose them, and they easily succeed by saying that he is an enemy of the Holy Fathers. It is a victory for despotism to present itself as a target of the shots of irreligiosity and so in this manner provokes it sometimes; but it trembles when it sees itself attacked by virtue.

Who but a person of science and the eminent virtue of St. Ambrose would have dared to whittle away the glories of a triumphant emperor, treating him as a criminal, reprimanding him for his cruel despotism and subjecting him to public penitence? After a cruel massacre in Thessalonica, the great Theodosius approached the temple like a wounded bleeding tiger looking for shelter in which to rest a moment, evading the horror caused by the sight of the palpitating remains of his victims. The saintly prelate met and stopped him with the terrible sword of the divine word, like the guardian angel of Paradise, whose fruits are kept in the sacred temple; and that prince, whose voice led the Roman eagles to conduct death to all the land, subjecting it to his empire, humbled himself before the priest of the Lord, in whose face virtue shone as a beam of eternal light. Listen, to the vigorous phrases of the most eloquent Ambrose:

With what eyes do you dare to look, oh emperor, at the temple of the one who is Lord of us all? How can you attempt to raise to God your hands, which are still steaming with unjustly spilled blood? How can you dare to touch the sacred body of the Savior of the world with those same hands stained in the butchery committed in Thessalonica? And how could you dare to receive that precious blood in a mouth that, in the fury of passion, pronounced the unjust and cruel words that have caused the spilling of blood of so many innocent? Leave, then, and see how you add one crime to another.[10]

These terrible words frightened emperor Theodosius in such a way that he left weeping; and submitting himself to an eight month-penitence gave satisfaction to offended humanity and served as an example to all who govern. Would the harshest curse from the lips of irreligiosity have caused such a positive effect? No, my friend; the rebuttals of the irreligious are like the puns of comedians, they lose all their strength as soon as we recall the role they play. Despotism has never been held back by the mordant remarks and abuse of the *presumed* philosophers; on the contrary, it has always acquired more vigor to continue its oppressions, rather like a runaway horse that increases his speed and does not respect any object in his path, while greater is the clamor of those who imprudently unbridled it. Yes, the saintly restraint of religion is the only one that can subdue human passions when power guarantees impunity; and those who intend to destroy this sacred link leave the human race completely defenseless against tyranny, which makes fun of the laws and scorns the declamations of the misguided. They try to use the laws as barriers when they themselves have voided them of virtue and reduced them to pompous phrases that lack consistency, in the manner of balloons with which children have fun.

Not so the words of the just. They indicate their divine

---

10. See Theodotus, *Ecclesiastical History,* chapter 17.

origin, and no matter how great the power and grandeur of mortals may be, a sentiment that they cannot manage to silence does not cease to repeat that heaven is more powerful and grand; and the strength to resist is lacking where resistance is useless. Just as the lightning bolt of Olympus stops the warrior, whose courage was always sound when he was attacking his equals, and makes him tremble, so does the voice of the just move the exalted wicked, whose perverse intentions were always promoted by the efforts their unfortunate victims made to distract them. Irreligiosity, knowing its danger, has always managed to allow the confusing uproar of human passions to prevent this celestial voice from being heard; but since it is eternal, it allows itself to be perceived during the resting periods of its fatigued antagonists. The irreligious, then, hears the reproval of his irreligiosity, the despot hears the sentence against his sin and the tyrant hears the celestial decrees of his extermination. Nevertheless, with stubborn perseverance, disguised under the name of power, these miserable ones continue in their sinful attempt; they again excite the passions, so as not to hear that divine voice that condemns them, and their delirium increases so much that they think of each other as enemies when they all have the same origin and aspire to the same ends. There is no doubt that the irreligious, the despot and the tyrant are three types of rebels against divinity whose motive is pride, and all turn to break the links that unite people with their Supreme Being. The irreligious breaks them by denying his existence; the despot breaks them by scorning divine commands; and the tyrant (who is a destructive despot of a high degree), breaks them by usurping Divinity and making himself owner of people's lives and arbiter of their belongings and future.

It is therefore evident that irreligiosity facilitates the necessary means to despotism and tyranny, and we can say that it prepares the way in such a manner that it leaves no obstacle of any kind. How could there be an obstacle, if such links do not exist and the being that could constitute them does not yet exist? The despot and the tyrant are free of all cares and ought not even to think of such disputes. What horrible consequences derive from this principle! And what do we say about those intent on implanting it?

DIFFERENT CLASSES OF SOCIETY
SUFFERING FROM IRRELIGIOSITY

I repeat this a thousand and one times, Elpidio: with an ignorance equalled only by their perseverance, the irreligious have managed to ridicule religion and discourage people from reading the works of the masters of virtue and the art of living; the irreligious have neither done in the past nor do in the present anything but favor tyranny. It is impossible for a tyrant to establish himself in a virtuous nation. These are monsters from hell and can only be nurtured and flattered by the infernal hydras: but in the midst of the sons of a just heaven, in the midst of true Christians, they find themselves abandoned and die of hunger. It is necessary to have rogues and fools in order to have tyrants, and it is not the works of the Fathers of the Church that can form such elements. They are formed by a multitude of justifications of a ridiculous Pyrrhonism, which with the erroneous title of philosophical works are to be found everywhere, drawing applause from a crowd of *brilliant fools,* who with all the refinements of cultured society exceed the barbarity of jungle savages. They are formed by a portion of scoundrels dressed as clergymen, who with shame to their sacred ministry and with tears from true ecclesiatics, strengthen irreligiosity by their total apathy, and perhaps are the first irreligious. They are formed by a multitude of sashed and unsashed monkeys, which they wrongly call the military, only because they are dressed as such, though they do not care for the honor of their uniform; and so they permit its dishonor, and change it with ease, because their purpose is none other than to gain without worrying about the means. Among these *illustrious traitors* to the cause of the nations that support them there is hardly one who is not irreligious; and how could someone not be who profanes a profession that protects justice and national rights, a profession wisely introduced into society to control crime and give strength to its laws? How, I repeat, could one who abuses such dear responsibility not be a loathsome irreligious? Lacking in public trust he establishes himself in the ministry of despotism and infringes upon all divine and human laws. Is there anyone who believes that in such an evil heart there is a single spark of the sacred fire of religion?

With what sorrow they see themselves mixed and alternating with this *decorated mob,* whose audacity and impunity are based on the abuse of the arms placed in their hands to defend the country; with what sorrow they see themselves part of a corps of deformed members of society; the true illustrious military people, or, better said, the only military people who, to the acclaim of their fellow citizens, march in the path of honor to the temple of glory!

Known more for their virtues and important services than for distinctions and insignia of class, they receive the esteem of all good people but are very soon attacked by the monster of irreligiosity who fears that their example could provide the nations a saintly militia. It therefore makes use of every means, and these honorable military personnel are made by their uniformed companions to look like foolish dreamers, slaves of despotism, like people governed by the clergy, whom no one can count on for anything noble. They should say, for nothing irreligious.

The results are, therefore, that since the nation lacks the support of a just militia it sees itself in the hands of the despots, which send their *famous assassins* to kill and destroy at will, as long as they manage to secure the chains that oppress humanity against the will of the Supreme Being. Irreligiosity raises numerous favorite sons, and places them in high destinies trusting its cause to them, a cause to which they are always faithful, just as they were unfaithful to the noble cause of justice and saintly freedom, which are irreconcilable with irreligious sentiments and the ambitious goals of these cowards. Yes, I repeat, of these cowards. Because they do not know organized courage, which is the only virtuous one, we see them surrender to fury or to condescension and weakness, being in both cases completely won over by a degrading passion. They do not have that saintly valor that is fitting for a dignified military, which is like an angel of justice sent from heaven to maintain his rights over earth when the laws have lost their power and are not obeyed through perversity or the people's foolishness. That courage that does not fear death by justice, but does fear imposing it without it; that courage undisturbed by the threats of crime, but always humble and sensitive to the voice of virtue. How few military people do we find nowadays who possess this saintly courage! And what is the cause of such loss if not irreligiosity? Who but this monster from Avernus has placed at the hands of the despots those devastating furies, with which they subvert innocence, ridicule justice, extinguish wisdom, destroy liberty, desecrate religion, and, in a word, annihilate everything?

Obedience is the first law in a good militia, but despots would not dare give wicked orders to the military; and if they were forced to act unjustly, they would never go beyond the demands of obedience and would never have the barbaric pleasure of adding new cruelties and greater injustices to those attempted by their perverse commanders. The nations would see in them brothers who attacked them with sorrow and only out of necessity, but not tigers that take advantage of the occasion to devour and who wish not to put an end to killings. A just army is always comforting to a nation, just as a wicked one is always a misfortune.

Rogues and fools are also formed by the bad example of others in the same class, who to dishonor religion take the most sacred insignia as a mark of their cunning irreligiosity. Yes, they take the adored cross of the Savior of the world and carry it over their hearts precisely to indicate how much they detest it. These notorious irreligious persons, whose intrigues and schemes against religion and whose infamous means in acquiring such decorations are well known, call themselves *knights* of such or other cross, and dishonor the true *knights*, who are good men, deserving by reason of their virtues and heroic actions such as illustrious distinction as the cross of the Lord, which a grateful nation has placed over their hearts indicating honor and saintly patriotism. These are the crosses that the nation considers legitimately bestowed, but the majority of them have been desecrated by this ridiculous force. We Christians use the sign of the cross to drive away the devil and to prevent his entrance, but it would seem that many of these false knights wear the cross over their hearts to prevent his exit, for fear that the devil himself may be horrified to live in such a heart and try to escape. How many of these *knights of the crosses of exit* you must know, my dear Elpidio! Irreligiosity varies greatly with its disguises and is never more dangerous than when it hides behind the veil of virtue and the very religion it wants to destroy. Under the most affable names of heroism, nobility and other similar titles, it fools a multitude of heedless ones and excites the most terrible passions. They who have been victims of ambition become ambitious themselves when virtue is missing, and in this way irreligiosity provides satellites to despotism, increasing the number of these knights of *the cross of exit.* You laugh? And why should I not give an order so vast and notorious its proper title? Without a doubt, noting irreligiosity in the diverse classes that compose the social body, you will expect me not to pass over in silence the judicature and all its aggregates; but permit me to say nothing about these merchants of justice, legal thieves, corruptors of morals, oppressors of the poor, swindlers of widows, assassins of all honor and enemies of people's happiness and peace. Mixed with these are people meritorious for their science and virtue, who as true instruments of justice diffuse comfort when they diffuse innocence and oppose crime; but these beneficient beings are so unusual that they become like the monster of a class, which seems to be perverted by nature. How happy the nations would be if irreligiosity had not corrupted such a useful and necessary state! But what a misfortune when the interpreters and guardians of the laws are its unpunished violators! And do you think that a truly religious learned person could be so, or that a truly irreligious could not but be so?

The observations I have just made do not seek to discredit the classes to which they refer. Quite the contrary, my sole purpose is to indicate how these classes suffer the influence of irreligiosity, which is always a strange body that does not mix with the other parts. The greatest torment to inflict on a good person is to confuse him with rogues; and even more so when certain insignia adopted by society as essential to a class make the distinction between the good people and the bad impossible, thus creating this misfortune. An honest military man must dress like all the rogues of his class and enter his ranks; an ecclesiastic deserving of this name wears the same habit as the wicked who unfortunately are of the same ministry; and hence the result is that discredit is general, and the entire class suffers when only certain individuals should.

Here lies one of the gravest wrongs produced by irreligiosity. All the classes of the State are corrupted by it, all of them lose their true prestige, which consists of the appreciation and trust of their people, and they keep only the appearance of prestige, or better said, the privilege of wearing signs or decorations that have already become ignominious. The good are ashamed to wear them but are compelled to do so, and the bad try to profit as much as they can from this vain splendor, convinced by the testimony of their conscience that they cannot expect anything from a people that loathes them. Society, then, remains void of virtue and reduced to a great theater in which diverse classes of frauds play diverse roles for the money they are paid. In such a theater, not in a well-organized society, ill-fated despotism can present itself with great insolence and audacity, assured of being suffered by the lack of trust that exists in all classes, which are the bases of the State, and thus the people cannot find any defenders of their rights among them. On the other hand, they are persuaded to believe it impossible to counteract the action of so many and such perverse corporations. True patriots of the nation moan when they see so much deception, but they cannot remedy it, because to live in society one must belong to a certain class or be useless, unless we speak of an extraordinary person who belongs to his own singular class or has no need of any.

This is the reason no political system, be what it may, can last in such a nation. A system of government is like an architectural plan, which when well done makes a great building; but it supposes that the rocks are solid, for if these give way the magnificence of the work only serves to make its ruin more terrible. There is no doubt that political institutions and civil laws serve to protect and motivate, but they are not enough to consolidate nations. They are like clothing that protects the body and frees it from the cold; but if the body is infected, clothing cannot heal it. A social prudence, the product of morality and wisdom, is the true support of the law, which in turn acquires all its vigor against the perverse. And who could be so demented as to think this prudence can be found in a society of irreligious? No; they will never acquire it, since they have undermined its foundation, which is virtue, with the result that no system can consolidate with them. Only despotism can establish itself with such elements, because it is not a system but barbarity; and therefore it needs rogues and barbarians, which are found in abundance among the irreligious who inundate society under diverse denominations.

Oh Elpidio, what dismal ideas rise in my soul from this sad picture which I have begun to describe, and which I cannot continue: the pen slips from my trembling hand and a cloud of tears blurs my eyes . . . My imagination takes me to very distant regions and my spirit travels through immense fields covered with darkness, which interrupted at times by soft rays of celestial light show horrible precipices where thousands and thousands have already died, and other numerous tribes run heedlessly to the same end. Oh, would that this divine light spread itself uniformly and constantly over the surface of the earth, so that these terrible cliffs would be discovered—these mouths through which hell vomits its furies over the earth. Would that they receive the reflection of the rays of the sun of justice and return blind and confused to the gloomy hell from where they came; would that these disguised monsters be seen in full light, and not be confused any longer with the perfect beings whom they try to imitate in vain.

THE HOPE OF A FREE CHRISTIAN SOCIETY

How happy society would be if, restraining passion and obeying divine law, people would be animated with sentiments of justice and mutual love! The diverse classes would not then be armies that prove their powers and employ all their means to destroy themselves; on the contrary, they would be numerous and well-governed families, which, being part of a perfect social and noble body, would retain mutual interest and appreciation, as if motivated by the same spirit. It would always be a matter of trying to cure the evils and not increase them with a cruel hypocrisy that takes the name of devotion. People would not destroy themselves for mere desires: as brothers and sisters they would first try to preserve themselves and the general well-being of the great family. Unjust pretentions, insults, scorn, mordant satire, offenses and affronts would disappear. Envy would flee from the land and discord would not dare show its horrible face; peace, the daughter of innocence, would extend her happy kingdom, and free from worry, people would work in agreement for the promotion of social well-being. The sciences and arts would see themselves nurtured by those who, having cleared away the clouds of worry, could perceive their beauties and appreciate their treasures. Instead of beasts that make use of them to destroy the weak, human frailties would find artisans of goodness, in whose hearts they would excite just religiosity and from whom they would receive a soft correction and an efficient remedy. Virtues would appear once the hurricane of arrogance ceased, and under a sky that shows the glory of a God of mercy, a great family would live peacefully and happily, uniting its voice to those stars (work of the omnipotent God) and to the spirits that already live securely in the fountain of love. This would be a nation truly free, enlightened and fortunate; this would be, in a word, a Christian nation.

It is not vain imagination, it is not a mere effect of my religious sentiments; I place the cause in the hands of the enemies of my belief; I establish as a judge that same irreligiosity that so hates and fights it; but such is the evidence of the facts that from its wicked lips I expect the most just of sentences. Let the pages of the Gospel, that Sacred Testament of the author of Christianity, open and each word will bring out a thousand virtues and will destroy a thousand sins. Even the unbeliever, who denies his divine origin, knows that charity moved the pen from the first to the last syllable of this saintly book. Passions are not flattered by it in the least, but rather are always restrained. People are all represented as equals, and without any right, nor the slightest pretext to be unjust; vices are corrected without consideration to the persons, and nature never seems mistreated, but always guided. Good deeds are encouraged with rewards and vices are threatened with eternal punishment. Frankness and generosity, the devaluation of worldly goods, sincere friendship, pure love, peace and happiness, obedience without lowliness and authority without arrogance, science with humility, richness without avarice, poverty without envy, suffering with heroism, greatness of the soul, the importance of ideas, to sum it up, all the celestial gifts, come forth from this divine code. Could this not be what is best for the happy nation I have described? Can there be a truly happy nation without this code of health? No, it is the only one in its nature and origin; it is not the work of people, who are not the possessors of happiness; it comes from the hands of the only Being who can give it. The tyrant trembles when he opens it, but the free person finds pleasure in reading it; the criminal becomes fearful and the just comforts himself with its presence; this is the code, it says, of the children of heaven; these are the laws of the city of peace and happiness; this is the fruit of the tree of life; these are the tokens of the most saintly betrothal, in which a fortunate flock unites with the most beneficent shepherd, by whose side it rests without fear of attack from butchering wolves.

Several times I have thought, Elpidio, about the analogy between the Catholic Church and free societies, and I have always concluded that Christianity and liberty are inseparable; and that when the latter sees itself persecuted, it finds refuge only in Christian temples. On the threshold of these sacred asylums remain the works of human pride, and only the work of God enters the human person. Therefore, saintly religion receives all its children with the same affection, grants them the same prerogatives, invites them to the same banquet and does not in any way uphold the distinctions (just or unjust) that the world has established between them. It speaks to them in a language both loving and severe, to reprimand their vices and preach love and justice to them. A celestial council, in which saintly liberty reigns united to a just obedience, forms in the saintly temple, and people learn equality without losing their individuality, since the rich and the poor, the wise and the ignorant, the powerful and the weak, and even the princes themselves, along with their subjects, form a family, all considering themselves subjects of the same law and free from oppression and injustice. The august mother of this unanimous family says goodbye to her children with the blessings of heaven, recommending peace and benevolence to them, mutual charity, which, more vigorous than the law, makes up for their defects and keeps the nations in perfect harmony. She implants social obligations and advises them never to lack mutual love; that far from persecuting each other they should help each other, as sons of the Celestial Father, who loves everyone, sustains everyone and protects everyone. She tells them, in summary, to preserve outside the saintly place the Christian sentiments they have nurtured inside it, and upon going back to the world not to forget that they have lived in heaven. Yes in heaven, because of the spiritual union with the God of heaven, because of the sublime idea and celestial virtues they have received as a free gift in that august house and before the throne of the Eternal One.

With such sentiments true Christians leave the saintly temple, and if they retained them, do you think, my friend, that they could be despots? Do you think that they would tread on the laws, infringe upon rights, destroy peace and spark war? It is evident, therefore, that Christianity is irreconcilable with tyranny and that any true Christian society is truly free. A Christian nation forms an immense temple, whose extension does not diminish its order but rather increases the sacred fire of love, increasing the number of virtuous persons. Liberty fears nothing when virtue is assured; and power is used with approval, and without obstacles, when justice and not perversity guides those who command.

Irreligiosity tries in vain to present the spacious plans of illusory societies; in vain it inundates the globe with visionary books in order to make up for the beneficial effects of saintly religion. The base is weak and the social giant cannot establish himself on it. There is no perfect society without perfect love, and an irreligious society can never be perfect. The perfection of love depends upon the object loved and the constancy and way of the one who loves; and there is only one perfect being, and that is God; only one constant way, and that is the unalterable light of religion; and there is only one just way of loving, and that is by referring all to the Supreme Being. Could irreligiosity do this? She toasts us with pleasures too suddenly embittered, with a science too soon disproved and with magnificent power that vanishes with one blow from virtue, disappearing like a dense cloud in a contrary wind, leaving nothing but the memory of its ridiculous arrogance. It cannot be the principle of just love and well-being; it cannot be the foundation of a free society; it can only nurture the hydras over which rests the despicable throne of tyranny.

FINAL OBSERVATIONS ON THE HUMOR
OF IRRELIGIOUS MASKS

Let us interrupt these serious thoughts to have some fun remembering the foolishness, the gestures and contests of the *sages of social debates,* whom you have many times observed.[(46)] Imagine one of these *philosophical frauds* entering a great event, so swollen with pride that it lifts him from the floor, which he barely touches with the tip of his little shiny fitted shoe, in such a way that he could run over fragile crystal without breaking it. The elegance, composition and adornment of attire, curled locks and perfumes indicate the time he has spent dressing; and the well-rehearsed and mysterious looks, symmetrical steps, and stylized gestures and movements complete the signs of spiritual superficiality and an idle life. No sooner does he sit down than he lets it be known that he is a philosopher and a true-blue *liberal,* and without any other proof or guarantee other than his word, he assures us that there cannot be liberty while there are fools that believe in religion and that it has been invented to maintain despotism. He repeats enthusiastically the names of some famous irreligious persons, but does not quote from their works, since he has not even read them. He talks of the contradictions of the Bible (which he has never opened) and speaks against idle clergy (he himself being a prototype of idleness). He ridicules everyone, without noting that he is a model of ridicule. The guests fix their eyes on this *refined fool,* who, taking the soft mockeries as just praises, continues vomiting *sublime foolishness,* and after having wasted time, leaves the gathering, thinking he has discovered the hidden secrets of the deepest philosophy and provided a great service to the cause of liberty.

If these crazy *serious-comedian-philosophers* were treated as such, it would matter little to society that they continue in their delirium; but unfortunately they find many as foolish as they are, although not as vain, who do not perceive their madness and follow their advice using them as models. I consider them as the most efficient agents of despotism, since they do not seem suspicious to their unwary enemies, although they cannot hide from experts who, being so few, scarcely cause concern. These *wise figurines* are like mosquitoes, for, being weak and insignificant, they manage with their first bites and with great presumptuousness to preoccupy the most populous society, and to interrupt the most useful works. We should, therefore, scare them off with a puff of indifference and contempt, but never actually hit them in order to prevent their bite. After they play a second political-religious trick without being noticed, they will forego a third, realizing that it is a bad idea. You well know that these *political chameleons* thrive on the air of vanity, and when it does not find support, they leave baffled. How much ground despots would lose if these *erudite jugglers* found another profession!

Only the one who cannot be a slave is truly free, and this prerogative is only fit for the virtuous. Enjoy it, Elpidio, for heaven has granted it to you for the comfort of good people and the glory of the fatherland.

THE CAUSE OF IRRELIGIOSITY

In my search for the causes of all irreligious behavior, I think I can narrow them down to two specific kinds: the heart and the mind of human beings.

Vice is like a cancer which renders insensitive the organs it invades. This is why a sinner hears wise counsel with indifference and witnesses virtuous behavior with detachment. Eventually the wise and the virtuous will disturb him and he will wish to get rid of them, but realizing it is impossible to do so without doing away with religion, he declares his animosity against it without truly inspecting it. This person will not take the trouble to examine religious doctrine, because he will not abstain from pleasures which cannot be compensated for by spiritual sentiments, so weak or nonexistent is his sensibility. Persistent neglect of remorse greatly reduces its effectiveness and judging its nature by the results, the person begins to question its reality. This is the first step to irreligiosity.

The person inclined to vice dares not to confront the good, which previously he only neglected, and his audacity will soon lead him to the temple of *pompous ignorance* that assumes the name of philosophy. Here he encounters the idols his depraved heart adores, idols that have taken sacrosanct names as if to do honor to the truth in the very attempt to deceive. This, Elpidio, is called the "temple of reason" just because reason is confined

73

there; incense is offered there to the monster of evil, despicable usurper of the august throne. Soon the unrestrained person finds his place among such foolish idolators, all the while believing himself to be among philosophers.

From now on he no longer thinks reasonably, but submits to *irreligious dogmatism* just to escape the religious one. The similarity between his new ideas and his heart's desires weighs heavily in favor of the former, and having reached the point of wishing to be irreligious the person achieves his aim. He begins to avoid as evil thoughts all religious ideas and dares not to examine them for fear of losing his delightful way of life. Let me repeat, my dear Elpidio, he is an irreligious dogmatist who mocks religious dogma, and he is chained by irreligiosity as the faithful is by faith. But, what difference between these two chains! An infinitely wise and just Being reveals sublime truths through indubitable signs, through works beyond the range of created power, and because of all of these, he expects a faith all the more *reasonable* for its most solid base. All ideas opposed to this undoubtably correct doctrine can now be held only as undoubtably false, while any sane person, any true philosopher, can and must believe without misgivings, aware as he is that his greatest freedom is that from the danger of error. He worships the goodness of a merciful God who warns him of the abysses into which he would have fallen.

Quite different indeed is the position of the irreligious! He rejects because he does not understand; through his own experience he has realized he cannot understand everything and has sensed the narrow limits of his mind. Yet his reason cries out warning him how shaky are the foundations of his unbelief and reminding him of his ignorance to annoy his arrogance. He complains about the restraint imposed on his reasoning by a benevolent religion, like a child who complains about the loving firmness of a mother who will not let him run toward a precipice; to make his insanity complete, he permits irreligiosity to deprive him of any guide and to blind him with a host of disordered passions while inviting him to run ahead. Heavy indeed are the chains that anchor to earth a spirit born in heaven!

In this miserable situation the person can be aware only of

earthly objectives and will think there are no others. Action proves the existence of objectives, and earthly ones alone will move his impassioned soul to action. And so he rates as absurd the fiction of beings that give no sign of their existence, and as a show of sad weakness the crowding of one's mind with vain intimidations against earthly pleasures. No matter how unfounded, this way of being seems well grounded to him, and he renews his determination to carry on his sinful life all in the name of science. Now his chains have been clamped fast and the unhappy person no longer attempts to break them; rather he likes them, to his great misfortune.

However, some rays of divine light occasionally lighten up this dark prison and let its horrors be perceived quite clearly, but the irreligious cannot endure it and he shuts his eyes in the weak state he calls his nature. His pride stirs up a cloud of disordered passions and restores the cherished darkness, and with it that fatal laxity settles in again. Then he conceives new plans and uses new tactics to block the light that disturbs his pleasant dreams, and he proclaims himself the enemy of whoever attempts to dispel darkness. This is the source of that hate all irreligious people feel for the religiously minded, whose presence they find frightening even as they look down on them with haughty contempt. They think they would be happy again if only this false light of religion would no longer disturb them and so many deluded people would cease to insist on transmitting it. To fool themselves all the more convincingly they consider the discomfort and remorse that occasionally disturb them as the result of poor education and childhood habits. They struggle with their heart until it gives up and quiets down.

Nevertheless, they know well that such false calm cannot last unless reflection is curtailed, hence the endless round of entertainment and the loose life of these pseudophilosophers. Entertainment is necessary in prison. The best way to endure it is to pretend it is not a prison but, quite the opposite, the palace of freedom.

Let us follow the steps of this poor slave of his passion, and we shall feel more and more compassion for his miserable situation. He becomes easily irritated by the slightest provocation and so he is unable to reason precisely and objectively. He experiences continuous fury unmitigated even by light humor, and since he cannot obtain his goals he lives in a pitiful state. Stubbornness takes the place of prudence and the consequence is irreligiosity. No doubt, Elpidio, this abominable sin does not present itself clearly to the irreligious because he is always suffering under brutal conditions—which he calls philosophy— that is to say, under an apathy born of the insensibility I have spoken of before, or in a state of frenetic agitation that transforms him into a *respected fool.* That is, he becomes a stone or a beast and for that reason serves only as a monument of ignorance or a model of anger. You know well that if these moods become habits, they take away religion as well as science.

No doubt you will answer me that there are wise persons who are not religious, and that then my observations are not true. Let us examine this point, my dear friend, and do not accuse me of animosity, because my soul is free from this passion, being filled only with appreciation and compassion for a great number of my fellow citizens who suffer under the most dangerous of sicknesses, the one that appears as a state of perfect health.

You well know that a science is not a mosaic of different or even opposite types of knowledge, with no connection among themselves; these knowledges, rather, must be integrated in a beautiful picture where truth is represented with lasting, bright, pleasant colors, never irritating to the eye. This is why it is not science that provokes arguments; on the contrary, disputes emerge when science is not present and they are useful only as raw materials to be tested as potential parts of a whole.[47] Remembering these ideas, examine the work of the irreligious and you will see that nothing is found in it but the constant assertion of irreligiosity, like the fool's constant repetition of his own theme. You will notice that they do not agree among themselves in any respect; you will see that their writings are a tapestry of disputes or negations, evident signs of ignorance. "Truth" nevertheless pops up from their lips while frequently they affirm that nothing is known, becoming as ridiculous as the old pyrrhonists.

As a consequence, my friend, you will find a great disparity between the scientific and the religious works of irreligious persons. You will perceive more soundness and order in the former, because there they do not play in a foolish key and so they have time for tranquil meditation. But the penchant for daydreaming about religious matters makes the irreligious lose much time, even when it comes to matters that are not religious, and for this reason you will see that among philosophers and mathematicians very few are irreligious. Even though today it is ridiculous to speak about Voltaire, let me remind you how poor is his *Newton's Philosophy,* which contains from time to time quite a lot of nonsense indicating nothing other than a very superficial knowledge of its subject. Those who have wasted their time, *and something more,* by reading his works will certainly not have found anything suggesting great knowledge of natural science, nor of any other branch of science, but literature (not of great quality) and the very unfortunate diffusion of pyrrhonism and irreligiosity.

Do not think that I intend to undermine the esteem that man have for irreligious literary works. Deception on this matter is unproductive and, when it comes to Voltaire, I could rather cite Pyrrhon, who was as evil or even worse than he; nevertheless, Pyrrhon performed an act of justice by stripping Voltaire of all vain splendor acquired by his calculated and aggressive wit, and portraying him as a second-class but eminently arrogant genius. But instead of considering the scientific merit—real or feigned—of those unfortunate victims of irreligiosity, I will limit myself to observing that irreligiosity takes root in this fashion: its ideas are exaggerated by the impulses and delights of a vain glory. Behold new chains, behold, my friend, an obstacle for the true enlightenment that is always the fruit of impartiality. Nothing is more pleasing but what increases this presumed merit, and since people rarely watch at leisure objects that do not please them, there necessarily results an aversion to the study of religious maxims and a delight in the sophisms that refute those maxims.

The irreligious, then, takes a most imprudent step forward in his pursuit of sin, and he dares to state that there is pleasure only in irreligiosity, that the delights of virtue are chimerical, that happiness is irreconcilable with the deprivations that religion has invented; these ideas eventually alienate him until, like a somnambulist, he roams aimlessly, unaware that he is

being misled by his own monstrous imagination. Only a powerful shock will free him from this ridiculous and pitiful enslave-
ment. But since it is impossible to discover this efficacious
agent except in the very religion he despises, his sickness remains incurable, the remedy rejected.

THE EFFECT OF SADNESS

In such unfortunate circumstances, the irreligious becomes prey to something no less harmful than indifference or
anger: oppressive sadness. Do not ignore, Elpidio, the fatal
impact of this passion upon personal morale, and then you
will undoubtedly agree with me that sadness cannot go hand
in hand with true religion, which is the purest source of joy.
The irreligious's sadness is produced not only by the uncertainty of his fate, but by the absence of what we can call
nourishment of the spirit, acquisition of truth. The unbeliever
becomes disgusted by his very irreligiosity and, unable to find
truth, cannot obtain happiness (it would help his own argument if others had not found truth either). But, Elpidio, observe the difference between the sadness that sometimes as-
sails the just and the sadness that overtakes the irreligious,
and then you will know more clearly the origin of both kinds
of sadness.[48] Giving in to one of the temptations of human
nature, the just gives himself over to sadness, but only as a
shelter and a barrier that compels him to return soon, without
any reluctance, from the misfortunes of this corrupted century
back to the delicious peace found within the human heart.
Displeased with the horrible way of sin and human miseries,
the just returns with holy constancy and surrenders himself
unalterably into the arms of a compassionate God, from
whom even his most hard-hearted enemy could not separate
him. The just is more confident than ever in blessed happiness
when he realizes that he can retain this happiness even in the
midst of all types of tribulations; these tribulations are to his
soul as clothing is to the body; they can disguise it, but they
do not alter its nature or deprive it of its robustness. But for

the irreligious these tribulations increase his irreligiosity, and like opprobrium, he is ratified in it. There is nothing in his heart that can console him because his sadness originated within himself. The world offers him nothing but total emptiness, and taking this fact as tested by experience he is confirmed in his own stubbornness. Unaware of his own delirium, he is confirmed in his irreligiosity. He does not relish acknowledging that he does not know, he does not manifest any doubts, but firmly maintains that everyone else is a fanatic. Such is the fruit of irreligiosity rooted in sadness.

Another source of irreligiosity is the pleasure that sarcasm and harsh censure give to the sinner. Since religious subjects have nothing in common with worldly ones and are surrounded by a mysterious aura, they provide buffoons with enough material for thousands of anecdotes, lies, and jokes, which the irreligious knows are unjust, but enjoys anyway, especially when they have produced the intended effect. Some of the irreligious get this malignant habit, and like mischievous and incorrigible children, they do not miss an occasion to mortify the believer with some jeers or ridiculous calumny. Sometimes the religious also respond with falsities that instead of convincing the irreligious provoke his exasperation. This is a great incentive for irreligiosity and an almost insuperable obstacle for just philosophical freedom. One can easily see that this irreligious type acts more out of revenge than according to system, but these ideas nevertheless become so familiar to them that they finally adopt them thoughtlessly. Suddenly they become truly irreligious when they had started out only as buffoons.

Young people tend towards this type of irreligiosity, because it is somewhat appropriate to their way of thinking and character, some of them reject this vice when they reach maturity. However, these are not very common cases. Usually we observe that the *irreligious habit,* which cannot be called by any other name, continues producing lamentable effects throughout a whole lifetime unless, by the extraordinary power of divine grace, a conversion takes place—the most difficult of conversions since the irreligious habit is the most deeply rooted illness.

CAUSES FROM THE MIND

Now let us talk about another type of cause of irreligiosity, which we can call *ideological,* beause it originates in the mind and produces only a hardness of heart that hinders religious feelings at the same time that it gives in to all kinds of sin. In general, all the irreligious are immoral. But sometimes one witnesses the extraordinary phenomenon of very righteous people, or at least those not guilty of any kind of scandal, who, nevertheless, are not religious. These examples are very lamentable and they do more harm than the corruption of irreligious persons because they serve as a shield to protect the sin that always seeks to defend itself and prove it is not a cause of irreligiosity. What a horrible monster is this that even sin is ashamed for having engendered it and pretends to disown it!

Take note, Elpidio, that there are two kinds of influences in the moral system which, like strong winds, blow human longings here and there. When these winds are rooted in sensuality and begin in the heart, even though they are make-believe, they raise a cloud to darken the mind and make the person vulnerable to sinful pleasures; the *dissolute irreligious* is then in place. At other times irreligiosity starts by a network of ideas before any action takes place or even any assent is given to those ideas by the person. These ideas bring about a hallucination that does not allow the mind to perceive abstractions and spiritual beings; but the mind can still perceive material realities and basic principles of public morality that both the law and public opinion support.

When free from strong passions, a person can lead his own life in relation to the things he perceives but he cannot regulate what he is not able to reach, or what he has erroneously determined is an unquestionable truth. Consequently there is irreligiosity that is accompanied by certain *social justice* and by a sense of honor which resents the slightest attack or disdain from public opinion. Without realizing it, these irreligious are practicing believers and they have never abandoned their inclinations, which, without the guidance of religious ideas, would merely be *honorable silliness.* As I said in my last letter, the unbeliever who follows public opinion and morality in spite of being able totally to disregard them is a most ridiculous fool. In fact, he is handing over to his enemies the arms with which to destroy him, that is, the means to convince him of his folly if he is genuinely candid or perfidy if he is merely feigning.

What is this network of ideas that leads to irreligiosity? All those ideas that form a religious system. Religion is not a system because it is not the work of humans, and although it can truly be systematized, religion is not necessarily limited to these purely human projects. Dogmas are not deducted from one another like geometrical truths, and one cannot establish principles by which to reveal religious mysteries. One could only perceive a certain conformity among the dogmas, enough to prove that there is no contradiction among them, but one is never able to demonstrate them by purely natural means. Knowing the existence of God, for instance, one cannot infer the idea of the Trinity, and this known, one could not then infer the idea of the Incarnation, nor from there deduce the idea of the sacraments.

It seems, my dear Elpidio, that since religion is part of the divine science it is not discursive, for as you well know God has all things present before him and therefore does not deduce; only ignorant creatures need to learn by deducing some truths from others. Religion cannot form a science of evidence in man as in God; it has only the most sublime certitude and scientific character, based as it is on the infallibility of the principles from which it proceeds. As a result, as far as we are concerned, religion is a network of facts and nothing more. Therefore, the formation of religious systems is a purely human enterprise, and when one tries to give them divine character it leads to infidelity, since they are frequently in open contradiction with the facts.

This *human religion* runs the risk of all systems, and you know not one is free of grave difficulties. True religion does not admit any doubt or discussion: if you do not believe in God, there is no need to talk about religion; if you do believe in God, there is no need to talk about doubt. I have always said that the nonbelievers who are not atheists are silly, and those who are atheists are stupid. This silliness and stupidity are not perceptible by the miserable who suffer so many illnesses, because their subject is not perceived by the senses and cannot be analytically compared. From this fact results the great difficulty of trying to convince one of these irreligious, whom we could call *moral* since they have not muddied themselves by the indecent and visible vices that degrade other nonbelievers. They begin by deluding themselves, believing that their good moral standing is indicative of the uprightness of their principles, and they worry and have a ridiculous animosity toward any efforts to convince them. The corrupt irreligious is continuously urged to abandon his irreligiosity by the testimony of his conscience and the force of the *sensible arguments* that oppose his conduct; but whoever commits only an intellectual mistake is a far sicker person because nothing can excite a response.

Unbelievers do not perceive that if religion could be the fruit of their arguments it could not have more authority than theirs, which do not satisfy even them, and that the most evident proof of the divine origin of our dogma is that very incomprehensibility they lament so much.

Observe, Elpidio, that among these irreligious endowed with *civic virtues* there are some who only say that they cannot believe, but who cannot find the reason for their unbelief, and there are others who present a lot of difficulties and have at hand a thousand answers for all the arguments in favor of the religion. The difference in their conduct proves the diversity of their cause. Some deny because they do not perceive and others because they have formed erroneous ideas; but, either way, the evil comes from a disastrous mistake, which is to assume that one cannot affirm what one cannot perceive with clarity, and that as a result the very nature of the mystery induces one to deny its existence, or at least to view it with a prudent skepticism. How many wrongs has this reasoning, which looks so well founded, caused and how absurd it is when analyzed impartially!

Reflect, dear friend, and you will see that it is the most ridiculous sophism. There is no doubt that only one affirms what one perceives, nor could one do otherwise even if one should want to, as long as one does not speak as if delirious, not knowing what one says. But this undeniable truth barely applies when one refers to the nature of the mysteries and not to their existence. The intellect perceives the possibility of acts superior to its capability, and then it also perceives the existence of such acts, convinced by clearly perceived proof. And so it is that the intellect never affirms as without knowing. But when it comes to the nature of incomprehensible objects the intellect cannot state anything as a result of its own efforts; on the contrary, it confesses its incapacity. This is how everything comes from an erroneous application of a principle, the very solidity of which deceives even more and is the cause of more pernicious mistakes.

We will be more convinced of these truths when we observe that in fact even the incredulous themselves admit mysteries, though of a different nature. The argument I will propose is commonly known, but little meditated, and yet I could affirm that it has always been neglected, so that as a result the irreligious have said that it is no more than a refuge of religion from the risk of being exposed by the bright light of philosophy. So darkness has been spread under the pretext of divulging culture and clarifying mortality. If good sense and the impartiality of judges prevail, I do not doubt that following reflections will convince any true philosopher.

The human person is a mystery in himself, and if he wants to be sincere he should confess that he does not know himself, nor does he know how he exists or how he works. Yes, because of this ignorance, he dares to deny his own existence, then creates a new mystery, since he is a skeptic, whose possibility the intellect cannot understand and whose existence would be unbelievable were it not confirmed by history. To deny the existence of truth is to confirm its existence, and knowing your liking for the holy Fathers I will quote the incomparable St. Augustine, who expresses this thought with his usual determination: "Suppose, he said, that the Truth does not exist. Will it not be true that it does not exist? But this cannot be true if the Truth is nonexistent. Therefore truth always exists."[1]

Actually, my beloved Elpidio, skepticism is a bigger mystery than all those that surround us in the order of material

---

1. St. Augustine, book 2, Soliloquies, chapter 2.

beings and in the moral world; only lack of reflection can authorize it. As a result whether the person believes or denies, he will always admit a mystery in every one of his intellectual acts, which, well analyzed, will bring him up to a certain point; but once past the limits of human comprehension, once entered into the region of the infinite, he finds himself in darkness, because weak natural light is not enough to reach and brighten those immense regions. Why so much resistance from the irreligious against the religious mysteries? The same St. Augustine gave the answer to this phenomena, which consists in the fact that natural wonders are more popular than religion's, though no less incomprehensible. The person comes to believe easily what is perceived frequently, and the newness of a mystery is the greatest obstacle to its credibility.

Irreligiosity is, in many cases, the wrong application of a principle and of erroneous ideological combinations. It will not be long before a truly educated person gets out of such a mournful condition through meditation, but the fool gets more confused and more convinced of his mistake the more he reflects. This moved me to write on another occasion that the wise are like the sun which helps disperse the dark clouds.

There is nothing more dreadful than an ignorant person pretending to be a philosopher in religious matters, but in any case the quasi-wise are very dangerous insects. A total ignorance, if it is accompanied by sincere humility, is a predisposition to accept the sublime truths that the Almighty reveals to people, making them the custodians, not the owners, and far less the authors, of that invaluable treasure. But a humble science not only predisposes to receive the divine light but helps to conserve it. As a peculiarity of the natural sciences, some argue with ignorance that the sciences conduct to unbelief, so this being, they would not be incredulous if all were philosophers.

THE RELATIONSHIP BETWEEN SCIENCE AND RELIGION

There are some natural sciences that are not worthy of the name except insofar as other sciences are applied to them, and such as these are minerology, zoology, and botany, which serve only to present a collection of natural wonders. What could be the result? To know much better the wisdom and power of the Creator and to prepare ourselves to admit many other incomprehensible facts, but always with proof that they have the same ultimate cause. Here is the evidence that these sciences, instead of belittling, favor religion. There are other sciences whose object is quantity and they are known under the generic name of mathematics, and because of the clarity and solidity of their demonstrations they remove any sophism from our minds and make us perceive the great potency of beings, and the infinitude of their cause, giving us a continuous lesson in religion. These are, therefore, but evident proofs of our impotency, compared with the workings of nature and the infinite wisdom in the movements that so harmoniously guide the great system of the universe. What could there be in such sublime calculations and in such profound studies that could be against religious belief? There could be much against ridiculous superstition, but this is proof that the study of sciences, far from supporting the unbelievers, confirms the believers.

As for physics and chemistry, one needs to be very ignorant to suspect that they could support unbelief. These sciences place the human being in close contact with nature, demonstrating to him that scientific knowledge is not only limited but is linked to a mere series of facts, even if some of them present themselves as principles of others. The true and primary causes are unknown to us and, speaking candidly, none is more disposed to accept the mysteries than the physicist and the chemist. Through their study and conviction, these scientists know that these deep and incomprehensible but undeniable realities are more common than the general public thinks. The irreligious expression "I do not believe in it because I do not comprehend it" cannot come from an educated physicist or chemist without his heart immediately intuiting this fallacy and his mind convincing him of his error. In fact, the irreligious have never presented any credible proof based on the above sciences.

What is most remarkable—if not most ridiculous—is that in order to attack a mystery, other mysteries are brought up, turning the attack into a real defense. And in order to censure those who believe without understanding, the irreligious comes forth with the same belief, even though his subject is different. Understand, my friend, that the irreligious does not cease to wonder about the infinite means of nature and its incomprehensible secrets, that he never stops attributing to nature the effects that religion attributes to the supernatural. The irreligious never promises to open these secrets or dares to tell us of his discoveries. He believes, then, in the great power of nature, based in what we could call *natural authority,* for the irreligious does not want to admit a divine one. He is a true believer even though he is not religious.

But, you might ask, "how can we reconcile these doctrines with the experience of so many irreligious who have a deep knowledge of the natural sciences?" This question could be answered with another one: "How can it be held that the natural sciences form the irreligious if there are so many eminent religious scientists?" Nevertheless, I want to answer you directly, pointing out that these irreligious scientists do not say, and if they say they do not prove, that it is science that has induced their incredulity. There is little doubt that a trained mind might sometimes be in danger, but this is because of the abuse and not the use of the intellectual capabilities of the mind. Murderers are usually strong and in good health, but we cannot generalize and say that good health makes the murderer. Is it not more correct to say that murderers abuse this precious gift which they ought to use for their own good and that of their neighbors. We can say the same with regard to the spiritual faculties and the forces that are used against the truth. It can never be said that they are the cause of such an enormous sin.

It is proven that the irreligiosity that issues from the mind, without consideration of the heart's malice, is an effect of the combinations of inexact ideas, this error being the result of lack of attention or of misguided fantasies. It is also proven that the irreligious who presumes to be so, as a result of wide and deep reflections, is a *mad philosopher,* who having repeated his theme for many years persuades himself to believe that experience is in his favor and treats those who do not believe as he does and who refuse to approve his mania as dupes and inexperts. It has always been said that Cervantes wrote a work suited to all times and conditions, though his subject was chivalry; believe me, my friend, each time I am more convinced that this compliment is well deserved and that the extraordinary genius of Cervantes considered all the dimensions of the human person. We have Quixotic kings, Quixotic tavern keepers and philosophers, who no matter how overthrown, beaten, or duped, never abandon their strange madness or drop the magisterial and ridiculous tone to which they are accustomed.

Irreligiosity, like every other monster of the abyss, cannot live in a pure atmosphere but prefers ignorance as its pasture. Let the customs be purified, enlightenment diffused, errors destroyed, and the irreligious will disappear, or at least will be reduced to a few, and will not harm society or lessen its beauty with their deformities. They would be like scattered weeds in a flowering garden, unnoticed, or if by chance they were discovered they would not alter the pleasant impressions the whole garden had made in our souls.

What a happy state is that of a moral and educated people! What undisturbed peace! What fair friendship! What unbreakable union! If I saw irreligiosity harassed by science and virtue, running to hide in the caverns of hell where it came from, I would be forced by the effect of divine mercy to deprive myself of life in order to avoid the risk of losing so much happiness, lest by misfortune this product of Averno should return.

Being deprived of such a blessing, I console myself by writing to a friend, who, free from common contagion, perceives the beauty of holy religion and the fantasies of its opponents; as a friend whom I cherish, receive this letter with my deepest affection.

THE MAGNITUDE AND TREATMENT
OF IRRELIGIOSITY

The earth is covered, my beloved Elpidio, with the fatal shadow of ominous and perfidious irreligiosity which, spread out everywhere, perverts, destroys and annihilates the miserable people who cherish it; and the large number of victims is a sign of the great power that sacrifices them. No class or condition is free, no place or time is immune to its cruelty, nothing distracts it, no barrier stops it; it despises everything, outrages everything, overthrows everything, tramples on everything; and irreligiosity, barbarous, untamed, daring and insolent, boasts of its successes over virtue, science and religion, which, tied to its detestable cart, groan over a soil they have vainly tried to overwhelm with benefits.

THE ART OF DETERMINING
THE SCOPE OF IRRELIGIOSITY

In my previous letters I have already pointed out the causes and effects of this cancer of society, and now I intend to make known to you its extent. A lot of people measure this extent by the number of chatterers who, unable to draw attention in another way, have decided to present themselves as irreligious persons; but this calculation is very wrong, because these miserable ones are not the whole and perhaps many of them only appear to belong to that number. They are more weak than degenerate, and when they forget the role they want to play, they give very obvious indications of their farce.

Others calculate the extent of irreligiosity by the number of works that promote it, and this calculation would be correct if half of the works were not a product of greed, and sometimes of hunger, but were a conviction of intelligence.

I suppose you know, my friend, that in France (a nation famous for both its good things and its ridiculous ones) the occupation of writer has been for a long time like the occupation of a carpenter; he is at the disposal of whoever wants to employ his services to make a piece of furniture, inquiring nothing but the price to be paid. Many of these writers compose a very pious novena for a religious society and immediately thereafter write the most irreligious of books on the orders of a bookseller, who perhaps prints both works only as a mere speculation. I was not unaware of these facts, but I got proof, thanks to our common friend's report . . . , who took in his hands one of these novenas and knew about the author thanks to the information of the bookseller himself.

I know very well that his easiness of speaking against religion, this indifference in writing for or against it, and the interest itself of speculators in the publishing of irreligious works are proof that pious feelings no longer exist in them; and unless we take into consideration other causes, I would also call that judgment very exact; but I will always distinguish the result of necessity from the results of a habitual state of the spirit. If we speak of a *material religiosity,* which we might better call a coarse joke, I agree with that way of thinking, as I do if we speak of *formal irreligiosity,* or a real and ingenuous admission of irreligious principles; but I must assure you, in defense of humankind, that irreligiosity is not so common as it is claimed. I repeat that irreligiosity is found in all kinds of people, and thus it presents itself with an exaggerated power; I repeat that its ravages may be seen everywhere, and thus many people think its action is general; but notice, my dear Elpidio, that it has always been a disgrace and a good fortune for the classes to be appropriated with good or bad denominations on account of the conduct of a lot of people; but, nevertheless, it is insignificant concerning the whole.

In my first letter I tried to call your attention to this point, considering it is a trick of despots to exaggerate the progress of irreligiosity, which, since they are real, serve as a base to the fiction that serves the interests of politics. Would you say there are many virtuous persons where many pretend to be virtuous? Then you must also say that there are many irreligious persons where many present themselves as such. I am fully aware that piety is lost through the mere fact of flaunting one's irreligiosity, but we must understand it as a matter of morals (it cannot be just if it is perverse), not as a matter of reasoning. That is the reason I remind you, contrary to my practice, of the two scholastic terms of *formal irreligiosity* and *material irreligiosity,* because they surely explain this subject precisely. Through conviction, although erroneous (what we might better call hallucination), irreligious persons do not easily abandon their irreligiosity; it is necessary to defeat them; but *fashionable puppets* dance in any manner and are more reprehensible for their misbehavior than for their ideas. It is known that the least doubt *held with obstinacy* by our mind about a dogma makes us heretics, and that, regarding the everlasting life, it brings about the same effect as the full denial of a revealed truth; but it is undeniable that irreligiosity has not taken root when the mind does not trust in its opinions and admits, at least as something possible, the existence of mysteries.

It therefore follows from these remarks that obstinate irreligious persons are not so many as some people, timidly or astutely, want to suppose; most of them are speculators who would not try to repress the religious feelings of their hearts, but and rather would try to foment it if they found some interest in it. The corruption of all classes of society usually upsets the minds of the devout in such a way that they consider it as a hopelessly sick person, and perhaps as a moribund, who can only be the object of tears. How many evils are derived from these ideas! It is not a matter of attracting but avoiding irreligious persons. It is not a matter of healing but abandoning them in their serious illness, which the devout justly consider very infectious. Consequently, the number of irreligious persons increases, because they consider themselves as invincible, or because, considering themselves members of a different faction or party, which is presumed to be very extensive, they incite much more the speculators' wish to become members of so powerful a family. I am speaking on the basis of my own observations and not theoretically. I am certain, Elpidio, that one of the means irreligiosity uses to extend itself is the assumption of its extent. You will notice undoubtedly that this trick is used by all parties, whether political or religious; and it works because of the natural tendency of people to come together, which causes them to desire to be members of big associations, at least if no opposing interest presents itself, which on religious matters is impossible, according to worldly ideas.

It is impossible to enumerate, even approximately, irreligious persons, because they have neither temple nor badge; they form an army without banner or uniform or emblem; they are noticeable only because of the harm they bring about here and there in society. They become like the guerrilla, whose number and operations never can be set; and so it is often supposed that a territory is full of them even if only a few are passing through it. Hence the great anxiety these enemies of virtue cause to good people, who suppose virtue is attacked everywhere, and really it is; because the contagion is worldwide, inasmuch as it is observed in all classes and all countries. If people became persuaded of the possibility of healing this formidable illness and of the fact that the apathy of good people causes the increase of irreligiosity, you would see, my friend, irreligiosity considerably diminished, if not extinguished.

THE ART OF RELATING TO THE
IRRELIGIOUS IN GENERAL

How, therefore, must the irreligious person be treated? According to the maxims of the Gospel. With charity and gentleness and, at the same time, with firmness. This firmness must show itself not through persecutions—which reason and experience prove are useful only to stoke the consuming fire of irreligiosity—but through a noble and determined character on the part of believers; through a holy contempt for the attacks of this monster; through Christian courage which instead of irritating the enemy attracts and ties him down with the bonds of respect, esteem and consideration. It is necessary to let enemies who cannot be attracted in that way go to their ruin, although the plan of healing must always be continued, and if they are lost it will be their fault. Let us pray to God to move their hard hearts with his mercy, and, as for us, let us be satisfied with the fulfillment of our duty, even if it is fruitless; and if in the end the devil takes them away, believe me, Elpidio, he will not be taking someone else's property.

Nothing is more contrary to conversion than the insult, and unfortunately we see very religious people using it when they attack irreligious people. They look ridiculous when they try to imitate the roguery of their enemies, and they think that by making those who believe in religion laugh they will convert those who deny it. These are not evangelical means, but only satisfy human passions and avenge insults. I am fully aware that some people have very different reasons and only intend to do good, but without a doubt they mistake the means. To be quick to believe everything that is said provided that it is against the people we want to oppose is a fault of pious persons no less than of irreligous persons; and when a mistake is proved, more solid reasoning loses its force and the enemy finds an obvious loophole. This word reminds me of a teaching of Saint Augustine which, if taken into account by all who have to deal with irreligious persons, would avoid many bad times and do much in favor of religion. "You must distinguish," says this holy Father, "between God's work and the devil's work in a criminal; man is God's work and sin is the devil's work. Let us love man, therefore, and hate crime." By no means must we, dear Elpidio, hate any work of the Supreme Being; and we must deal with irreligious persons as with brethren who are unfortunate enough to suffer from a spiritual illness, or rather who are dead, and who can be brought back to life only by grace, which is all our interest and aspiration.

Personality puts obstacles in the way of conviction, and so private controversies, in which almost always particular individuals are offended, seldom bring about good results and usually give rise to countless evils. When you attack vice without ascribing it to vicious persons, nobody wants to be counted as such and therefore nobody appears to be offended. In the same way, if one class is attacked, making a distinction between those who deserve eulogies and those who do not, no one fails to claim to be part of the former group, and everybody shows signs of contentment (some in fact, others falsely) with the just punishment that public opinion inflicts on the criminals; but if the attack is general and without distinction, or individual and marked, it surely exasperates and brings about only obstinacy. This teaching must be applied to all kinds of controversies and in all cases in which social interests collide, but much more in religious matters. It is unlikely for someone who suffers a rebuff, disdain, or sometimes contempt during a visit, only because he is irreligious, not to come out with the resolution to continue in his irreligiosity; but maybe he would have detested it if instead of rudeness he had received courteous and charitable treatment. I know very well we must avoid having anything to do with irreligious persons, and I hope this teaching will be put into effect; we must fight against their *irreligiosity* but keep social relations, which we must not cut with rudeness. It is very good to avoid having anything to do with such people, because the danger of being mortified by their stupid remarks or corrupted by their immorality can rarely be escaped; but when it is necessary to have something to do with them or when by chance they get together with believers, they must be treated as human and, if deserved, as gentlefolk; and nothing is more ridiculous or more contrary to the spirit of the Gospel as to mortify an individual in society when he gives no cause. It is true that St. Paul tells us not even to eat with them, but that is understood in the case of being in danger of perversion, as in the times in which the faithful of whom he wrote lived, and when you seek to get familiar with them, which always leads to vice.

If an irreligious person aspires to propagate his irreligiosity, believers do not have to suffer him patiently, and they are authorized to oppose his depraved intentions. This can be done by shunning his company, warning him about his mistake, or punishing him with a just contempt. The first way is the most proper, but it is not always possible, and in that case, when it comes to scantily instructed people, the third way is the most convenient. No punishment can be more severe nor more adequate.

Nothing mortifies an irreligious person more than silence, if it is accompanied by certain signs which prevent him from believing that it is lack of conviction or a lack of rationale that is being used against his arguments, or rather against his vague assertions, for it is known that all his arguments are only vague assertions. I speak from my own experience, and maybe there are few persons with so wide an experience in this matter as mine. My profession, and the various incidents of my life, which are not unknown to you, have put me in touch with all kinds of people for many years, and I can tell you that I have dealt with major irreligious persons and major fanatics. On serious reflection, I have adopted a plan consisting in not answering them except with a special countenance: a few smiles and a few vague monosyllables, which indicate that I could say many things if I did not consider them incapable of an open and unbiased discussion and if I did not know their aims. I have tried to indicate my respect and consideration for their persons, my good friendship and condescendence, so far as I could, without compromising my principles. Believe me, Elpidio, in that way I have set my thinking before them, and perhaps I have brought about more results than by means of endless discussions, which are intended to be endless, the passions always finding a way to keep them so. I can tell you that sometimes various irreligious persons have tried to despise me and were not able to do so. Their faces let me know that I possessed their hearts, and I was glad not to take note of their nonsense. In these cases, I have always remembered a piece of advice and an admirable comparison taken from Saint Augustine. If we approach the bed of a sick person who is running a high fever and may be delirious, perhaps he will receive us with rudeness, despise our advise and even throw the medicine we offer him in our face, but we would be silly if we took offense at that action and abandoned the patient. Why? Because he is sick. Well then, says the holy Father, all sinners are seriously sick.

You will tell me that silence explains nothing, and it serves rather to deepen unrefuted mistakes. You are wrong, my friend, if you think so. Certainly, silence explains nothing, but it is not so inert as it seems. Irreligiosity comes, as I said in my previous letters, from corruption or hallucination; and in both cases, a wise silence serves as antidote, because it demonstrates to the pervert that we know him but, out of charity and prudence, do not despise him; and it demonstrates to the deluded person that his reasoning is so groundless as not to deserve an answer, which is stimulus for a more careful examination as well as for self-conviction, the most solid of convictions. We must not lose sight of the fact that most irreligious persons make a great effort to be so, and therefore their irreligiosity is something arbitrary that ceases to exist as soon as they want it to; if the will is won over, very soon the mind is attracted; but if the will is exasperated, you must not think that the mind is convinced, or at least considers itself convinced.

Take note likewise, my friend, of the fact that most of the religious controversies stirred up in social gatherings are tricks used by some idlers sinfully to amuse those who are weak enough to praise them and laugh at their jokes and audacity. Many ladies are guilty on this point, because certainly many of these buffoons would stop their sport if they encountered, instead of support, a just rebuke from the ladies, a rebuke they can make without danger, because society, which ties them down in so many ways, grants them at the same time permission to do and say anything they want in these and other similar cases. Unfortunately, they follow a misguided plan, because they either praise these blasphemers, fearing to be taken as prudes and exposed to mockery, or they show signs of restlessness and scandal, which is exactly the intention of these crooks. But if ladies, maintaining their composure and serenity, paid no attention to these simpletons and prudently let them know that you cannot imply scandal where there is none, or plead ignorance to admit mistakes or perversity to imitate criminals, but that an educated and virtuous person attracts no scandal and only feels sorry for those who try to spread it; if these wicked and unpleasant conversations did soon be banished.

You have heard a lot about religious freedom in this country, together with its social harmony and admirable peace; and in spite of your great talent, as I know the effect brought about by distances between peoples and the various customs in the judgment of people, I am afraid you have not acquired right ideas on this matter and are influenced by the exaggeration of some people and the prejudices of others.[49] It is not irrelevant to present the facts. As these people are considered a model of religious tolerance, it is necessary not to get wrong ideas on it, because later it discourages imitators when experience shows it has not reached, and perhaps never will reach, an imaginary perfection, which they take for granted.

Many think religion has little influence on these people, or at least that it does not alter the peace of the spirit; that everything is different and there are no religious rivalries and grudges here. This way of thinking encourages irreligious persons, who assume it is the most convenient society for them; and it encourages religious persons, who assume it is the calmest society. None of them are mistaken about the facts, but they are mistaken about the circumstances. Irreligious persons have an open field and religious persons have security, but everything is purely external and it is not so much an effect of the law as an effect of the public view. Irreligious persons know they are detested by believers, as in any other country; the former know the latter are their most bitter enemies. The different sects are as hostile to the Church of God as were the Arians and the ancient heretics, and as Englishmen were, are and will be. If any one of the sects could oppress the other ones, it would renew the time of Henry VIII and Elizabeth; and if irreligious persons had enough forces they would present the bloody scenes of the French Revolution to us in America. You will ask me: what is there in that country which is so much celebrated? A *social moderation,* fruit of education and experience, by which people respect one another even if they detest one another, and they never interrupt the harmony of a meeting with personal insults. If, unfortunately, an unpleasant episode takes place, or somebody fails in what we may call this general discretion, the offended person receives quick satisfaction in the behavior and expressions of the public and is calmed down, and the rest of society then remains quiet and unanimous with regard to civil behavior, though divided more than ever in its religious feelings. I know very well that many persons who are respectful with me as I am with them would say there was one less devil on earth if they heard I was dead; but I am also sure they would never take the liberty to insult me in order not to put themselves in a ridiculous position in the eyes of the majority. Here is the force of public opinion.

Until people get this *habit of respect,* this social condescendence, they will never imitate the United States of America, whatever their system of government may be. We adults are like children, who cry when somebody makes fun of them and never miss the chance to take revenge on the aggressors. The most wise institutions, the most judicious writings, and the most heroic models are not enough to keep peace if you cannot be in a get-together without exposing yourself to insult.

To apply these remarks to the matter in question, I will say that irreligious persons must be managed in the same way in private society as in this country. Sensible people try to keep them far away from their homes, but if they go there, they are treated with the greatest respect. If they dare to mortify society with their nonsense, failing in their duties with regard to the courtesy and welcome they have received, they lose their right to all consideration; and soon they read in the eyes of those present the judgment of contempt, if by this time the head of the household has not already indicated to the irreligious persons their abuse of his hospitality. That is, my friend, the great mystery of the religious calm of this model country.

It is necessary to become accustomed to moral objects as we do to physical ones: we see healthy or sick men, perfect or vitiated trees, precious or ordinary stones, and the sight of this diversity induces us to make different judgments about their merit, but it does not cause uneasiness or arouse strong passions; that is the way to deal with good or perverted men, with wise or ignorant men. The opinion of them is varied, but it must not affect us. Allow me to give you a personal example, because after all I am writing to a friend. Often in the street I meet an outstanding irreligious person, an ardent writer, who usually tells me frankly he is an atheist. Sometimes I have almost given him Father Lammenais's biting answer to another such scatterbrained person: *Long since I desired to see an animal of that species, and I am very glad to have satisfied my desire.* But that was not in keeping with the system of the American society, and so I always answered him with a smile, and after a friendly conversation, we parted. I knew he kept laughing for having entertained a dupe, and, for my part, I keep laughing for having met a *tame bear* who claims to be a man.

Experience will prove to you, Elpidio, that this is the best plan of behavior with regard to irreligious persons, and that all unwise opposition only serves to aggravate the evil. I am not unaware that it is a duty to defend the truth and an act of justice to instruct the ignorant, but it must be done according to the advice of prudence, because we must not cast pearls before swine. Whenever it is known that an individual is willing to admit the truth and is seeking after it in all sincerity, we must tell him the truth and rescue him from his mistake, if we are qualified to do so; but if we are not, it would be wisest to send him to a competent person or to give him books to instruct him. A poor defender makes a case bad and loses the best one. The same goes for religious matters; believe me, Elpidio, it is a misfortune for religion to be daringly upheld by some chatterers. As a rule, they distort it and make it appear as horrible and full of contradictions that exist in their silly answers and not in fundamental teachings.

I do not think it is possiible to make rules to decide these cases. I think the same happens in this matter as in medicine, that all remarks appearing in books are almost worthless if the physician lacks a certain common sense, which cannot be a result of art but of talent, tactfulness and other personal attributes. It is necessary not to be influenced by captious expressions and ridiculous protests which a lot of people use to prove their good faith, while at the same time they plot the most treacherous attack against religion. Personal and local circumstances must guide us in this interesting and very delicate undertaking, which if it comes to nothing brings about sometimes incurable evils, because irreligiosity takes root, boasting in its victory. It would be absurd and ridiculously vain to hope to convince and almost always convert irreligious persons each time you enter into a religious dispute with them; therefore the failure cannot be attributed to imprudence. Conviction comes from many circumstances of the mind that wants to be convinced, and, above all, from a heavenly light, not from men; and regarding conversion, it comes from grace, and it is always mysterious. Saint Paul himself preached to crowds and only people well disposed to eternal life believed. Nevertheless one who begins an imprudent controversy is responsible for its evil results if he observes clear signs of its fruitlessness and danger. Note, my friend, that people, when they want to educate themselves and not defeat nor make a fool of their opponent, do not dispute very much but ask only a few questions and calmly hear the answers. You will note sometimes a certain reservation that shows itself no matter how much they try to conceal it, but this silence and affected moderation cannot be confounded with the sincere behavior of a really unconcerned spirit, who tries to instruct himself. These are the only symptoms that may be indicated to guide us in the inquiry on the state of sickness or improvement of these spiritually sick persons.

Above all, my dear Elpidio, it is advisable not to encourage the rudeness and perversity of many rogues who, as I noted in one of my previous letters, usually enter into religious controversies only in order to make fun of religious persons; and, believe me, these are the most common kind of refuters. When they leave the gathering or their opponent retires, they usually laugh at their own reasoning, or at least they have so little interest in their opponent as to pay attention only to the unpleasant sensation they caused and to the expressions and gestures of their antagonists. I remember a funny but at the same time very wise story told by a clergyman friend of mine about a friar who rid himself easily of these fools by asking them to explain Christian doctrine and its foundation before entering a controversy about it, because, as he told them with very good sense, nothing is more ridiculous than to discuss something about which you know nothing. You may deduce that none of these gallants or, as Feijoo called them, these "theologians wearing a tie," dared to embark on such an explanation; and the good friar, after perceiving their embarrassment, pulled a gold coin out of his sleeve and offered it as a prize to the person who explained the matter. He laughed as he put the coin back in its place, telling them they had the same right to talk as every mad person, since experience had proved that they spoke not in wisdom, but in madness. How many times have I remembered the good friar!

I dare to advise my brothers in the priesthood to be much more careful than laymen on this matter, although they have more means to defend the cause of religion. It is necessary to remember that we start at a disadvantage because a lot of people think we promote only our interest and that it is not the loss of the souls but of our comfort that grieves us. However enormous these calumnies may be, we see they are very common and are received by people from whom we do not expect so much injustice. Therefore, all our heat in the controversy is usually presented as proof by irreligious persons of a hostile disposition in our spirit, and with the highest hypocrisy, those who detest the Gospel invoke it only in order to calumniate the ecclesiastics, trying to show them as not having feelings inspired by the Holy Book. There is still an even greater danger: irreligious persons are not very careful with the truth; they do not find it difficult to make up anecdotes about these controversies and they manage to hold ecclesiastics in derision. We must not lose sight of the fact that even the most reflective persons are influenced by so-called personal impressions, because they are brought about precisely out of consideration for persons. It follows from this that if the ministers of religion seem ridiculous because of some simpleness, or if they are maliciously ridiculed, the Church always suffers the consequences, because *ridicule*, spreads like a poison and brings about disastrous effects. Very few are instructed and wise enough to respect the worship even if the ministers are not respected. It is impossible, therefore, to calculate the harm done to religion and public morality by those who, out of a criminal condescension and sometimes with perverted aims, encourage with their laughter the buffoons who enjoy demonstrating their unconcern by making fun of ecclesiastics. Even disregarding purely religious considerations, such a behavior in relation to the ministers of the worship always does harm to society. These ministers, for their part, must avoid these situations anyway, because the Church gains nothing from their sufferings;[1] rather, the cause of religion loses ground.

Religious persons usually become so annoyed by the nonsense of irreligious persons that they spend their lives filled with bitterness. This bitterness is undoubtedly very well grounded if it comes from sorrow at the sight of so many despicable people in so horrible a state, and shows a really Christian soul; but if it comes from personal sufferings as a result of the attacks of these furious persons, it is far from being a properly religious feeling; rather it is an evident weakness and concealed pride. Half of the people who complain about irreligious persons perhaps would not remember them if they were rid of their insults. But Christian charity is not like that, my dear Elpidio; it suffers with a certain inexplicable pleasure if that suffering can contribute to the welfare of the others and the glory of God.

Allow me, my dear Elpidio, to transcribe a paragraph of the incomparable Bossuet in his very eloquent sermon *on the unity of the Church,* in which he considers the afflictions of righteous persons because of the spread of irreligiosity. Picture one of these tormented spirits and address him with these words: "You will tell me: there are so many irreligious persons; their number is infinite, and I cannot live in the company of them. Where are you to get to? You will find irreligious persons everywhere, they are everywhere mingled with the good ones; someday they will mend their ways, but their time has not yet come. What must we do in the meantime? Part company with them in our hearts, reprimand them freely in order that they mend themselves; and if they do not mend themselves, tolerate them out of charity in order to confuse them? But, we do not know God's counsels. There are wicked persons who will mend themselves and it is necessary to wait patiently; others will persevere in their wickedness and since God tolerates them, should we not tolerate them? Some are destined to permit the exercise of charity in some and punish the crime in others. They will get out of the way as soon as they finish their work . . . do not

---

1. " . . . *buscados* e *innecesarios* sufrimientos."

anticipate the judgment. "Love your brother," St. John says, "and you will not suffer any scandal." "Why?" asks St. Augustine. "Because he who loves a brother tolerates everything in order to keep unity."[2]

The harm would be less noticeable if the spirit who moved Bossuet's pen would move the hearts of the people who complain about the multitude of irreligious persons; but unfortunately it is noted that most of these grumbling persons want to find an object for their grumblings and they pretend to grumble even if they do not find it. There is hardly an illustrious person whom a multitude of *pious fanatics,* always in plenty, do not imagine as the worst irreligious person; and other *wily fanatics,* or assumed fanatics, do not calumniate in the most wicked way. These calumnies serve to plant a concern, innocent to a certain point, thanks to the religious persons' fear of the spread of irreligiosity; they do not realize that they sometimes get to such a point that they fail in justice by suspecting, or even believing without basis, that everybody is irreligious; and fail in charity, which asks not to consider them incurables until all of one's spiritual resources have been exhausted. These calumnies also bring about another effect that is even more disastrous, namely, that they lead irreligiosity into many persons who are far from it. This evil is very serious, because it is very senseless to create irreligious persons while you defend religion; and believe me, my dear Elpidio, that is very common and has deprived the sciences, the arts and the whole of society of many useful members who have become harmful.

THE ART OF RELATING TO IRRELIGIOUS YOUTH

With regard to the youth, I think its irreligiosity is judged with the highest haste.[50] It is real in many cases, but in others is only nonsense or rather childishness; so we must not lose hope for its correction, nor become anxious in spirit about a youth's pranks. When I was young, I thought it was vain of the elderly to hope that the way of some of these bewildered people, who

---

2. Bossuet, vol. 2:63–64.

mortified society with their blasphemies, would be mended in the future; but time has proven in many cases that their hopes were not very groundless and that prudence, at least, is noted in them even if they hold the same ideas. I do not mean by that to advocate the abandoning of youth and permission for all its excesses under the pretext of a future mending, nor do I intend to excuse it. I only want youth to be treated, on religious matters, as children who annoy when they are up to mischief. In fact, the first offers of understanding are as shaky as the children's first steps. Nevertheless, this weakness with regard to perception of objects always goes with a great strength and resolution to act, and thus nothing puts obstacles in the way of a young person who begins to be important in society. The best way to get, if not a reform, at least some moderation in the religious behavior of youth is to lead them with gentleness and by loving means to peace and joy. Notice, Elpidio, that youth is inclined to justice, no matter how much some deceiving and thoughtless persons persist in contradicting it. And thus no matter how much a young person may be indulged in pleasures and irreligiosity he always shows signs of gratitude for efforts made to improve his situation if he perceives no intention to oppress him.

The great secret to relate to youth, taking advantage of its talents and good disposition, lies in the investigation of the individual character of anyone and regulating our conduct accordingly. If we are in opposition to a young person but want to bring about good results, our effort must be almost imperceptible; it is necessary for the young person to correct himself. Nature shows its strength in the tender years, and passions then are very strong; reasoning is not very trained and as experience is almost nonexistent the young have not acquired the habit of moderation proper to the elderly. The fact is that young persons take delight in fights of all kinds, and resistance serves only to increase their efforts rather than to dominate their inclinations. Many educators usually make a mistake on this point, as they think they have won a victory over the young people's inclinations, when the latter, out of fear, do not show those inclinations, that is, when they have acquired sufficient cunning to defend themselves with premeditated skill and tactics. This mistake has brought about many deplorable effects, which show themselves obviously when the oppression stops and the corrupted nature makes the filth of crimes so long held back appear freely. This is the reason, my dear Elpidio, that many young people educated in poorly managed schools indulge in all vices, and especially in irreligiosity, after they go out of what they consider a long period of imprisonment, and why they frustrate the hopes of their loving fathers, and turn fruitless all the lessons of their wise teachers.

The object of this digression, which you perhaps think is untimely, is to say that it is poor sense to attack irreligiosity in the first stages of youth, when passions begin to set free; this poor sense in managing youth at the most dangerous age of life is the cause of the demoralization of many of them; something that is inexplicable to thoughtless persons, who say in great surprise: "He was educated in a college!" But they do not mention the college nor the people who managed it. To tell the truth, my dear Elpidio, very good colleges, as far as this point is concerned, are so few that wise persons, instead of being surprised about that apparent phenomenon, will find a very natural cause in the same fact that makes it extraordinary, and would say that such a young person is irreligious precisely because he was educated in a college. Many years ago reading the very wise *Treaty on the Studies* by Rollin opened my eyes, so to speak, to this matter; and believe me, since then I have not stopped making observations which confirm the bright ideas of that learned teacher and wise director of youth. In many colleges, or rather in most of them, the interesting subject of religion is entirely neglected, inspiring thus a certain contempt, or at least a certain indifference, to it; and in others the professors try to inspire the pupils with religion by force, by dint of punishments, which only brings about a mortal hatred for those who impose it and a complete and indelible aversion for the object that is the cause of punishments. We should not indulge young people in matters of irreligiosity, but it is advisable that they perceive only our annoyance and hear affectionate suggestions instead of opprobrium, and that they be led with gentleness to the religious practice they should not miss. I can tell you from experience that young persons always love when they know they are loved and whoever gets their love may surely manage them as he likes, because they get a good idea of things proposed by the loving person and examine it without any reluctance or worry, or rather with inclination to virtue. These little irreligious persons must be managed in a particular way for they go to the bad if treated according to the common rules of rewards and punishments. For my part, I assure you I never gave a reward or a punishment because of religious practices. The rewards are useful to form hypocritical speculators and to plant in the young people's hearts a purely human religion, because they get accustomed to pleasing people and put their faith in them and not in God, so that in the end the words of the Gospel may be applied to them: "they received already their payment."[3] Punishments, on the other hand, destroy truly religious feelings and also bring about hypocrisy of a different kind, reserved and in a certain way fierce. It is therefore obvious that all religious constraint only serves to destroy religion, which must be promoted only with the elevation of heavenly ideas and the charm of virtue and constrained only with the horrors of crime and the anger of an avenging God. Even in this case a lot of prudence is necessary, because a never-ending sermon becomes an old story, especially for young people, who cannot bear for long such serious thoughts. If you want a young person not to have any religion, talk to him continuously about it.

I should like, my dear Elpidio, those who direct young persons not to forget a weakness which must be avoided. There is no child who does not want to be big in body, and there is no young person who does not want to be great in ideas and feelings. And as children take all opportunities to practice lifting weights and to show off in one way or another that they are nearly in a perfect state of nature, because all their physical capabilities have already fully developed, so young persons who already think they have reached a state of perfection, or are nearly in that state, aspire to demonstrate that they have also reached a state of intellectual perfection; and so they undertake great tasks and think they are able for

---

3. " . . . acceperunt merceden suam."

any scientific work. As they know that very noted people have combatted against religion, and they say those attacks show strength of spirit, nothing pleases the desire of the young to show intellectual perfection more than to enter the fray as determined champion. Religion has been taught to them from childhood (although most of them only learned to know it existed), and their mothers, in keeping with their rights concerning children, usually took them to the temple to practice some religious exercises. They are persuaded that the first step they must take to show they are *men*[4] who are not tied to their mothers' apron strings, as it is usually said, is to begin to talk not with frankness but with audacity on matters of religion. It is much better for them to find opponents; they consider their own value by the attention paid to them and thus think about themselves as consistent men.

A great prudence is necessary in such delicate circumstances not to break the string and temper it at the same time; to neglect this interesting matter would be the greatest of absurd things. Many people decide to humiliate them by reminding them of their tender age and lack of experience, in a way more offensive than effective; and I assure you that those who behave like that do not know the human heart nor all the resources of vanity. On my part, I have followed a different plan and I think the experience authorizes me to recommend it as useful and reasonable. I always have tried to treat them as they want to be treated, namely, as trained people; and as they dare, so to speak, to show themselves at the gates of the shrine of duty, I make sure they enter it. By treating them as persons with experience, I communicate my own experience and allow them to believe they have deceived me by presenting my ideas as if they were theirs; and so I usually convert them into my collaborators, while they imagine they have gone far, since they even surpassed the frenzied actions of youth's folly. These *beardless old men* are in general very useful, and the society which has a lot of them is happy, because in fact in the end they know we acted cunningly with regard to them. By then they are

---

4. *"hombrecitos."*

trained and are able to assess the merit of such a useful strata-gem. I have never desired to be an enemy of young persons, much less to enter into controversies with them; on the con-trary, I have always tried to show them I love and respect them; and I always have taken advantage of their ideas about me and used them as an effective tool to make them accept my ideas and follow my advice.

But how difficult it is to go on with this arduous undertak-ing! The slightest imprudence destroys the whole plan and gives it the appearance of a despicable fallacy, even if it is a wise means to keep the truth and avoid countless evils. In such a case, instead of getting good results we obtain the unbridling of the passions of the pupil, who thinks he now has the right to take revenge for something he calls an ill-intentioned deceit. He imagines that we are afraid of him, that his reasoning is unsolvable and our defeat would be inevitable if we did not take such ridiculous precautions. Sometimes, because of a teacher's imprudence, a religious *quixotism* is created; and af-ter such enormous harm, it is very hard or almost impossible to make up for it. Young persons are ingenuous and resent more than any other age group any intent to deceive them, and are therefore suspicious afterwards of those who want to become their friends.

Some young persons whom both of us appreciate because of their integrity and religious principles alarmed me when they were in the dangerous age, from fifteen to eighteen years old. This time of life demands much attention and prudence on the part of the people who take care of youth. Seldom does a young person in this period not give more or less noticeable indications of a regrettable irreligiosity, and I have already indicated how to manage it. It is advisable to take some precau-tions to make corrections unnecessary, and I think that one of the most important precautions is to distract the young person's mind and to devote them at the same time to solid studies, but not religion and morality. Purely speculative subjects must be avoided and they should be nurtured with a select amount of practical knowledge. For this reason, I think it is advisable to lead them at this age to music and drawing, mathematics, phys-ics, and chemistry.

Although I do not understand much about medicine, I think the practice of some renowned professors who in certain cases of delirium soothe their patients with opium, supplied sometimes profusely but always with the highest prudence, is well grounded. I have been told that the aim is to stop entirely the use of intellectual powers to give time for strengthening the physical ones without an excessive action of the nerves. After the patient comes back from this sleep, the doctors make sure that there is nothing to remind him of his old mania; on the contrary, they give orders to treat them as if they had never suffered any illness. I have been told the professors have healed many people. I think we must do the same thing, my dear Elpidio, with regard to what we may properly call *irreligious madness* in young persons of the age in question. The best course is to keep them from thinking about such sublime subjects until able to do so with soundness, when they have abandoned their mania. You know very well that music is the best narcotic for young people, and this is the reason to consider its study, like that of the other fine arts (but preferably that one), as the best way to prevent or heal such a disastrous evil.[51] I remember hearing often from one of my teachers, who in the interest of youth is at the head of one of the most reputable literary institutions of my country, that nothing reassured him so much as the sound of an instrument in the hands of one of his pupils. "This sound," he said, "indicates to me what the one who produces it is thinking, and perhaps the pupils who are around him, and while the boy is playing the instrument I do not need to take care of him. I vouch for his body and soul." How often, Elpidio, have I remembered this wise remark, which I keep, among other things, as a priceless treasure, whereby I am enriched by someone whom I will remember until my death! By the same reason, I think the study of mathematics, physics, and chemistry should be fostered as an antidote against the corruption of youth and irreligiosity in the dangerous years. It is clear that while a young person is solving a problem of geometry, his mind is out of this world, in a very useful dream, because he avoids harmful subjects and at the same time concentrates on solid truths, which he applies without fear of erring, and gradually he becomes accustomed to not indulging in wishful thinking or enjoying controversies that are good for nothing. That is the great advantage, the great remedy for those cases in which, in social relations, young people are in the midst of unwise persons who raise religious controversies. A young mathematician soon finds that these chatterboxes have no order in their ideas and that their language is ridiculous. From here usually stems a very opposite effect from the one intended by these pedants: instead of making fun of the young people, these make fun of them. God forbid that we fall into youths' hands. They throw stones or pull one's leg—they are always the same.

It is evident that physics and chemistry distract more than any other subject, and it is easy to prove that a young person who is conducting an experiment does not engage himself in anything harmful to religion and morals, and if some irreligious thought comes to this mind, it fades quickly and effortlessly, because the sensations caused by physical subjects are more pleasant. When a young person begins talking nonsense in matters of religion, I consider it the wisest of means to supply him with the necessary things to study the above-mentioned sciences and to propose to him all kinds of rewards without discovering our intention, otherwise out of contradictory temper, which young persons like so much, those very sciences that are the delight of thinkers and most useful entertainment in afflictions, which are always provided by human society to sensitive souls, would become unpleasant for them.

I have always deplored the delusion of many parents who consider their children's dedication to the study of natural science a waste of time. They do not perceive the profit, because it is not valued in money. What a disastrous mistake! As if the intellectual and moral perfection of their children were worthless. Yes, I repeat, Elpidio, the moral perfection, because there is no doubt that many young persons would dare to be completely irreligious if they were not practicing and entertaining themselves with the very pleasant study of natural sciences during this dangerous age. Seldom will you find a young person, well gifted and instructed in those sciences, who degrades himself by starting indecent talks or who scandalizes with irreligiosities, but you will find many of these kinds of young persons who act as a check to the others, not because they become preachers but because they set an example—and that is real preaching, and very efficient. They are satisfied because they are capable of entertaining society if they wish to do so but do not need to call attention to their knowledge, and they are not so foolish as to importune with irreligious nonsense, which their hearts accustomed to righteousness could never approve.

At other times, I have regretted what can be properly called the venality of sciences, because its services are sold only for money, and they are appreciated only as a means to get it. Therefore, they are called *career sciences,* because they constitute the individual in society and give him means of sustenance. No wise person may oppose those careers, because it is fair to receive compensation for long studies and inconveniences and it is wise to assure sustenance in order not to suffer or be burdensome to anyone; but at the same time, regarding things from this point of view, the same personal interest is harmonized with the scientific one. There is no doubt that a young person with a trained spirit and a heart freed from strong attachments, and rather inclined to the peaceful emotions caused by the contemplation of nature, will always be more able to make progress and receive esteem, which greatly influences the common good. Notice, my friend, that you can find many perverts who have gotten rich with the help of wicked means, but you will never find one of them who got a fortune with the help of licit means, and therefore with popular appreciation. People, no matter how corrupted they are, know when there is interest how to treat the irreligious better than wise and religious persons.

THE ART OF RELATING TO IRRELIGIOUS WOMEN

How regrettable it is to notice daily the progress of irreligiosity where it is least expected: I mean the fair sex! This is the most dangerous class, because of the privileges which society has bestowed on it and because of its very great influence. Pains must be taken to manage this family, because if neglected it will cause the ruin of the people. Perhaps my pretension to set rules for the management of women will make you laugh, because they have no other law but their passing whims and are only constant in fickleness. That is the common saying, and they use it to do just what they like; sometimes they take it into their heads to cause enormous evils, and afterwards they remain as calm as if they had scattered nothing more than a bouquet of flowers. Thoughtless men have whims, and four schoolgirls put them to shame. These schoolgirls seem capricious and unstable but that is pure affectation, because as a matter of fact they are more constant in their projects than the most firm and determined of men. The privilege of causing harm through the spread of irreligiosity cannot be conceded to any sex, class or condition; on the contrary, so horrible an attack should be prevented through wise means. I have always believed that through ignorance, which is called concern and politics, women have been put out of action and at the same time have been made unhappy and given the ability to cause many misfortunes. Nevertheless, the determination to reform society on this point would be very ridiculous and it is only advisable to take necessary precautions to prevent evil. I have noticed that many ladies foster the irreligiosity of men as they approve and gladly hear their blasphemies; and I want you to notice, my dear Elpidio, that they, too, are usually irreligious and blasphemous themselves.

Sometimes this horrible crime comes from the frivolous character of many women, who, in this case as in many others, are usually the victims of a desire for praise; at other times it is the effect of falling in love, to please the person whom they love (if this person unfortunately has no religion), and seldom comes from a perverse heart, or from the several reasons I have indicated in another of my letters. These remarks may guide us in the management of such harmful, irreligious ladies, since they must be treated in a different way, according to the cause of the evil, and any mistakes in this respect may have unfortunate consequences.

With regard to women who are irreligious out of sheer vanity, it is necessary to consider that most of them come from a desire to present themselves as above their sex, which is always weak and religious, and to approach the virile character, which they envy. I do not know, my dear Elpidio, if you have noticed that this kind of woman is more numerous than some thoughtless men perhaps think. Many people imagine that women are very happy with their privileges and only envy the physical forces and the social representation of men; but that is a great mistake, because there is at least in many of them a desire to place themselves on an equal footing with men and a regret that they do not belong to literary societies and to all kinds of boards in which the enlightenment must guide society. I might mention, among other examples, the famous Madame Stael, who has astonished France and, I might say, all of Europe with her works. Those who dealt with her assure us that she could not hide her sorrow that she could not be a man or manage herself as one of them, and even though she kept the habits of her sex, she always presented herself as if she was not one of her own sex. I cannot count her among irreligious women, because she had intellectual resources to imitate and surpass the wisest men and never needed irreligiosity to call attention and get applause; but there is a host of very ignorant women who, having the same passion and lacking the means possessed by that illustrious woman, give themselves to all delusions of incredulity, at least apparently. The foolish and ugly women are more exposed to this misery, because mediocre women, unable to change their faces and being slow on the uptake, have only the resource of grace, or of the unusual. Regarding grace, it is very difficult to get it without talent; and the unusual entails the ridiculous, unless because of particular circumstances, it has gained admiration. They think irreligiosity fulfills this objective, because there are famous irreligious persons and many irreligious persons in the gatherings who at once second these contemptible women, only because they are useful as supporters and to ridicule. That is the secret of many *ugly and foolish* irreligious women.

What is the remedy then? Not to praise them. This is the best punishment and the best cure; but, at the same time, it is necessary that they not understand that we know the cause of the illness. This would mean declaring them ugly women, and I wrote on a certain occasion that women never forgive those who give them such a name. Without a doubt, it takes common sense to let them perceive our disapproval but not its cause; but this reserve is so necessary that, if it cannot be attained, or if we are afraid of embarrassment, the best course then is to avoid dealing with them; if necessary, silence may be the only course left. My dear Elpidio, do not insult any woman, because all of them, in this case, become vipers whom you never will subdue. The surest way to ratify them in their irreligiosity would be to put them in need of defending themselves against the suspicion that it is only a resource to make up for the lack of talent and beauty. In these circumstances, a woman never gives up, because it would amount to a confession that she knows herself a fool and is aware that she is ugly. The mere sound of these words makes a woman jump, and never say it in her presence if you do not want to have a rough time.

It is very important for the advance of religion, to take advantage of these women and to cleverly involve them in the defense of sound doctrine, which they would gladly do because, in fact, their irreligiosity is only speculative, and they are encouraged by the esteem you have for them and their talents. You will tell me that this leads them to a detestable hypocrisy, but I answer that it is to turn them from real hypocrisy, and that the other one is apparent, and in this way you prevent them from doing harm and destroying themselves. I do not doubt that vanity is the string we pull, but praiseworthy works can be produced without mixing the poison of vainglory. It will therefore be their fault, and not the fault of any who induce them to do virtuous works, if they lose merit because of feelings other than real piety. Sometimes we are forced, my dear friend, to make use, so to speak, of the enemy's weapons to defend ourselves and destroy him; and this will never be a treachery but rather must be considered a wise and heroic action.

With regard to women in love, I can only say they are crazy and must be treated as such. It is undoubtedly very lamentable to hear them talk nonsense, but it must be expected that their absurdities will last as long as their love madness. There is a great obstacle for the reformation of these unfortunate women, which is that they consider as an attack against the object of their love everything you say in support of the religious principles that he detests or at least does not admit. You may deduce how difficult it is to be convinced when you are in such a state of mind, and thus it is advisable to avoid controversies with girls in love. This situation is very dangerous; if you are not cautious in the management of these irreligious women in love, you produce in them a daring and uncontrollable character, because the check of religion is lacking and they have the incentive of one of the most powerful passions. It is advisable to make them understand we do not want to begin controversies or insult them. We should not insinuate we know the cause of their irreligiosity, and whatever may be the cause, we must intend to heal them with gentle means. If our suggestions cause annoyance, it is advisable to give up at once, because we waste our time; we should not abandon them but wait for another chance. Experience proves that this kind of delusion ends when the circumstances change, since they either marry the irreligious or very soon become bored with irreligiosity, because they notice its effects; or they are abandoned and their hatred becomes implacable. Then they detest irreligiosity for the opposite reason from the one which drew them into it. Whereas before they were determined to please, later they persist in offending those whom they held in so much esteem, and they desire only revenge.

Women who are irreligious out of perversity of heart—I mean those who are not guided by love or vainglory, but who do not have any bridle for their disorderly passions—are worse still than all irreligious men, and their correction is very difficult. Gentle means seldom bring about an effect, and strict ones almost always exasperate. The only course left is to convince them about their moral faults without letting them enter into speculative matters or taking notice of their blasphemies; and when they are certain that we know the facts which prove their slackness, they give in and blush for shame, because they are aware that our indifference in the refutation of their errors comes from our knowledge of its voluntariness and shameful aims. If we cannot convince them of their perversity, it is advisable at least to let them know our judgment even if they will be furious, because they have no other cure; and as long as they are concealed perverts they will be obvious irreligious women.

There is fortunately a great difference between immoral men and women, because the latter rarely pass for immoral unless they are prostitutes, and the former often boast of their slackness. Thus it is easier to keep women in check by the force of public opinion; and if they think we take their irreligiosity as a signal of disorder, they stop at nothing to make that impression disappear, beginning with not causing a scandal with their nonsense and ending by forgetting it all, thus regaining common sense; and virtue comes back to a heart in which before there were only horrendous sins. These cases are very rare indeed, but as they are possible and have taken place, we should have hope that we may cause a repetition.

Undoubtedly, you will take as a joke that I drew your attention for so long to women's irreligiosity, because this subject does not deserve the slightest consideration; not among philosophers, who always consider them as children, nor among the majority of men, who have bestowed upon them the privilege of talking as they like, since their words are not given consideration except if they refer to love. How they deceive themselves by this way of thinking! We hear this language very often, but it is always refuted by experience, which demonstrates that society is ruled by women; and thus their slackness, in every sense, always brings about the most unfortunate effects. By the misery of human nature, men never want to be excelled by the sex they improperly call the weaker sex only because of its want of physical strength (the result not so much of constitution as of inertia); and, on the other hand, having made the lamentable mistake of considering the irreligious ones as strong souls, it so happens that the irreligiosity of women has amounted to a danger forced on a lot of people. Among these are those called people of the world, not because of their experience but, on the contrary, because they do not know it and become its slaves. You hardly find one, even among the more moderate, who does not introduce himself as irreligious or at least as indifferent to irreligiosity when he is in the company of ladies *in name only,* who flaunt their incredulity. Without resorting to private anecdotes, I may remember a public fact that obviously proves the foundation of my remarks.

AN ANECDOTE OF AN IRRELIGIOUS WOMAN
—FANNY WRIGHT

Perhaps you have heard about a devil dressed in women's clothes whose name is Fanny Wright. This devilish creature presents herself as the mother of irreligiosity, since she practices and teaches it by all means. Some persons who have seen her assured me that she lacks beauty, and even, we may say justly, is ugly. It is said she speaks several languages, but I am not certain whether she speaks in languages other than English in public; and being blunt, or rather cheeky, she has constituted herself as a public teacher of immorality, preaching in theaters and other public places where thousands of persons gather to hear her. She has visited this country for a second time to sow the seeds of irreligiosity, which will be very difficult to destroy, and has returned to England to continue her scandals. She preached against all beliefs and when she thought her followers were very *careless,* that is to say, very drowsy, began to preach openly against the more essential points of morality. Nevertheless, she did not dare to do it with as freely in public as in private, because she feared exposure herself to what finally happened, in spite of all her precautions: that is, some of her letters against matrimony, of a low and seductive kind, were printed, and she fell in universal contempt and abomination. She has perverted many people and given opportunity to many others, already perverted, for presenting themselves cheekily as members of a new sect, which boasts of not belonging to any belief, even though it does not dare to say it has no morals. I have been told that this refuter of matrimony finally got married! We realize thus that there are all sorts of people and every absurd thing is possible. I intend to give you an idea of this modern heroine of irreligiosity in order to prepare the field of your observation for my indications, and for that reason I must tell you the story, to a certain extent secret, of the great influence of this despicable woman.

Every person who does not trust in outward appearances knows very well that this pernicious woman is, and always has been, a mere tool of several irreligious persons and especially of a certain individual who is supposedly the author of all the harangues or depraved lessons that have done so much harm. This fact proves that irreligious persons know very well the value of a woman in their party, and believers must learn to avoid such antagonists. The stratagem was well known in two noteworthy occasions. In the city of Philadelphia the use of one of those so-called churches, which are useful for everything, was granted to this irreligious woman. There was an extraordinary gathering to hear the blasphemies of this scoundrel; but among those present was a young lawyer with very different intentions, because he was determined to ridicule this perverted woman and let her know that she was only a vile tool, as I have told you. After she spoke with the greatest eloquence, defying everybody and offering an explanation for the most difficult points and a refutation for arguments considered as powerful but which she treated as foolishness, the funny young lawyer asked for permission to speak and began his talk, singing the praises of the talent of the prodigious defender of irreligiosity, and as soon as he thought he had attracted attention—even she heard him gladly—he began politely but firmly to refute her in such a way that everybody waited for her answer; but she went out as soon as she could do so. Maybe in a moderate woman this action might have been considered as delicacy, but in this cheeky woman it proved her incapacity and that she could speak only from memory of the lesson given by others in writing, which was exactly the suspicion of her refuter. In the city of Boston a wearisome trick was played on her by a man of knowledge disguised as a handcart man. When the haranguer was in the strongest part of her talk the good man entered the room and playing his role as a rustic interrupted her to ask a question. The worried woman tried to ignore the man with contempt and continued her talk; but the questioner interrupted her again with another question, more difficult than the first one, and the audience's laughter suggested to the speaker that they were aware of the matter. She gave no answer and went out of the room and in a few hours she left Boston, where surely they treated her better than in some other places.

Here it was proven by experience that when irreligious persons unfortunately find a woman who adopts their principles and has the courage to defend them, they never fail to use her to get, by the use of such infamous means, something they would never get by themselves. If the person who directs this unfortunate woman had appeared in public, he perhaps would have never gotten applause—rather the audience would have detested him—but as a woman was presented, given the rarity of that fact and the privileges of her sex, she was heard with pleasure and sometimes cheered. Do you think that her lesson was attended only by depraved men and women without virtue? I must tell you that I am certain that many honest and talented men and many virtuous women were there to hear her. If they intended only to refute her errors, they would not be so reprehensible, but I am certain they were there only to amuse themselves. An unfortunate distraction, which fostered irreligiosity and made the uncautious people believe that the number of her followers was great! I remember having very serious talks with a friend who participated in that joke. He told me many times he was firm in his beliefs and only went there to hear the irreligious preacher out of amusement and to see the extent of her cheek and because, in fact, she spoke the English language very well and her speeches were eloquent. But I asked him whether it was possible to calculate the immense harm done by the presence of men of merit in such gatherings. Is it not a mistake to foster the pride of this woman, making her believe in her unequalled talent and that her objections deserve the attention the ministers have not paid?

In fact, I think that by a special Divine providence not only the priests of the true Church but also the ministers of the various sects agreed, without previous talks, on the plan to follow regarding this heroine of darkness. No one deigned to attack her writings or harangues, and all of them tried to give to the incautious people, with contempt, the answer to her captious objections. This contempt brought about an admirable effect, because people knew that silence was a wise measure by which not to leave a margin for greater scandals. We also took into consideration that a dispute would have produced much money for the speculators who moved the machine, and this pecuniary interest would make all controversies endless. We will always lament the corruption of customs caused by this unfortunate woman, but at the same time we will have the consolation of not having increased the harm with unwise measures but rather of having defended religion in a noble and efficacious way, without anybody, not even the most irreligious person, suspecting the slightest weakness. How many imitators we find of Fanny Wright everywhere, less cheeky, but not less perverted!

There are those who suspect that the famous preacher, in spite of the unselfishness she pretends, did not stop casting glances at the *pesetas* she won in plenty because of the imprudence of many people who like buying everything that is harmful; and so her irreligious writings were sold, although they have no literary merit. This is one of the most formidable difficulties for young women with some talent and self-interest; and, undoubtedly, vanity is her fault, always a dangerous and destructive one. A woman desires to have the means to satisfy her passing whims, and at the same time she would like to be considered well educated, and that is not very easy unless she had an extraordinary character; but she can get those means with little work, succeeding in easing her conscience, devoting herself to irreligiosity. This is usually more advantageous than prostitution and does not bear so much dishonor among people, and thus many women usually constitute themselves as mere tools of perverted men, becoming real slaves. Fanny Wright belongs to this kind and has been noteworthy because of her boldness.

I desired to make these remarks in order to prove that the irreligiosity of women usually comes from the irreligiosity of men and that the only means to manage these irreligious women, as I have said, is to let them know that their misery is not concealed to us, and that we value their word as we do their passions, that is, at nothing. Thus, we manage to make them angry with themselves, and if vanity is lacking or lessened it is not difficult for them to follow the advice of sound reasoning and morals. It is necessary to treat them in their line, as we treat prostitutes in theirs, because in both kinds of loose women sin has the same cause, even if both defects are not always found together. I do not know if you have noticed that unbelief is not very common in prostitutes, but rather they are obstinate persons in their crimes with the vain hope that they will mend themselves; and when they are in deadly danger they ask to be reconciled with God and His Church. I do not remember having found one incredulous prostitute. Where does that faith, even if it is dead, come from? From grace, which although not sanctifying, prepares to sanctification and excites the person's soul continuously to draw itself out of so miserable a state; but there is also another cause and it is that unbelief would not bring any advantage regarding the temporal aims of these miserable women. And so they do not care about thinking on points of religion, because even if religion did not exist, they would be treated in the same way by society. As for the remorses of conscience, irreligiosity cannot ease them, and a lot less if they know their depraved origin, because that is a recourse that comes after the commission of the sins they try to continue. Therefore, the situation of the *honest irreligious women* is much more lamentable than the situation of these immoral ones, since the world sometimes gives very honorable status to those perverted women, who cause much more harm. A prostitute has no influence to induce a woman to become one of them, but a decorated and applauded irreligious woman exerts much influence over young women and gets them carried away to dissipation.

Until now, I have likened two kinds of women as if they were in fact different; it will not escape your insight and sound judgment, Elpidio, that they form two species of a general class, divided into public and concealed ones, into downgraded and applauded ones. It may be stated as a rule, with very few exceptions, that irreligious women are dissolute, or are prepared to be dissolute, and only are stopped because they have not yet lost the habit of respecting virtue, which they consider as a human invention and a lamentable weakness. The remarks I made previously on the causes of irreligiosity must be kept in mind, and more so when we are forced to deal with irreligious women, who, shielded behind the prerogatives of their sex, usually conceal a very unbridled immorality under the veil of enlightenment. I have always felt sorry for the simple persons who allow themselves to be fooled by the talks and jokes of these perverted women, succeeding in their foolishness by marrying those women, which is the last disgrace possible for a man of honor. I should like, Elpidio, the young men to be aware of the harm these dangerous women can cause them, from whom can be expected deceits of all kinds, because they have talent to practice the deceits, decorum and prestige to hide their wicked things and no ties with virtue, and so they succeed in becoming accustomed to a sinful life.

The story of most women who became renowned because of their irreligiosity even though gifted with very brilliant talents certainly proves, my dear friend, that the things I just told you are not vain conjectures but lessons of experience. Remember the favorites of the most renowned irreligious philosophers or pseudophilosophers of the sixteenth century. I do not want to mention their names, no matter how abominable they are. You will become convinced, by the stories of their lives, that they were unaware of honor and only had many means to affect it. In later centuries, and even today, we find one thousand examples to prove the same thing, and it is almost impossible, indeed, to find one that proves the opposite. How much would morality gain if men of sound judgment succeeded in being heard when they spoke out against these impostors! But unfortunately, in almost every person, and much more in people of letters, you find a fatal tendency to excuse the defects of women of any talent at all, and, moreover, these women succeed in becoming dangerous on account of their infinite resources to do harm and remain unpunished.

This is one of the main reasons for the authorization of the iniquities of irreligious women in the courts of kings, where a lot of pretenders are always ready for adulation, even if its object is most infamous. There is no one who dares to stand up to these malevolent courtesans, who usually manage the monarchs from afar, without presenting themselves, and dispose of the tranquillity and sometimes of the life of the most modest people of society. Fear is the real cause for this favor, and it is very difficult, if not impossible, to find brave men who challenge all persecutions and are not afraid of anything. The majority follows a very different way and thus it happens that society in the high courts presents more refinement, but at the same time much more refined malice.

Here is another considerable difficulty in the reformation of customs and the restoration of social order, which can never be kept when it is in the hands of irreligious persons. It is known that the minor cities and especially the province cities always take the court as a model, and that the spirit of imitation becomes extreme. It follows from this that very soon you find *provincial women philosophers* and cheeky irreligious women, who consider themselves as pupils of the ones who deprave the capital; and the speculators, who think they bring themselves near the throne by pleasing these indecent women who move those people surrounding the monarchs, do not stop celebrating the *enlightened provincials* in order to be recommended and profit by that. So is the world, Elpidio, and I hope everybody knows it. It is more noticeable that the most worldly persons are the ones who know the world least, and with such pretensions their correction is very difficult. They receive blow after blow and disillusions follow one after another, but they have such a vain idea of their merit and experience that they always put their ignorance down to chance.

The fate of these miserables is pitiable, and even more if, abandoned by those who might remedy their misfortunes, they not only succeed in considering themselves enlightened but have a title by dint of experience, as it is usually said, for becoming guides of society. It is very dangerous to stand up to these teachers, and all the more since they gave themselves the title which is very difficult to have it revoked. It is more advisable to present them no arguments but facts, and some hints of their causes, leaving it to their reasoning to infer the facts that will convince them. I do not approve by any means the plan of those who think they can take advantage through adulation, paying tribute to the mediocre talents of some irreligious persons, in the belief that they will then hear with more interest the truth that they deny without adequate examination. These frauds, in addition to being illicit, always bring about an opposite effect, because rarely is there such a fatuous person who does not know when he is being praised more than deserved, although there are many people who like these exaggerated praises only because they suppose a trickery in the panegyrist, who serves the interest of the praised person even if he does not convince him. The result in these cases is that the admiration comes from ignorance, and you can perceive, my friend, that one who thinks in that way will not be willing to follow the advices of a fatuous person whom he has succeeded in deceiving. Frankness is always necessary and especially if you are dealing with persons of some talent; it follows from this that if they succeed in observing that in fact we have made no mistake regarding their merits, and do not treat them with unfairness or pay them undeserved honors, they will form a good opinion of us, and this is the best disposition to hear us without animosity.

We should live with the irreligious in such a way as to induce them not to be irreligious any more. This remedy, which you have always applied with great skill, is the one I should like to see spread in the whole world and especially in the country that both of us love, and where you, as Titirus in the shade of eternal spring, surely do not forget your Melibeus, who, far from the country, waits for the harshness of a severe winter.

THE JUST AND UNJUST COMPLAINTS
OF THE IRRELIGIOUS

The purely human interest of religious persons is mixed with the holy interest of religion and added to the furor and blind stubbornness of the irreligious; there results from this combination the most horrendous monster, whose cruelties afflict the whole natural order, disturbing propriety and dishonoring philosophy. Attacks are made by both sides and we need to examine them with the calm of Christian charity and good logic, in order to proceed justly and not count ourselves among the deluded.

JUST COMPLAINTS

The irreligious complain with reason of the cruelty with which they have been treated many times, of the haste and the anxiety with which many religious people have run everywhere with the decided determination to find nonbelievers to fight, of the atrocious slander caused by the prejudice and ignorance of many who hear it with pleasure and let themselves be dragged along by those who manifest a false zeal, which is only an infamous vileness. They justly complain of the hypocrisy of many speculators, who pretend to be quite religious only to better hide their irreligiosity and get as much as they want by declaiming against the irreligious. They complain of the robbery which has repeatedly been committed under the pretext of religion. They complain of the darkness which ignorant, and sometimes very perverse, people have spread, under the pretext of the diffusing of the light of faith, whose foundations they pretend not to know. They complain of the iniquity to which the use of religion as an instrument of politics has been put. They complain, finally, that the just and caring means of which I have spoken in my previous letter have not been used with them.

These complaints are so established that all the efforts that have been made to silence them until now have served only as fuel to vengeance, which has caused so much evil. The offended one always expects satisfaction and can do no less than be exasperated when he receives a mere dishonest apology for the most scandalous assaults, or an artificial excuse, which not only does not lessen the enormity of the sin, but even prepares the spirit to expect this to happen again. One must confess that this has been the unjust and mistaken conduct with which many people who are in other ways reasonable and of good sentiments have acted toward the irreligious. These people believe that if the irreligious manage to prove injustices in the adherents of religion, they will be filled with pride and will be more obstinate; but they do not realize that this pride and obstinacy will be much greater when the irreligious discover new injustices as the religious attempt to exonerate themselves.

The irreligious, then, are persuaded that everything that is said against their irreligiosity has hatred of their persons as its origin, and although they are mistaken about this, one must admit that, at times, they are justified in their error. They cannot reconcile with the Gospel the lack of charity that they observe in the conduct of many in respect to themselves; and, they take those who pretend to be believers as either hypocrites or ill-intentioned people who, in spite of believing in the Gospel, do not follow its precepts except for the satisfaction of revenge. In both cases, the complaint is most just.

UNJUST COMPLAINTS

But many others are unfounded and only prove that the disarray of passions does not allow reason an impartial examination, or that the irreligious pretend to hide their depraved intentions under the veil of justice and humanity that they invoke. I will reflect upon some of these, because it would take too long to consider all the complaints; certainly the irreligious have tried to justify their arguments, with the aim that some be believed, and that all of their complaints together delude the unwary.

The irreligious are accustomed to complaining about the reserve that believers use in regard to them, the believers at times going beyond the most complete scorn because of a mere intellectual fault. This is the most ridiculous ruse, since the same ones who use it show by their conduct on other occasions that they know their weakness and lack of principle. Observing the same irreligious people in the diverse states of politics is enough to convince us. Let us suppose that, alleging freedom of thought, there were a boor who started preaching on the streets of New York about the necessity of reestablishing the former government of England in this republic; do you not believe that, aside from what the authorities might do, the preacher would get a comeuppance from the people, and that perhaps the irreligious would be the first to give it to him? Would the one who preached the necessity of establishing a republic in Vienna not run an equal risk? Let us think in the same vein about religious matters and the affair will present no difficulty at all. Everybody could be irreligious, and while irreligiosity is in the mind it cannot be an object of our analysis; and thus it is that, speaking precisely, no one suffers except for what he does and could have avoided. How can there be a right to demand that a religious society approve of the attacks made against it? Let us suppose that there were a people entirely composed of irreligious folk, would these people approve of religious people who were going to preach and proselytize? Each complaint is, then, totally unfounded with respect to the scorn with which the irreligious are viewed.

I am not talking about persecutions by law, about which my opinion is well known; I am only talking about that which could be called *social rejection,* which exists and will always exist among both nonbelievers and believers and is more powerful than all the laws. The country in which I reside confirms my observation, and better evidence of it cannot be found. If *mutual respect* is preserved, society remains quiet and orderly, as in this country; yet attacks are no less intense because of it, nor are its effects less acute. When one carries on without courtesy or prudence, both the peace and harmony of society are destroyed. If the irreligious are more numerous, believers suffer; and if believers prevail, the irreligious are afflicted. It depends on the same nature of things and it is observed in all matters of opinion, therefore those who think in the same manner naturally will join together, and those of contrary opinion only respect each other out of social considerations; yet one would be very foolish to claim a right to a trust that one would be unwilling to grant. I am really convinced that the complaints of the irreligious in this matter are nothing more than a means of conjecture, for they try to enchant believers by recollecting, hypocritically, evangelical doctrines and human rights; they imagine themselves persecuted and they invent a thousand stories, only to achieve whatever they want by means of fear and vanity.

A religious person feels the spiritual ruin of another in such a manner that he would suffer it all rather than cause it; and the irreligious, who see this good disposition, always consider themselves compelled to sin and are scandalized by the least opposition against them. The religious are also vain when, mistaking weakness for prudence, and moved only by the desire to be popular, they support the unjust complaints of the irreligious only to be regarded as generous and unbiased. This is a very grave fault and a most unjust attack on the right to think—a right that everyone is so sensitive to protect. By means of a moral compulsion that at times is equal to a physical one, they wish to force believers to give up their ideas and accept those of the irreligious, so as not to appear their enemies. How many have become persecutors through the desire not to be their enemies! Put vanity (which is the most insidious of all passions) into action, and the most sensible persons tend to sacrifice their feelings so as not to incur a hated and an intolerable reputation. They become in fact (although not in their hearts) the cruelest enemies of their fellow believers and at the same time proceed with greater firmness against them, and in the end the believers become persecuted only in the vain pretext of impeding the persecution of the irreligious, who in turn ridicule the foolish who fall into this trap and bestir themselves to lay out other more dismal traps.

What persecution are we talking about? Why do we give this detestable name to the use of one of the most sacred rights—to give an honest appearance to the most unjust attack? The believer has an unquestionable right to proceed according to his ideas as long as they do not infringe upon social laws or evangelical precepts. Admitting or not to private confidence or intimacy, putting personal and family interests in someone else's hands, should be an act that is entirely free and not subject to investigation or inducement. Since in the opinion of a believer, irreligiosity is the foremost sin and the origin of many others, he has a right to proceed according to these principles with regard to his choice of trustworthy persons and members of his family. No one has a right to be trusted; thus no one should complain for not being chosen.

This question, Elpidio, is of the utmost importance and I could give you more examples of unfortunate families who, in trying to avoid the unjust complaints of some irreligious persons, trusted them and in the end were destroyed. You well know that a more extensive explanation would force me to enter into the private lives of people, which I detest; but I hope from your prudence that you infer all that I could say, not with airy proofs, but rather with facts as evident as they are lamentable.

I only wish that the unfortunate ones who take social complacency to the point of sacrificing their religious feelings would meditate a moment on the degrading and ridiculous role they present to the same nonbelievers they wish to please. Yes, as soon as they attain their goal, these same ones who cunningly complain consider those who have been led by their advice as either hypocrites who have pretended to be believers or as weaklings who have sacrificed their beliefs for human considerations. In both cases the role is very dishonorable.

This evil is of such great importance that it affects even the most prudent persons, and it spreads throughout the most enlightened countries. I do not need to convince you that indifference in religion is equivalent to irreligiosity, because the one who insists that the choice of what is believed does not matter truly does not believe in anything. This *indifference* may well be called *religious irreligiosity,* even though these terms contradict each other, since they pretend to preserve some religion when they only preserves a true irreligiosity. There is a great multitude of these irreligious people in this country, and since they cover themselves with a shroud of religion, their complaints are heard by people with much interest; and even many of the enlightened, though they perceive the plot clearly, fall for it, defending religious indifferentism with their example, if not with their words. Observe, Elpidio, how shrewd irreligiosity is! The people, most practical in matters of religious freedom, become the enemy of all religions at the same time that all religions are protected by the law; vanity is the real source of these arguments.

There is not a single conversation in which you do not hear frequently repeated: "I am not concerned, I am liberal and flexible on religious matters." If this means, "in religious matters I do not insult anyone in society," it would be equivalent to say "I act like everyone in this country, except a small number of unwise people"; but the meaning is a different one. The true principle that they try to inculcate is a dogmatic indifference, or better said, dogmatic nullity—holding all dogmas to be good as long as a person believes them.

You may infer that those who think like that while they pretend to belong to a specific religion are no more than irreligious hypocrites covering themselves with a vestment of piety and frankness. This is the great tactic and astuteness with which, by means of complaints, irreligiosity lamentably triumphs.

In effect, there are many people in this country who, judging in a very different mode, use the absurd language that I just mentioned only because it is fashionable, and the one who rejects it is labeled as prejudiced and is exposed to the complaints of countless people, very *religious* they say, but of a different creed. Sad fanaticism in the midst of so much enlightenment! If any one of these people is asked if the objective is to destroy religion and promote irreligiosity, they become very offended, even though they do not do anything else but propagate a principle destructive to all dogma and religion. If irreligiosity would take off the religious mask, it would be hated by the same who now are praising it as wisdom and refined charity. Observe how powerful are groundless irreligious complaints when the believers are either so gullible or ignorant that they believe such complaints just, or so weak and tolerant that even knowing they are unjust, do not dare disregard them.

CIVIL RELIGION IN THE UNITED STATES

This country is always looked upon as a model of perfection, and even though I am one of its admirers, at the same time I would not like to see some delude themselves and lose the important lesson that they may learn in this country they so much laud. The faults of great people have always been the best corrective for mending the average; and by the same token, the imperfections of advanced countries should serve as an antidote to the poison that may be introduced into other, less experienced countries. Anyone who is not stupid, or deluded, will perceive that the principle of civil religious tolerance has been degenerating into dogmatic or purely religious tolerance, from which results a new religion, which has no name (and it is difficult to find one for it). When I am among friends, I call it the *religion of the nothings;* and since the pen has already slipped to communicate my jest to you, be patient and allow me to reveal my thoughts.

The people to whom I am referring do not wish to be counted among the irreligious, and in fact many of them are not. Nor are they considered to have an attachment to any religious sect. They have not formed the religious monster propounded by Jerieu, that is, a church formed by all sects; instead they defend each and everyone's independence and fight the unity of the Church. If you ask me what these people are, my answer is that they are deluded, or they are irreligious; but if you ask me what they *seem* to be, I think I can say that they are people who, while they think themselves religious, are in fact nothing; and this is why I call it the religion of the nothings. Unfortunately it spreads more and more, serving as a cloak for the irreligious, who do not mind covering themselves with it. They recognize it as the best disguise—the most suitable to gain the esteem of the truly religious without assenting to the dogma or discipline of any religion. That is why they do not cease to praise this system, or better said, this social religious conduct, and they complain bitterly when they encounter someone with enough firmness to refuse to play the fool or the *religious charlatan,* one who acts according to the circumstances, seeking only to please, without realizing or caring much about the degradation they incur to sensible people, even when they are not irreligious.

Besides their religious complaints, the irreligious have the fatal practice of being offended by any minor circumstance that does not satisfy their wishes, and they cause much disquiet to many religious people. These are a new kind of complaint, even though they make use of the religious feelings they find in some persons. We could call them social complaints, or perhaps *philosophical complaints,* since enemies of true philosophy have the boldness to call themselves philosophers and have fashioned themselves as apostles of irreligiosity. If it is your misfortune, Elpidio, to deal with this family, you will observe that they are always complaining and protesting injury. Forget any hope of pleasing them; plan only to fulfill your duty, for they are most ungrateful, always complaining. Consider them maniacs. We should not be perturbed by their complaints nor become vain from their praise, because one will follow the other as soon as they find that they have not gotten all they hoped for or plundered the mine. Ingratitude is their principle, and we should not heed it, for we are not so naive as to expect something different from people who are looking for anything they can get.

The result of this is that they are in constant disagreement among themselves, which proves that it is not precisely for religious considerations but because of frustrated expectations. They proceed like what they say they are, that is, *pure animals* of a kind much more perfect than the others we know. Consequently, their norm is sensitivity, and anything that does not gratify it is bad; and gratefulness, when separated from the vanity that produces a sensitivity to the homage and applause of our neighbors, has no power whatsoever in their hearts, much less in their minds. They complain just as a lion roars for food, or other kinds of animals give other signs.

ANECDOTES FROM THE LIFE OF ROUSSEAU

Knowing that you have read the *Memoirs of Marmontel* I want to remind you of some passages that support my observations. The wretched Rousseau, who was always lucky enough to be ridiculed since he could never hide his conceit and cunning, consulted the rogue Diderot about what side he would take in the famous program proposed by the Academy of Dijon, that is to say, whether he should defend the sciences as useful to society, or whether he would become a defender of ignorance. Wanting to laugh at the presumed philosopher, Diderot advised him to attack the sciences, telling him that in this manner he had the merit of singularity, because without a doubt all his opponents would take the ordinary and rational way of defending the sciences. This advice, given solely for the purpose of mocking the conceited and duplicitous philosopher, was so in keeping with his character that he did not hesitate to accept it: here is the defender of ignorance trying to obtain the award of wisdom. Do you know that the Academy bestowed it to him? In this case, I am of the same opinion as La Harpe: that illustrious society appeared much more imprudent and ridiculous than the dunce it so capriciously rewarded. The glories and dishonors of this Genevan, however, are not my main concern, so I will call your attention to the false character of the irreligious, and therefore to the groundlessness of their complaints when we guard against them. I know very well that you never can deduce a universal proposition from a particular case, and that the nonsense of one person would be proof of it in the rest of his class. I therefore want to give a single example, an observation that I think is founded on an infinite number of cases to which you, Elpidio, could undoubtedly add many others. The words of Diderot that Marmontel quoted, as told to him by Voltaire, deserve to be cited:

I was in prison in Vincennes, Diderot says, when Rousseau came to see me. He had made me his Aristarchus. One day while we were taking a walk he informed me that the Academy of Dijon had proposed an interesting program, mainly: *If the reestablishment of sciences and arts has contributed to modify the customs.* "What side would you take?" I asked him. "Affirmative," he responded to me. "This is the asses' bridge," I retorted. "All common talents will take that same way and you will only find common ideas while the opposite way presents to philosophy a new rich and fertile field." "You are right," he responded after meditating for a moment. "I will follow your advice." From that moment, Marmontel adds, the character that he should play, as well as the kind of mask, was decided.[1]

This is an example of the sincerity of the irreligious and of the desire to find truth and promote philosophy. They are in fact only a mask and nothing else. "Not in vain," said Voltaire, after he heard this anecdote: "This man is fiction from head to toe, in body and soul: it pleases him to represent sometimes the stoic and sometimes the cynical; he will belie himself so many times till his own mask will give him away." And, may I ask, did Voltaire not have a thousand masks and could this not be used to give more weight to my observation?

Let us continue to observe the Genevan philosopher in his ridiculous role in the hope that his miseries will correct his unwary admirers. Determined to fool the whole world, he realized he had to add an air of mystery to his farce, introducing something of the supernatural and divine in the lowest of impostures. Let us hear how he refers to his marvelous inspiration in a letter to Malesherbes.

I was going to see Diderot, who was in prison in Vicennes, and I had the *Mercury* in my pocket, which

---

1. Marmontel, *Memoirs,* book 7, 223.

I took out and started to glance through on the way. I found the Academy question that gave motive to my first writing. If there has ever been a sudden inspiration, undoubtedly it was the one I felt towards this reading. I felt my spirit bathe in a thousand lights and a network of very vivid ideas presented itself with such force and confusion that it put me in an inexplicable disorder. I then experienced such bewilderment as if I was drunk. I was being oppressed by such palpitations that my heart was swollen and being unable to walk or breathe, I lay down under a tree, where I spent half an hour in such a state that when I got up I realized my clothes were sopping wet from the tears that I unconsciously poured out.[2]

From this profound and mysterious meditation Rousseau wants to make us believe that here is where the *eloquent foolery* came from that flattered so many ears but hurt so many hearts.

Could there be a greater fraud? Is this the same man who has so often declaimed against impostors, who established as a modern Heraclitus never stopped complaining and condoling himself with men's delusions? My friend, decide what we shall do about such complaints. Indeed, his friends did let him know, and, if I remember correctly, after he pulled one of his tricks on Duclos, Duclos asked him: "Are you mischievous or dumb?" "Neither," cried out Rousseau, "just an unhappy man." "Keep your eloquence," said Duclos, "to use with others. As for me, I know value and I cannot fantasize." The complaining philosopher was left completely bewildered, his intrigue exposed. How much would society benefit if all imitators of this silly pedantic would be treated like this!

ANOTHER ANECDOTE FROM VARELA'S YEARS IN HAVANA

Forgive me, dear Elpidio, if I bother you with the narration of an incident that, in a way, I can call personal and that

---

2. Rousseau (taken from a letter of his to Malesherbes).

shows that the author of *Emil* is not the only one in madness or perversity. I was a professor at San Carlos in my dear Havana, and among other fools (a group that always follows me) there came into my room a man about thirty years old, thin, pale, weak and badly dressed. I could not help but notice from his appearance that he was sick. After a few moments of conversation I realized that his soul was even sicker, for he was very irreligious, and I went on to notice that this person was one of the *Frenchified.* Ignoring then my political tendencies, even though he could not ignore my religious ones, he started to tell me how he abused each party and how in his travels with the French Army he could always get a bed even when the bishop could not. As you see, Elpidio, the good opportunist had everything he needed for his game. Nevertheless, no matter how he tried to present himself as a brute, I could not forget that he still was a man, so I treated him like one, trying to comfort him and help him without hurting his feelings, which in wicked men are very strong because they are so proud. He offered to sell me one of his works, leaving the price to my discretion. I paid him twice its worth, but I could not hide the gift from him and he insinuated that I was trying to favor him. No doubt I was taking the chance of having happen to me what happened to the Count of Aranda, the Spanish Ambassador in France, who was insulted by Rousseau in a similar case. Fortunately, I escaped from this danger. He came back a few days later selling a much better work, which I later discovered was not his but came from a generous man who did not have anything else to give him (having given him much), and who told him to sell it and use the money for himself. He could not sell it in school, and for no other reason he came to my room, swearing and crying against the ingratitude of people. I remember that he said, among other things, that he was in the same situation as the famous *Juan Santiago,* who was abandoned by people and persecuted by fortune. I said to myself, "and as wicked and possessed by the devil as the original from whom you are a copy," but I did not want to answer him one word. He left my room without saying good-bye and with a desperate look. I did not think I should let him go in this condition, I followed him to see if I could placate his fury. He stopped in the cloister where I talked to him for a few moments. If he had been thinking, he would have known his insanity, but his passion was so strong that he could not control himself and he eased his pain with new and ridiculous exclamations, with grimaces that in another situation would have made me laugh but now only made me sad to see how wickedness can degrade the human person. You can imagine that he left the school swearing at the unjust manner in which he had been treated, since he had not received the ninety dollars for the work he was trying to sell, despite the fact that I bought another from him for an exhorbitant price.

I went back to my room feeling very sad because of the incident I had just witnessed; also I was considering the ingratitude that irreligiousity leads to and how unjustifiable the complaints of the irreligious are. I said to myself: "How many people would this wretch deceive with his eloquence! How will he describe this school where he has received attention? How many will believe him because of the tendency nowadays to believe everything that is said against the priests! In this way, I said to myself, many institutes have been slandered and the complaints of the irreligious should only be seen as signs of their slander. The more they complain, the more certain it is that they have slandered. I wished in those moments to have all of Havana's youth there in order for them to receive a practical lesson on the worth of the irreligious and the credit of their words when, with great hypocrisy, they say they are persecuted. If the narration of these facts has bothered you, I hope you will forgive me, considering that it affected me in such a way, notwithstanding the fact that it took place many years ago. I cannot forget it so, without knowing how, I have been a little careless in mentioning it in this letter, but friendship seems to give me the right to be sincere.

Enough of anecdotes, you will say. I hope there will never be another one like this to tell; but as long as they are repeated everywhere as we can see in daily life, it is convenient not to forget them, since they are practical teachings that at times are better than books. The harm that irreligiosity causes when it is presented as an object of compassion is incalculable. It is therefore necessary to unmask it and make it show its real face in order to deprive it of the means to deceive people so hypocritically. Youth, impetuous by nature, is carried away by fiery emotions when it sees science and virtue persecuted; and since there are hardly any irreligious people who do not pretend to act in a wise and virtuous way, unjustly persecuted by superstition and fanaticism, they profit from their complaints and harangues, thus inducing young people to commit horrible abuses. True enlightenment is a shield against the sarcasm of pseudoscience that has spread so much darkness all over the world. Because of this we should promote the right kind of knowledge in order to destroy deceitful feelings that transform the human heart into a blind and ridiculous tool of perversity. Oh, Elpidio, what a rare virtue is fortitude, even though so many claim it! I believe fortitude reveals itself in nothing so much as when it resists the feelings of self-love when, fooling ourselves, we give the latter charming names like humanity, justice, and science. Many endure fear but very few will not surrender to adulation. the irreligious take advantage of this human weakness and this is the secret of the power of their groundless complaints. Let Heaven allow us, my beloved friend, to see the true *strong souls,* among which yours has a prominent place, proliferate.

THE FUROR OF IRRELIGIOSITY

I would not want, my dearest Elpidio, to present to your imagination terrible images that cannot but move your sensitivity; but the horrendous picture of the furor of irreligiosity causes such an impression that, in order to look for some consolation, I have determined to tell you in this letter the very sad conclusions that I have arrived at about this *powerful misery.* Irreligiosity fills mortals with horror, and they are humiliated at the same time under the hand of a vindictive God, who permits it as punishment for such daring sinners. The person believes himself superior to everything when he cares about nothing, and what is a source of peace and joy in the virtuous person is a source of anxiety and sadness in the irreligious, whose situation I have already considered in previous letters; but I want to go now into some details, whose examination yields a thousand proofs that irreligiosity is the most horrendous of monsters and the most pitiful of all calamities.

The irreligious is enraged at the sight of a religion in which millions of happy persons find consolation, persons whom the irreligious has in vain attempted to portray as deluded, since conscience tells him that illusion is incompatible with true happiness, and that time, which has finished with all illusions, far from destroying holy religion, confirms and propagates it. Pride comes to torment the irreligious and more than once repeats the sacrilegious exclamation of the leader of the famous unbelievers of the eighteenth century: *can it be possible that so many of us philosophers cannot destroy the work of twelve poor ignorant men!* The irreligious marshals all his talent and makes new efforts, which being futile are only good to increase his furor. The sight of a temple, which for believers is a source of consolation, excites in the irreligious a mortal hate for those who contribute to it; and since these believers are innumerable, the irreligious becomes the enemy of almost all people, and terrified by his isolation he curses his existence. The irreligious desires to have a happy life, but knowing that the duration of one's life is not enough to see evils (as he calls them) eradicated, evils so old and rooted that they have sneered at all the efforts of the greatest philosophers of all ages, the irreligious falls in the greatest despair, because he gets nothing in this world and the other world is for him a chimera. My dear Elpidio, infer his furor, infer his hatred against religion, and you will not be puzzled by his attempts to destroy religion.

How miserable! And even if he were to destroy it, would peace come to dwell in his heart? No, my friend. His furor would only increase. It is of such a nature that it does not calm down, as in other cases, with the destruction of the hated object; and this particular circumstance lets the irreligious foresee an origin whose knowledge he wants to avoid by all means. Indeed, he proves a divine origin in religion, since the sadness for having destroyed it cannot be avoided by any sort of human effort; and when a vain philosophy, fascinating his spirit, persuades him that he has diffused enlightenment, an unknown but commanding voice cries out against such an irreligious assault. The irreligious starts noticing that all is not reduced to this world, and that sparks of a light of a very different nature descend from the other world. Behold a new cause of furor. His deception is certain, as is his humiliation, but his pride is so great that he resents being humiliated even by God himself. He does not want anyone to be superior to him and aware in his heart of all these guilty feelings that are proof of his being somehow inclined to admit that there is one superior to him to whose laws he is subject, he turns as a tiger against himself, and would like to devour his very entrails so that they would not torment him in such a horrendous manner. The irreligious becomes an enemy of God, of men and of himself. Only objects of hate and furor exist for the unfortunate. Life is a torment, but death is a much greater one.

The irreligious begins to know that religion is never destroyed, although some of its supporters may be seduced, and he begins to know that, when the tree of irreligiosity is believed to be more firmly rooted and more leafy with vices they call delights, a breadth whose origin he cannot know, cuts the leaves off, scatters its finest branches in the air and bends its erect trunk. The hand of an all-powerful being lets itself be felt everywhere and his corrections do not have the same effect as those of a loving father on an obedient child, but are those of a just and relentless judge over a proud and stubborn delinquent. His crime confuses him, but his confession confuses him even more. It is impossible to hide it, it is folly to maintain it, it is a humiliation to hate it; and among these powerful and contrary feelings the irreligious finds the greatest despair. Being a tremendous evil, it produces a hate toward all those who provoke it, and this is the way the irreligious directs his sweet furor not against his fellow unbelievers but against believers.

A REFLECTION ON THE TOMBS OF VOLTAIRE AND ROUSSEAU

This idea reminds me of an observation that I have repeatedly made about the tombs of the two coryphaei of irreligiosity in the last century. You shall know, my Elpidio, that the temple of Saint Geneviève has been profanely made into a pantheon, and that among the many irreligious men that have been placed there, the two tombs of Voltaire and Rousseau are across from each other. Perhaps you do not ignore that the *naive philosophers* who take care of the profaned temple and show the foreigners the sepulchers of the different personages say, with great emphasis, as soon as they arrive at Voltaire's: "le tombeau de Voltaire," and at that moment they all doff their hats. Then they go to the tomb of Rousseau and they pay the same honors. What fanatic irreligiosity! What a flagrant contradiction according to the principles of the unbelievers! The Catholics are naive because they venerate the relics of saints, and they believe themselves to be very enlightened paying such homages to the remains of Voltaire!

According to Voltaire's doctrine, only inert matter remains; he thus did not have soul or, if he ever had, it perished with his body. And to say it once and for all, Voltaire is no more than a *name* without object, and it is to this *vain name* that honors are paid as to a real being. Can there be a greater stupidity than to attempt to honor an object that does not exist? More rightly should they doff their hats before his works. But laying this contradiction aside, I could not help remembering an anecdote from the life of Rousseau that proves how far he was getting along with the one who is now his neighbor in the sepulcher. He was once in his country house, which was precisely opposite Voltaire's. One of his friends told him (pointing toward said house) that Voltaire was there, and he responded, "if this is so, I think that even the air coming from that direction makes me sick." Voltaire, for his part, was no less sarcastic in his words against Rousseau. So, which one of them was so stupid as not to know the value of the other, or so perverse as to attack him? Which one of them deserves that submissive homage? Is it not clear that neither of them does? These two *little angels,* however, who hated each other to death while on earth and who never had a fixed doctrine, lie one across from the other and are equally honored as torches of learning and norms of virtue! As if virtue could coexist with personal hate and science with lack of certainty.

Undoubtedly you will accuse me of having made a digression, and frankly I will confess that I know it; but I believe that my motives are not hidden to you and that these motives can excuse me. I could, however, present the heroes I have dealt with as norms of furor as well as those of irreligiosity and pride. Remember when Voltaire in his old age jumped from the bed where he lay sick, and almost naked he was moved by rage to dance in front of his friends, just because one of them told him that the rascal Frederick emperor of Prussia, praising a young poet, said that he was a sun in its zenith, and that Voltaire was a sun in its setting. Although part of this fury resulted from his being a poet, because all poets are furious when their verses are at stake and more jealous of their poetic reputation than women are of their beauty, that is all that can be said.

There is no furor more implacable than the one that comes from a mocked vanity. Reflect upon the different occurrences of human life and you will be convinced of the certainty of this idea. The injuries that do not come together with insult are losses to which one easily adapts, sometimes the very vanity being a means for resignation; but when that vanity is dejected, unless it happens by way of virtue, it provokes a furor so constant that time only serves to increase it. From this it follows that when the soul of the irreligious finds itself deprived of all virtue, its furor is not comparable with the most terrible furor that can ever take hold of the soul of a believer. I have already observed in my previous letters that the virtues of the irreligious are neither real nor meritorious, but simply calculated by *secular ethics*. They do not exert in his soul the command of the true virtue, and so they cannot calm him. Laws say nothing about hate or vanity, because they only address the operation of the social order, personal security and mutual rights, since it is of no concern to the legislator that a fool bursts with vanity and that he hates everyone, as long as he hurts no one besides himself. It follows, then, that the virtue of the irreligious, always limited to the observance of the laws (when they cannot break it without risk), turns out to be of no value when it deals with objects not related to this sphere; and therefore, far from repressing their furor, they only contribute to augment it. Yes, my friend, to augment it, because seeing that not even this kind of virtue, which although superficial also demands some sacrifices, can reconcile the irreligious with himself after he has suffered a wound in his vanity, he hands himself over more than ever to rage and desperation.

Note, Elpidio, that the irreligious not perceiving in the same manner as the believer nor under the same relations, their furor is also of a different kind, or rather it is *more furor* than any other, since nothing acts as an obstacle except physical force. Objects only have a value relative to his person, and as far as they are useful. Therefore their destruction, when they are no longer useful, in no way affects the irreligious. The same evil that they cause is seen at times as a duty, not perceiving, much less accepting, anything related to a future state. Consequently they destroy and kill in cold blood, caring much less for other acts of less importance. The hand of an assassin who luckily keeps some faith trembles and at times refrains from striking, even though he might escape the arm of the law; but the irreligious who takes such feelings as ignorance and weakness, strikes without fear and finds only pleasure in giving free rein to his fury. The number of his victims matters little. The crime is only a voice and revenge is a delight. If hate succeeds in destroying the links that nature and education have established among people, nothing remains but an unbridled fury, which, not feeling any pain in the havoc it causes, repeats it with pleasure, not knowing the value of the word cruelty.

I remember that among the irreverent sarcasms of Pirron can be found his epitaph, which he wrote himself so there would not be any doubt of how he had spent his sad life, which no matter how hard he pretended to hide it was a continuous torment. This unfortunate one then said, "here lies Pirron, who lived without knowing what he was and died without knowing where he was going." It is horrifying, Elpidio, that a rational being could write such a confession of his ignorance and of his imprudence in refusing to recognize it, but rather on the contrary, allowed himself to be led by it. What fury can be compared to a soul in such a terrible state?

Imagine the heart of a person in such state to be like a moving and inseparable inferno where the miserable irreligious burns alive, who, were he not completely deluded, could know what he was and where he was going if he did not take another road. Surely Pirron is not the only one who feels this way, although he has had very few imitators in his ingeniousness in confessing them, and by the state of his tormented soul you can deduce the feelings of those similar to him, and you will know by a simple reflection that these miserable ones are the victims of an inexplicable furor.

I would not want to speak about the innocent blood shed by the unjust hand of irreligiosity, because nature itself, even disregarding religious affection, is moved by the sole memory of so many horrors. I am the first to lament the illusion of those who wishing to honor God have believed it necessary to kill people; but I also lament the perversity of those who try to prove that there is no God by killing those who confess and praise him. There is nothing more frequent than the invectives against religious persecution, which are always exaggerated and aggravated; but what we can call *irreligious persecution* is heard with indifference. This started in the beginning of the world and it is very simple to believe that it will last until its end. It will change its scenery, its means and its degree—but never its nature.

Why should we be concerned about irreligiosity? To learn how to suffer it and offer it as a sacrifice to a God of goodness, who was the most persecuted one; to avoid being ourselves the instrument or cause of this horrendous crime; to terrify the irreligious sacrifices with the same serenity and meekness of their victims; to indicate with a finger covered with the blood of those who found death for the glory of the author of death itself; to elevate in honor of holy religion indestructible temples, cemented in solid virtues, which, not being the work of humans, do not yield to their efforts neither do they perish with them. I implore your friendship, Elpidio, and forgive me if, in the profound sadness that oppresses my heart in these moments, I write strong expressions that may appear to allude to specific cases against my will. I expect your indulgence if by misfortune I let the mere human rather than the priest in me speak.

THE MARTYRS' WITNESS

The Church of God has always extinguished the fire of persecutions; she has submerged the enraged hosts of the disastrous irreligiosity of every century in the blood of her children and in a sea of tender tears. Permit me, illustrious martyrs of Christianity, to dare praise you, not to add anything to your glory but to excite in my soul the sweet emotions that your memories cause. Permit me to celebrate your unheard-of victory, won with the death of the winners and the life of the defeated. How many were born for heaven each time a few died for the world! You, oh Roman amphitheater, respected by history as a monument to the triumph of holy religion, you record, with your immense space and high walls, the innumerable witnesses of the martyrs' perseverance, meekness, and courage. At your sight the unbeliever vacillates as he recognizes that an illusion could not be the origin of so much and so rare heroism, neither could it snatch with its example so many victims from the hands of irreligiosity and sacrifice them in order to destroy them. The tree of the cross[1] is seen rising in your center, as in the paradise of life, and around it Christians raise songs of victory to the patient God, whose imitators dyed with their blood the grounds consecrated to the glories of the Church by her most feared enemies. It seemes to me that I see the infernal furies flee in horror upon seeing the theater of their cruelties converted into the new Eden of Christianity, and there, far away, they throw desperate looks over the new scenes of glory that have been the effect of their assaults against the spouse of the immaculate lamb.

But alas! The real suffering was not the pain and death of the martyrs, but the persecution of the Holy Church. This was the true torment of those just souls, as it is now the torment of a great number of believers when they see that while martyrs are uncommon the cause of martyrdom is indeed very common today. Irreligiosity takes a different road, to see if it effectively destroys the hated religion, and it appears much more furious, although more dissembling.

The rigors of persecution are not only suffered in jails and scaffolds, for the *philosophical mode* practiced by the enemies of Christianity is most cruel. But, why do the irreligious persecute the Holy Church? Only because its origin is divine, and persecution itself is an evident sign of this truth, which the irreligious pretend to obscure in vain. Let us examine the alleged causes, and they will be the best arguments to demonstrate the blind furor and unfortunate ignorance of the persecutors.

---

1. The amphitheatre, although ruined in part, conserves its walls, which are very high, and in fact there is a large cross in the center and various others around for the devotionals which the faithful practice with the greatest devotion. In this sacred place, in which the martyrs preached with their example, the ministers of the Gospel now ordinarily preach to the people.

ALLEGED CAUSES OF IRRELIGIOSITY

The perversity of many Catholics, and what is more painful, that of many ministers of the altar is alleged by the unbelievers, who dwell on this question and believe that their considerations have the weight of arguments. The actual failings are exaggerated and many others are maliciously feigned. But is this mayhem able to prove anything against the Church? On the contrary it follows that the Church is one and holy. Those members of the Church who do not observe her doctrine and infringe her laws are perverse; but those who obey her would never be able to be so. What a blindness! They want to prove that a law is bad because those who do not observe such a law are bad, those who kept it being just. Would this line of thinking not suffice to contain the furious persecutors of the Church? It would suffice, undoubtedly, if these persecutors were guided by reason, whose rights they applaud; but we see these presumed philosophers, who are guided by their unbridled passions, ridiculed daily. Is it not the greatest of injustices and the most unheard-of cruelty to attack innocence only because it is being attacked? The Church, as tender mother, laments the misguidance of her children, and is it not an injustice to increase her sorrow by imputing to her these very crimes she detests? The argument is ridiculous and the intention corrupt.

Those who publish the defects of *nominal* Christians make a public confession of the holiness of Christianity, which is not in harmony with them; and therefore, far from persecuting it, they should promote it if in effect their intention were that of correcting these defects. How hypocritical are the irreligious when they boast an extraordinary zeal for the virtue that they do not know and that they despise! These enemies of hypocrisy are the greatest hypocrites, since they reduce everything to a true speculation.

Observe as well, my dear Elpidio, that with their works they counteract their words, and they confess the weakness of their argument and the injustice of the furor with which they attack Catholics. As deceived as the irreligious are, they cannot deny that in fact there are among them very few who are not totally demoralized, and therefore if the argument based on the improper conduct of the believers had any value, it should have the same value in regards to irreligiosity, which should excite against itself the furor of the irreligious. Therefore, if this way of thinking were valid they could justify to themselves all the persecutions they suffer, and the furor undertaken at times by their enemies.

In order to underscore more clearly the weakness of this argument, or rather, of this pretext to address their fury against religion and against those who observe this religion, pay attention, Elpidio, to the great number of perverted men found among the irreligious and observe that if their perversity could be a just motive for their furor, they should start by reforming in order to have a right to speak; and on the contrary, they should only be furious with themselves. If you reflect upon the statements of the irreligious as regards immorality, you will see that they admit a retort and that we can always say *a story is told about you having exchanged your nature.*[2] In regards to hypocrisy, none is worse than that which consists in feigning what you do not have, and what you rather detest and attack. I suppose you know that almost all the irreligious are guilty of this kind of hypocrisy and can infer what right they have to our consideration, and what basis has the furor they boast under the pretense of an enlightened zeal.

Another cause the irreligious allege against the Church is the possession of temporary goods, and with great hypocrisy they remind us of the apostolic goods. I wish we could see them renewed, that the Church might lack nothing and the faithful, when they offer their gifts, might not believe themselves to be burdened, but pleased! The reply of Eneas Silvio, later Pius II, to Majerius of Maguncia, is very judicious: "You, who imitating the early Church, wish, he said, a poor priesthood, should also wish with it a poor people imitating the early Christians on both counts. Therefore it is necessary that you require people to beg with the clergy, as our forefathers did, or that you permit that both be rich according to the present times."[3]

---

2. *mutato nomine de te fabula narratur.*
3. See Schwarz, in Sardagna, *Dogmatic Theology,* 2:524.

I do not argue for excessive riches and much less for the *personal* wealth of individual members of the clergy; but it is necessary to confess that without pecuniary means we cannot always do good, and that ministry falls in contempt and is put in jeopardy where it lacks that certain dignity that society considers necessary. There is no doubt that the main dignity and splendor of the clergy should rest on their virtues, since without them they would never be able to command respect, much less be loved by people; nevertheless, having these virtues, the clergy will be able to make a holy use of wealth; and wealth in itself should never attract the indignation of sensible men against the clergy. The excess, in this as in other things, will always be reprehensible and the Church is the first to condemn it; but not for this condemnation must the faithful be persuaded that the possession of something more than what the apostles had is incompatible with the ministry of the apostles. We must, however, consider wealth as clothing, which we should divest ourselves of whenever it is an obstacle to the struggle, but which we can hold on to in other circumstances. Therefore, in the constant fight of the Church against the corrupted times, wealth should be abandoned if it becomes harmful to the true interest, which is the salvation of souls; and in this case, a poor ministry, with no defense but the cross, will always be victorious over all its enemies. Yet why do the impious get enraged and cry over the ecclesiastical riches? To possess these riches themselves? This is the true case, although I do not believe they want to admit it. If the wealth the Church would be deprived of were employed for the benefit of peoples and mainly for the benefit of the poor, nothing would be done above their real and natural application; since the Church never possesses wealth for any other purpose but than the spiritual help for the dignity of worship and administration of sacraments, and the material help for her favorite children who are the poor. Yet when these riches become pabulum for luxury and recompense for sin, you can infer, my friend, the nature of the zeal that sustains the plunderers. Unfortunately, in the history of the plunders that the Church has suffered through the centuries, I do not know if one can be found that does not belong to this category, and this argument of experience cannot be refuted with harangues, and it shows that the fury of the irreligious in these cases has as its source the thirst for gold, however much it wants to appear of another color.

The Church's aim has always been the people's well-being, not only in the spiritual realm but also in the temporal one in regards to peace and mutual charity, in other words, in regards to the eternal life, which is the only happiness. Consequently, the Church is the first to provide help in the great urgencies of the state and in public calamities; and the ministers of the sanctuary far from opposing alienation of the Church's wealth, should present it without any repugnance whatsoever, since in this manner the glory of God and the true splendor of the Church is advanced. I will always lament the stubborness with which some churchmen defend material goods, as if our holy religion depended upon them, without noticing that the sinister interpretations of which their zeal is susceptible cause a much more considerable loss in the real treasure of the Church, which is the love and respect of her faithful. If there are material goods to be used, let them be used according to the spirit of the Gospel. It is convenient, however, that the irreligious be aware that we know them and that their ill-founded furor always be faced with a barrier to restrain it; and this barrier may not be formed of materials other than real learning, charity and frankness.

Let there be no mistake: while people believe that churchmen are bent on being rich, people will regret that they are so, and inasmuch as they try to present truly religious motives, these will be paid no attention, and only the ostensible proofs of worldly interest will be noticed. A noble detachment lets those with bad intentions know that religion is not to be bought and that its ministers do not preach it as mercenaries but as shepherds of souls. The irreligious see themselves, then, in the need to confess that they are moved by the hatred of religion and not by justice. I say this in regard to those who are merely irreligious, but not in regard to thieves, who will grab whenever they can, without any ceremony or excuses; and against them there is no useful precaution, nor any other way than to hand over the purse as to highwaymen. It is known that when money falls in the hands of such a family, it disappears completely and neither the general public nor private agencies receive any benefit; but this is an evil that must be suffered in complete silence, since any claim makes it worse.

It is necessary to confess that many perverse churchmen suppose that the churches have been robbed when they themselves are hindered from robbing them, making an illegitimate use of their funds, and they attempt to increase these funds to have them available for their use. I always remember, Elpidio, that when I was in the middle of a political storm, I had among my fellow coworkers a churchman of great knowledge and virtue, who used to tell me that many of our brother priests are like the *mourning women* who weep without feeling the sorrow, only to perform a job, while those who truly suffer rarely complain.

Dealing with this question with impartiality, I must clearly say that it is one of the many comedies that rascals usually perform, from which they get real profit, that is, *pecuniary* profit, in exchange for their fiction. Some put on the disguise of religion, others that of patriotism, and they represent their roles with so much earnestness that sometimes they mislead even the more sensible people. One actor cries "let the Church goods be respected," and internally adds "so that I may enjoy them," and another exclaims "let the churchmen be stripped of riches they do not need," but also says, "and let me share part of it." There is, however, one difference between these two kinds of speculators, and this is that the poor receive much from the faked religious, and rarely one penny from the faked patriot. To achieve their purpose some exaggerate the needs of the Church, others those of the State, needs that they themselves make up, and consequently they are sure of their existence and duration.

When you hear talk, Elpidio, of the national debt and mainly in Spain, be sure that the *bells toll to rob* and that this is one of the greatest *needs*. The true patriots never rob churches and the true churchmen never are unresponsive to the needs of the country, and if according to the doctrine of St. Augustine they can and at times must break the chalices and sell their gold to help the poor, they not only can but ought to break them to help the country that is the common mother, whose ruin would produce millions of poor. However, in the same manner that it would be a crime to sell the chalices to help the faked poor or even to help the real ones if they can be sustained by other means, so it would be in respect to the faked or real needs of the state. Give me good intention and I accept responsibility for good harmony. Let the religious patriots be in charge, that is to say the true patriots; let all be children of the Church; let them live as brothers, that is to say let them be Christian, and there will be money for everything and for everyone. The furor of the irreligious against churchmen because of the goods they possess is nothing other than envy and disguised greed, not worthy of attention; all that is necessary is to use whatever means to avoid its ravages.

How sad is the situation of the Church in such dangerous circumstances. She is being attacked in the most unjust manner, which is to blame her for the offenses of her own enemies, changing into accusations the most evident proofs of her holiness. Inasmuch as many with great hypocrisy feign to be believers only to commit errors against the very faith that they do not have; and in the name of religion they commit an infinite number of crimes against her, since her enemies want to infer that such offenses have their origin in the Church that mourns them. Would it not be fairer to infer the contrary, namely, that the Church is holy, since only those of her children who do not keep her commandments are criminals, and those who obey them are virtuous?

Should this not be a motive to protect the Church and not to persecute her? This truth is plain, but so is the desire not to notice it, and with such dispositions, we should not wonder at such evil effects. We observe that people of talent, and some of them of quite a bit of education and good logic, incur this defect which would be reprehensible in a beginner, and they have written a large number of works based on this ridiculous sophism, that their authors would not accept in any other matter.

It is a common saying that the persecution is against the churchmen and not against the Church, and with this and other nuances even more ridiculous that those of the most rancid scholastics the attempt has been made to quiet the believers' cries and imprecations. If a just determination to correct abuses would only be made manifest, we would not call it persecution, but protection of the Church against her most cruel adversaries, who are those who feign to be her children only to have easy acceptance in her bosom and to be able to wound her the more easily; but the furor of the irreligious is calmed only with the destruction of the persons, under the pretext that it is not possible to reform them, and without them it is clear that worship suffers and consequently religion too. The attempt to give an honest appearance to this persecution by saying that it is addressed only to bad clergymen is in vain, since irreligiosity says that all clergymen are such, and they would truly be bad if they were not attacked by said irreligiosity. We know, then, that all are persecuted, with the only difference that the vicious give an ostensible motive to be attacked and those whose conduct is not scandalous come to be much more hated because they back a religion that the irreligious want to destroy. Therefore it can be said that in a society where irreligiosity is generalized a clergy habit is an affront.

I would not want to enter into the examination of this mockery directed against the clergymen, because I do not know if the hardiness of the mockers is more deplorable than the weakness of those mocked. Many get exasperated to the point of incurring the same defect as their enemies, becoming enraged against them and giving pabulum to *personal* revenge disguised as religious zeal; others pact with them and join their army only to be ridiculed. Many clergymen brag of being liberals without being anything more than despicable fawners of a party of perverse people, who have the boldness to call themselves free people, as if the slaves of the devil could be such! Would to God that all clergy were truly liberal! But of those who pretend to be such, many are *libertine,* and others base their liberalism on an iniquitous weakness by which they make the most infamous concessions, sacrificing at times the evangelical doctrine only to gain the esteem of the world. These are nevertheless called clergymen and the Church suffers for them. I remember that a companion of mine, a clergymen of great merit, who was considered servile only because he was not crazy, said to me that, in his opinion, the strategy to adopt with these *pseudoclergymen* would be to open a free door for them so that they could leave the sanctuary, since they do not want to stay in it, and degrade them and plunge them into the secular state, where perhaps God would bring them to penance; and if they continued serving the devil, they would not be as damaging to the Church. I assure you, Elpidio, that I am not too far from the opinion of my virtuous companion.

Perhaps my suspicion has become a reality; perhaps I have given pabulum to human feelings when dealing with the cause of heaven. Enough, then, of dealing with irreligiosity, and may I see it destroyed. To conclude, I have a request to make of you; Do not ignore that if *inevitable circumstances separate me from my fatherland for ever,* you also know that the youth to whom I consecrated my energies in other times keeps me in its memory, and I am told that the new generation does not bear my name with indifference. I trust you, then, to transmit my feelings and to procure, in any manner, to stir both generations from the reef of irreligiosity. If my experience can give any weight to my reasoning, tell them that a man, of whose honesty I do not believe they doubt, and who unfortunately or fortunately knows the irreligious thoroughly, can assure them that these are miserable and warns them and pleads with them to avoid such a horrendous precipice. Tell them that they are the sweet hope of the fatherland, and that there is no fatherland without virtue nor virtue with irreligiosity.

Elpidio, we are not going to meet again, unless you come to visit me. Meanwhile, I am planning to send you another series of letters on superstition and fanaticism, if with God's help I keep my present health, since I am still in my forty-eighth year of age, and stronger than what I was at twenty. However, the unfortunate cloud of old age is lingering on the horizon of my life and further ahead I glimpse the lugubrious confines of the empire of death. Nature, in its *imprescriptible* laws, is announcing my decadence, and my good God is warning me that the loan of life that He lent me is about to be due. I throw myself in his merciful arms, without any merits other than those of his Son, and guided by the torch of faith I am walking toward the sepulcher in whose threshold I expect, with the divine grace, to make, with my last breath, a profession of my firm belief and a fervent prayer for the prosperity of my fatherland.

Goodbye, Elpidio! Goodbye!

II. Superstition

TRUE RELIGION AND SUPERSTITION: ANALYSIS AND CONTRASTING EFFECTS

Everyone slept, Elpidio, and a profound and majestic silence took my spirit from the present age and brought light to the past. Without the wonderings of dream, it seemed to me I saw not the trophies of death but its very defeat, as if an image of the future resurrection.[53] Among the thick multitude that glided through an immense firmament animated by a breath of life, I saw the great masters of science and virtue rise up after their lengthy rest, as the brilliant stars of the morning rise up among the waves softly moved by a gentle breeze, rippling through the dense darkness of a prolonged night. Though it was superior to nature I considered it as nothing. My being seemed to detach itself from it, absorbed as I was in the contemplation of a more exalted order of things. I saw the end of ignorance and misery in the fountain of health and wisdom. I saw the chains of passion broken and the spirit free and united to the only being who can bring about its happiness. What harmony! What peace! Oh that I should be able to express the sublime emotions of my soul on that unforgettable night, which poured over me a torrent of strength and consolation. This was a night that all my days shall bless, a night in which insomnia destroyed the image of death as if to mock it, always showing me the most beautiful image of eternal life, a night, Elpidio, that I wish had never ended.

HAPPY NIGHT—
A VISION OF A CHRISTIAN SOCIETY

I transported myself to that most exalted moment in which the womb of eternity was opened to give origin to time and to the most perfect creature, reflecting the image of its creator. This then gave rise to relationships that cannot be altered without altering the objects mentioned, and, since these cannot change because one is infinite and both of them spiritual, they must be *eternal*. One then finds oneself eternally obliged to obedience, gratitude and love at the same time that the Supreme Being is always merciful and just without being obliged. He is not capable of obligation since that always implies inferiority.

Obedience, gratitude and love presuppose a knowledge which, if it is not exact, makes all that homage ridiculous for having been paid to an imaginary object. Thus we see that the concept one has of the creator must be exact so that one's religion may also be exact and never be reduced to sham. But the exactness of knowledge is agreement with its object, and since the one is one and unchangeable, so the other should be one and unchangeable. Otherwise, it goes on to become error. The end result of this is that natural religion is one and unchangeable.

But mankind is aware of the vast distance between the cognitive faculty and the infinite to which one applies it. Thus one tries to go beyond oneself and search greater depths of this sublime idea of so perfect a being, and here one becomes aware of the insufficiency of natural religion to make one happy. At the same time one becomes aware that the infinite being can communicate to one the knowledge that cannot be acquired through natural effort. It is a *free gift*. Here then we have the *possibility* of revelation which, since it is necessary and possible, must be supposed to exist unless one blasphemes against divine goodness. But God could only communicate a single and unchangeable idea of himself and thus revealed religion must be *one and unchangeable*. The result of this is that religion, whether natural or revealed, must be one and unchangeable, and the plurality of religions is a philosophical absurdity.

DESOLATION. THE EVIL OF SUPERSTITION

Ah, my Elpidio, what sad reflections took hold of my spirit as it compared these doctrines with the history of the religious struggles within countries. How horrible the monster of superstition seemed to me in those moments. Superstition separated people from their God and God from himself; it embittered the human heart, brought unrest to families, burned cities, devasted nations and filled the globe with the victims of its cruelty. One can hardly open a page in history without noticing the ravages it wrought. It caused *knowledge* to moan, irreligion to glorify itself, energy to be dismayed, shamelessness to rise to high places, religion to decline, and it constituted itself as an infamous hypocrisy.

Whether a ficticious divinity is adored or an absurd worship is given to the true one, it is clear that the building cannot be stable and that its ruins ought to crush its builders. The truth that is hidden, or better yet, the truth that is not perceived at times, always recovers its rule and an enraged error destroys everything in its path. From this comes vengeance, from this come slanders, and from this come injustices of every kind, which very soon set society aflame, and people come to believe less in God the more they call for him.

For the superstitious, the idea of God is a torment, for having invented a god according to their own willfullness they cannot find in him sublime attributes that are the distinguishing marks of the true God. If the fiction persists in worship, this is not in accord with its object and brings only unrest and grief.

When the unity of religious sentiment is destroyed by superstition (which is always radically different from true belief and always diversified in itself, as is always the case with error), the harmony and holy peace brought about by the delight of a truly religious society are totally destroyed. Then people must seek refuge in tolerance as a measure of prudence, but this is also a sign of division and affliction. The prudent person says, "I suffer so that others will not think as I do, but this very suffering indicates that far from uniting me to them in ideas I prefer to displease them by openly showing my disapproval."

Now then, my Elpidio, no one ignores the fact that it is

almost an innate tendency of human nature to desire approval, or rather, to desire that all people may feel, like and
think as we do. From this come quarrels, and you know very
well that out of every one thousand individuals, only one is
not an arguer and even that one ceases to be so through study
and with violence. From this we can infer that superstition,
while it divides the powers of the human spirit at a most
essential level, such as that of religious belief, necessarily produces a general dissatisfaction, an upheaval in society and an
internal war which is more bothersome and dangerous the
more it is camouflaged.

Oh, if the earth were covered by only one family united in
one pure belief, would it not convey the image of heaven? No
doubt, there is but one family in heaven. There we find no
divisions. How *politically* and *morally* powerful must this
happy family be! How much would society stand to gain in
every sense if that *holy unity* and *purity* of religious principles
were reestablished. Pretense would stop; trust would be reestablished; men and women would work for the common good
of one another as members of the same family. Small differences in the way of thinking about points of lesser importance
would only produce momentary annoyance, which could be
readily reconciled with good harmony an esteemed *truth.* Thus
human miseries would never get to be the cause of division. I
am so convinced of these truths that I believe that a politician
who does not wish to sacrifice the common good to his own
particular feelings should always move toward unity of belief as
an effective bond for social peace, even to the point of leaving
all religious considerations out of the question.

I do not know if I dare tell you, Elpidio, that superstition
causes more damage to the nations than irreligiosity and heresy. The latter are well known enemies who normally, as they
say, do battle *face to face,* even though at times they may
disguise themselves. Superstition, on the other hand, is always
mean, infamous, and perfidious. It puts on a sacred mask in
order to undermine everything that is just and destroy everything that is correct. It seduces in an almost irresistible way
because it can scarcely be recognized. The infidel does not

believe in religion; the heretic is a *nominal Christian*,[1] who believes most of the dogmas but *obstinately* denies one or more of them. The superstitious person pretends to believe everything, but in reality he does not believe in anything since to adore a false god or to give false worship to the true God would be equivalent to real infidelity. The mere reminder of these doctrines should convince you, my Elpidio, that superstition, without yielding to the error of irreligion or heresy, surpasses them in meanness.

RELIGION VS. SUPERSTITION AS A
BELIEF AND AS A FEELING

I wish to present to you some of the reflections I made on this matter on the night I have already mentioned. I compare religion with superstition, considering them from two points of view, as *belief* and as *feeling*. I do not need to warn you that this distinction is necessary, because the same belief can be accompanied by diverse and even opposite feelings, and the same feelings can be associated with different beliefs. False religions as well as the true religion can be found in philanthropic hearts, and consequently it is clear that the identity of the feelings does not prove the identify of the belief. I told myself, however, that it was necessary to examine the relationship between beliefs and feelings and note their particular tendencies.

It is clear that religion *itself* can only be *one:* but religion according to human understanding can *vary* according to how each person see things or imagines them. Consequently, superstition is *human* religion, or the religion of the human mind

---

1. I call the heretic a *nominal Christian* because the denial of a dogma presupposes a falsehood in Christianity and destroys its divine character, leaving only a *nominal Christianity* and consequently *nominal Christians.* If I proposed to elaborate a dogmatic treatise in these letters, it would be easy for me to prove that to admit the possibility of introducing an error considered as a dogma by the Church would be to destroy in one fell swoop all the proofs of the divinity of Christianity and reduce it to a *human Christianity,* which is the only one *preserved by the heretics.*

when it is not in accord with the true and objective religion. Having translated the terms in this fashion, I have reduced the entire matter to analyzing the true religion or religion itself and religion in the human mind.

The divine character of the first indicates unity, consistency, loftiness, justice and immutability, because God is one, because in his works there is no contradiction, because God is infinitely sublime and just and because he is eternal and consequently unchangeable. A religion as a *belief* must of necessity produce mutual love as a *feeling*. Because love tends toward unity, leading creatures toward the Creator and towards loving him in them, such love is bound to be well ordered. This love should also lead to humility (a noble feeling that delights even the most arrogant), since the very loftiness of its object destroys the desire to be equal to it.[54] It makes every worldly height seem as nothing. In the presence of an Infinite Being human misery is thrown into disarray and the door is closed to arrogance. The end result of this should be a detachment from self and a holy courage, which is the origin of *respectful sincerity.* This is a courage that never offends and always edifies; a courage that always compels the very person it admonishes to love; a courage that makes suspicion withdraw, dissipates doubt, inspires trust and lifts up the heart.

Yes, my Elpidio, a truly religious man is one whom no one fears, except the wicked, and all respect, even the irreligious themselves. How noble and uplifted is this holy religion that presents itself to me. While giving self-evident signs of its divine origin, it also gives social happiness, which it ought to generate all over the earth. I regard it as the rays of pure light of the sun of justice, reviving the beings deadened during a long night of ignorance, doubt, fright, and lamentation.

As a necessary consequence of its perfect nature, this religion should have the constancy which crowns all perfections and without which nothing can be called truly perfect. I see in it the elements that ought to produce this desired perfection. Divisions always have their origins in hatred, in doubt, in arrogance or in mistrust, but these monsters have no place in the holy temple of pure religion, which despises them, rooting itself in the opposite virtues. It is necessary, then, that either religion should cease to exist in the very temple consecrated to it or that these monsters be eradicated from it if they have stealthily gained entrance.

Elpidio, I see so clearly the incompatibility of religion with everything that makes one unhappy, that I cannot be less than amazed as I remember the futile efforts that have been made through the ages to destroy religion under the pretext of making people happy. The regretable history of human miseries gives a very important lesson to those who study it with impartiality. The attempt has been made to substitute a changeable principle for one that is constant, a doubtful principle for a certain one. Instead of destroying the empire of disorderly passions, people have attempted to enthrone them, gratifying them in every way as if they did not have ample proof of their *tyrannical insufficiency*. Do you believe that I am talking only about irreligion? No, my friend, I refer first and foremost to superstition, which is the more deadly because it is perfidious. Here now are the observations I made about this monster as I compared it with the pure religion I have just sketched.

The deformities of superstition came before me at once. Superstition is a belief that is essentially diverse, since it is either the work of arrogance, which as a raging hurricane buffets the human mind with vehemence and disorder, or it is a whim that is as varied and diverse as ridiculous. Running through the history of this calamity, we can see that its permanent feature is its inconsistency. The different superstitions that in different ages have degraded people have no other converging point than *ridiculous inconsistency*. They fall or rise; they transform or modify themselves sometimes in very short periods of time. They do not have fixed principles or dogmas, and their own followers do not succeed in defining them. Thus an observer cannot make any sense out of them other than as dreams of greater or lesser duration.

No matter how little one may reflect upon this it should be easily understood that any religious notions that are so varied and inconsistent, far from reassuring and fulfilling the human heart, unsettle and torment it. There can be no peace or consolation where there is no uniformity and constancy. Yes, my Elpidio, the name for inconstant religion is invoked in vain and consequently it is doubtful and incapable of soothing our anxieties. To resort to a variety of religions only serves to increase misfortune as one becomes aware of the insufficiency of the only remedy which was believed to have been found. The very diversity inspires fears and its multitude produces confusion. This results in a never-ending fight of people among themselves and within oneself. From this result great upheavals and a plethora of evils in society. One of the consequences is the debasing of the spirit, which normally tends to give in to every imaginable wickedness, if for no other reason than to uphold every religious notion suggested by whim or treachery as divinely originated and therefore constant. That which was thought to be a principle of life is turned into a principle of destruction, and a false belief is disseminated, and this is the deadliest discord of all.

When the spirits are unsettled about matters of such great importance, they lose all prudence and give themselves to vengeance, which is even more cruel when its cruelties seem to be sanctified. Once the first errors have been committed, the arrogance of pride comes, asserts itself, in order to avoid giving in to correction, and little by little the superstitious loses all sensibility.

The human race reduced to such a deplorable state, one should not be surprised that it is plunged into ignorance and incivility, thus losing the splendor and the noble feelings that inspire true religion. Under the pretext that mysteries are always obscure, superstition has fabricated everything it has wanted to out of its own whim, as if the clouds that are enlightened by the Sun of Justice could resemble those that surround them and be penetrated by the darkness of the void. My Elpidio, there is in pure religion a divine clarity that shines through in the very mysteries, and the truly religious man never believes just to believe but because he ought to believe. However, the superstitious man does not present any rational explanation unless one holds as a rational explanation his whim or a series of whims, which he does not examine so as not to have to refute them. Superstition is a *sweet* illness that comes to be loved by the very patient and thus many difficulties must be overcome in order to cure it. When one believes himself to be religious, it requires a great effort to persuade him that he is an enemy of religion. At times the very attempt only succeeds in engaging and provoking the man to take violent measures which he may consider as just as the cause he defends. The irreligious man never denies irreligiosity, but rather boasts about it. However, the superstitious man denies being so, abhors irreligiosity and grows furious with those who accuse him of it. It is easy to perceive the horrible consequences of these dispositions of the spirit. However, permit me, Elpidio, to continue the parallel between religion and superstition so that I may show you my thinking about the diverse ways in which both make their influence felt in society.

Superstition is opposed to every reform and does not recognize abuses. His mind imprisoned and his heart fearful, the man is reduced to a state of simple insanity. In vain do the truly religious and sensible claim the necessary reforms for the common good of the fatherland and of religion. In vain do they protest and give proof of their sincerity and the religiosity of their feelings. A multitude of fools, led by a band of theologians more rotund than the three *o*'s in the name, comes to the front, screams insult, torments and persecutes, audaciously defending the cause of the devil.[55] This multitude presents itself as promoter of the cause of God and as its army against irreligiosity. There is no reputation nor honor that they do not attack; there is no scientific plan that they do not destroy; there is no work of learning that they do not condemn or at least make look suspicious; there is no measure that they do not take up to extinguish the light of reason, not realizing that this divine torch shines more brilliantly the more it is buffeted.

The truly religious are indignant at the sight of such conduct and attempt to unmask these *religious irreligious,* and in the end new difficulties arise. The good ones, out of their irritation, attack the superstitious, but not always with prudence. Thus many scandals are caused which give the basis for new persecutions and perpetuate hatred in all classes of society. Usually all this is reduced to a war of insult and slander, a multiplying of hateful names, which, when imbedded in the memory, always keep alive the flame of discord. Immediately the superstitious take refuge in Holy Scripture, as the heretics do. They quote texts right and left, doing violence to the texts, and they call everyone irreligious who does not accept their interpretation of these texts. They invoke the authority of the Church to back their own authority, and the people who are spectators in this theological joust alternately applaud the competitors and little by little lose every shred of trust and find themselves in perpetual anxiety.

THE IMPACT OF SUPERSTITION
ON THE MINISTERS OF THE GOSPEL

My dear friend, I want you to note another result that is also deadly, namely, that the wise rush in so rapidly to demonstrate their wisdom that at times they cease to be wise and fall into error; later on they persist in upholding error out of human weakness, which always resents being put down. This temptation, is very dangerous, especially among the clergy. I wish I were not able to tell you about examples of clergy who have fallen in this way. They are filled with shame as they hear the nonsense and observe the wrong ideas of a great number of their companions, and they want to separate themselves from them and show people that they are separated. For this reason they pay homage to the world and sacrifice the most sacred interest of religion on the altar of their vanity. They unconsciously lose the evangelical spirit and are reduced to a nominal clergy who serve neither the Church, which does not recognize them, nor the world, which dispises them no matter how much they have attempted to please it. This is the origin of all heresies with clerical authors, and this is the reason why many of them threw themselves into the abyss of irreligiosity.

Believe me, Elpidio, that I speak from experience. This is the greatest harm produced by superstition. The people distinguish these two classes of clergy, the superstitious and those fallen from virtue; they do not believe there is a third class, or at least they think that this number is rather small. The end result is that all clergy are objects of suspicion. What can one expect from such deplorable circumstances but the debasing of the clergy and the loss of a true religious influence for those wishing to exercise influence in the world. Discredited in this fashion, the clergy, far from propagating religion, becomes a stumbling block to its progress, and like salt that has lost its flavor, it serves only to be thrown out and trampled under foot.

Do not believe that I exaggerate when I ascribe these evils to superstition. What I write is the fruit of very lengthy meditations and well found convictions. I am firmly convinced that people know that we clergy are human, even if they deplore our faults and are scandalized when we commit them. They find consolation in the fact that as *clergy* we guide them with dexterity and the ministry preserves its dignity. However, people observe that there is superstition or irreligiosity in the ministers of the altar, and if they unfortunately and erroneously persuade themselves that all of us are tainted by these two monsters, there is little hope that we might be useful. Now irreligiosity is rare among the clergy and people do not always discover it in them; but superstition is not so rare and always manifests itself. From this we may conclude that superstition is the main cause of a great many evils and is a blotch that blemishes the sacred ministry. You will say that I write a diatribe against the clergy as one of its members. No, my, friend, I write in its defense. If I have to repress any feelings in order to write with impartiality, it is my love of my colleagues and my love for the priestly state, which I have enjoyed for thirty-three years, during which time there has not been a single moment when I have regretted being a priest and many moments when I have been proud to be one.

I repeat that I write in defense of the clergy and this is why I wish to demonstrate the deadly effects of superstition in many of its members, so that it can be seen that superstitious clerics are our *colleagues* only in the *cloth*. Even though they are in our ranks they do not belong to us. The ministry should not suffer any attack from those "ministers" simply because by virtue of an unfortunate ordination they can say they are such. It is necessary to let the weeds grow with the wheat because it is not prudent to uproot them, but it is expedient to point them out so that people may know them or at least know that they are good for nothing except to be thrown into the fire. No matter what malicious or superficial people may say, this weed is not very abundant compared to the total number of priests. The greatest harm is that people have not become aware of this fact, and our enemies work so that the people do not perceive it. Notwithstanding the fact that you know my sincerity, I am afraid that you may suspect that I now write as a *cleric* and thus I see a need to show evidence. Allow me to engage in a small digression, which may not be useful. It is always encouraging to take action when we hold the conviction that evil is not as widespread as we had figured, and especially if I demonstrate that all means are available to overcome it.

Like any other group, the clergy is composed of members whose functions and abilities are very different. There is always one group that directs the function of the ministry and the doctrines that ought to be presented to the people and another group that is purely executive. Do not think that I speak only about the Church in its general councils or about the dogmatic and moral decisions of its head or first Pastor. I wish to consider this matter in a more generic way, restricting myself to what is taught by the learned clergy. Even though this learned clergy is not infallible, they assure us that they explain church doctrines faithfully.

This ecclesiastical body, my Elpidio, has never taught nor authorized any superstition. Quite the contrary, it has written and preached against it. The very enemies of the Church have not been able to cite a single example except for particular instances, and even these have been exceedingly exaggerated. Church history does not give us evidence that the Church has had to condemn superstition as a fact admitted or taught the learned clergy, and what is more, the superstitious have always been foolish. Please note, dear friend, that clerics of this group have fallen into heresies and even irreligiosity but not into superstition.

It follows then that the doctrine of the clergy is not superstitious unless one attributes to them that portion of ignorant men who wear clerical clothes. This would be an injustice, or better yet, an ignorance similar to that which would be committed if we were to take that which is expressed by many ignorant soldiers as the general military opinion or the foolishness of many lawyers as juridical doctrine. If everyone who examines the doctrine and conduct of the clergy were wise and impartial, little would need to be done to defend them.

Regretfully, however, the *number of fools is infinite,* and to add to this misfortune fools are the first to establish themselves as judges. To these should be added the clergy fallen from virtue whom I already mentioned. One can easily infer the justice of the decisions of such a tribunal. Nevertheless they acquire enormous prestige. These clerics present themselves, and are presented by their cohorts, as the most select and most just of the clergy. In fact they sacrifice their ridiculous claims at the altar of truth. They excel in revealing secrets which they themselves make up. If, unfortunately, there is an orator who sings their praises, or an idle poet who writes a couple of verses applauding them, they swell with pride and, fools that they are, they end up lost. People then begin to call for a reform of the clergy, which is in need of it. They do not, however, perceive the direction such a reform should take. The first thing to be done is to boot out of the Church those ecclesiastical Quixotes, who do not know what superstition is even though they speak about it. Far from being capable of correcting *true* abuses, they only work to root them more deeply and introduce other abuses that are more deadly. At the same time they trample down dogmas, often out of pure ignorance.

Yes, my Elpidio, these wretched clerics cease studying about the Church, forget what little they learned and merely retain the title of clergymen, being as incapable of knowing the needs of the Church or of indicating the reform of true abuses as the would be of forming or directing a campaign strategy.

Not bothering anymore with those reformers, let us agree that superstition, even though it is disseminated among many of the clergy and is in need of correction because of the results that it can have, is not in fact present among the clergy whom the people should regard as their pastors in the different levels of the ecclesiastical hierarchy. You might say, "Are there not priests and even bishops who are superstitious?" There are, my Elpidio, and there are also sly ones who pretend to believe much nonsense and promote many superstitions because of what is in it for them. Nevertheless, neither the small number of pastors who are truly superstitious nor the sacrilegious speculators I have spoken about mean anything in comparison to the great number of true pastors, who with more or less instruction, more or less talent, come forth honestly to impart to the people sacred doctrine, pure, without disguise and without criminal intrigue.

The faithful have every means to avoid superstition, and if they fall into it, it is because of human weakness which always finds pleasure in vices. The same is true with this sin as with other: the sin is known, but is nevertheless committed, and if it is ignored, then ignorance is guilty. The Church of God has a very simple way which even the most stupid person can recognize, whether one is a heretic or superstitious, namely: *there is no dogma nor new worship nor legitimate practice which is not universal or in conformity with the universal principles applied by the Church itself to particular cases, places and circumstances.*

I have also said, my friend, that superstition cannot advance among the clergy if the simple means that are available to contain it are employed. Even though this is a subject that requires a lengthy treatise, I wish nevertheless to justify my assertion with a few reflections. The true ecclesiastics who, by misfortune, may not have completed the necessary studies or who may not have meditated on what they learned (and this is the most frequent case), since they do not have any interest other than the glory of God, cannot possibly find it in superstition. Thus they are open to the lights not of the corrupted world but of the learned world, and it is easy to bring the glory of God to the many true pastors because they have true *pastoral spirit.* The very attacks that are made on the Church may even serve the purpose of defending it, since many of these holy men will shed their excess clothing, so to speak, which might be cumbersome in the fight, and present pure doctrine with the pure spirit so that victory is certain.

The wicked who pretend to be superstitious become the objects of public contempt. This contempt grows the more people become educated. If this is not enough to correct them, it will at least help avoid their perpetrating any evil other than the pious thefts of money or honors which they do not deserve. It is impossible that the confusion between religion and superstition can last any longer, for even the most ignorant already perceive the difference between them. That part of the clergy who pretend to connect religion and superstition will find their pernicious effects neutralized and even destroyed by the great majority of thinkers.

All the difficulties on this subject will cease, my dear friend, after the restoration of the essential Catholic feeling that guided primitive Christians, that is, always to depend on God and never on mere human power. We see that St. Paul conveyed this spirit to the faithful, admonishing those who would say "I belong to Paul" or "I belong to Apollo" instead of saying "I belong to Christ." This spirit of Paul can bring heresies and superstitions to an end, since they are always the fruit of ignorance or of arrogance in individuals, and it will also avoid scandals, for no one will consider himself authorized to do wrong or despise religion because its ministers may be good or bad, wise or ignorant, sensible or superstitious.

THE IMPACT ON THE NECESSARY ROLE
OF JUSTICE AND THE LAW

What do you think of my long digression? Do you blame me? I recognize the justice of your criticism; I confess to be guilty of taking advantage of your *patience,* but let us proceed. Yes, my dear Elpidio, let us follow the march of the horrible monster of superstition and let us note, although just in passing, the ravages it produces in society. One of the most unfortunate results is that of obstructing the effectiveness of laws. Perhaps it may surprise you that I make this observation. I hope, however, to present it in terms that may place us in agreement with it by demonstrating that the civil order is disturbed and even destroyed by what we can call false religious attachments.

First of all I believe that we can be in agreement that every law in order to be a law should be just and every superstition is false and unjust. We see then that by their very nature, there should be open opposition between new laws as well as the observance of those already in effect and superstitious ideas and practices.

If superstition were to present itself as such, it would not be fearful. Since it presents itself as pure and sublime religion, however, it usually captivates spirits in such a way that the unwary consider as unjust and sacrilegious all laws that oppose it. Thus they make the legislature seem irreligious because they are not superstitious. Under these circumstances the ignorant mob starts to have no confidence in the government and detests its laws. It believes that religion is being attacked, when in reality religion is not offended in the least. Many wicked people who call themselves religious, use it for despicable purposes. You know very well, Epidio, that every law that is hated by the people is broken quite frequently; and that in a society of thinkers force does not have as much value as will, unlike the herds and other groupings of animals which are easily manipulated by staff, whistle and other similar means.

One can imagine what the wisest laws would be reduced to if the monster of superstition succeeded in making the people hate laws. They would no doubt be reduced to a few lines in a book that a few or no one would read, and that would produce no other effect than popular disgust. The courts would lose all moral force and they would be left with only physical force. However, the wisest laws are easily opposed when a mass of people are set in motion. For instance, all *pious mobs* are incited and brought about by people who seem most virtuous in the same way that many *patriotic mobs* are incited by the true enemies of the fatherland.

Once the people have lost their love for laws and have become used to breaking them, it is very easy for the superstitious to guide them at will. This is due to a principle almost inherent in the human heart, which exerts every effort to destroy that which it hates and to uphold that which it loves. This is especially true when people have already made sacrifices that they do not wish to render futile. People then reach such a degree of obstinacy that they are unable to reflect on anything but their purpose, which is to destroy the laws they hate and to replace them with superstitious tenets, for which they have risked so much and disturbed and disobeyed all authority. They make such disobedience appear to be an honor, and they find great glory in the persecutions they suffer, believing themselves to be martyrs of religion when in reality they are martyrs of the devil. If only they had read the doctrines of the Fathers of the Church and remembered what St. Cyprian, among others said: it is not the penalty but its cause that makes the martyr *non poena sed causa martirem facit.* They even give their lives for their errors, but this would not even bring them from the side of the wicked and obstinate.

Oh my Elpidio! How much damage these feigned martyrs have done to religion! How many tears they have caused to the true lovers of religion! Their irreligious efforts insult religion even while they pretend to protect it. Few of them really suffer because only a few delude themselves; most of them are sly and pretend that they suffer so that their own may open their purses and reward them; but when they are pressed, they run away so quickly. However, religion is at times so hated as the cause of these evils that the laws do not find any support, and therefore people, without any restraint for their shams become demoralized.

There is, Elpidio, another inconvenience of great importance which results from this infamous war that superstition declares on all the laws it believes are opposed to its depraved interests. That is, that thanks to a reaction to which the human spirit is prone, the good persons usually forget that they are so and thus laws are promulgated against the interest of religion under the guise of a need to suppress false defenders. This is the origin of almost every scandal and persecution that the Church and even more frequently the entire clergy have suffered. Church and clergy are two quite different entities because the first never ceases to be heavenly while at times the second lets it be known that it is earthly by the passions which dominate its members.

No sooner do some laws that are imprudent and contrary to the Church see the light of day than the just join their voices against them and the superstitious find an excellent opportunity to attain their designs. They take for granted that the lawmakers have no other purpose than the destruction of the Church and that no matter what the lawmakers do they wickedly lead everything towards this end. Thus people come to believe that all their civil officials are irreligious. What can one expect from such a deplorable situation but open war between lawmakers and the Church and between a people divided into factions that insult and curse one another? These are the beauties of superstition.

Once this ominous campaign has been started it is very difficult to end it. The unconcerned believe that if they show even one sign of weakness by compromising with superstition, this will become established forever, having been made bold by the victory; and the superstitious feel that a defeat would be irreparable. Both parties then begin to delude themselves and then look for flimsy reasons to justify their conduct. Some say that it is necessary to use harsh methods, even if they border on injustice, in order to avoid so many evils; even that it is necessary to tolerate a measure of insanity in order to awaken people from their deplorable apathy, make their interests known and in this fashion contain those who oppress them by pretending to disseminate religion. Those who follow this line of reasoning give themselves without fear to all their passions and they set the fatherland aflame by invoking patriotism.

On the other hand those who are no more exact in their speeches or more just in their operations claim that religion is being attacked and that it is necessary to defend it. If they commit any excess, it must be forgiven because of the nature of the cause they defend; because of the perversity and audacity of their opponents; because of the difficulty of suppressing the indignation of the people once they see attacked what they venerate and love very much; and finally because of the vast number of innocent victims who would be sacrificed for the sake of the irreligious. All these deserve not to be sacrificed even at the risk of committing some injustices.

With these and other similar lines of thinking both parties attempt to silence the cries of reason, nature and religion. Their disgrace reaches such a proportion that, as they get used to conforming their actions to their sayings, they succeed in blunting *moral sensibilities,* which are the fruit of reflection and conscience. Thus men are reduced to mechanical beings when it comes to *good sense,* but they are very thoughtful and skillful when it comes to the means of their cruel perversity. Should these deceivers not reflect in quite a different way on the principles of true religion, and should they realize not that neither religion nor the Fatherland can receive any benefit but can only suffer grave dangers because of their injustice?

Does it really help the fatherland to form enemies against it and take away all prestige from authority, which loses everything when it is perceived as unjust? Does it really help religion to break its most sacred precept, which is justice, and its divine bond, which is charity? Why do these wretched people not unmask themselves and present themselves openly as promoters of their own particular interests, leaving aside the renowned names of fatherland and religion which in reality they defile?

People would then be able to know them for what they are and would stop being fearful of falling victim to the disgrace they in fact deserve for their infamy. But this is not advantageous to their ambition and thus they find a reason for their reserve. I repeat, Elpidio, both parties operate out of their own ambition; let me present to you the basis for my assertion.

How well I know that money is lord of the world and that those who only have worldly ideas always think about money. Nevertheless, note that money is used as a means of obtaining pleasure and social recognition and the latter is the one which is valued most and is most pleasing. This then demands that greater sacrifices be made, sacrifices that all people are ready to make, some by just means and others by sinister and wicked machinations.

Very few hold pleasures in high regard if they go hand and hand with degradation, but many are pleased to endure the privation of pleasures if it brings honors. From this one can infer that the wicked who make up both parties, since they do not have goals other than worldly goals, become victims of avarice and even more so of ambition. The former serves as a vehicle of the latter, even though they may seem to be divided. Without specifying hateful references, you might observe, my friend, that in both parties there is always the claim of a *cross* or a *title,* either *aristocratic* or *democratic,* some sign of honor, which feeds ambition. From this comes *false modesty* in order to be the more praised; from this comes *humility* in some and *sincerity* and *detachment* in others according to the *nature of the party,* but for no other purpose than to dominate in the least

hateful manner; from here comes *political* and *religious* hypocrisy with all its consequences, which are always most deadly.

But you might say that I am unfair, assigning to superstition not only the evils that it causes but those fostered by its
enemies. I do not excuse these evils, rather in my letters about
irreligiosity I have attacked them openly; but this evil is of such
proportions that it can be divided between the parties and
make both abominable. Do the wicked claims of the superstitious not serve as a pretext for the irreligious? Do you believe,
Elpidio, that the irreligious would find much support among
the people if they did not find material to make forceful and
just harangues, depicting and exaggerating the evils brought
about by superstition and using it gradually to confuse the work
of heaven, the holy and immaculate religion. I have more than
enough basis to make these fools and wicked ones responsible
for the evils I have specified; and no matter how much I would
like to have a reason to excuse them, all I find are reasons to
support my assertion and deplore the misfortune of the fatherland and the Church caused and furthered by superstition.

Let us now consider, my Elpidio, a most grave evil that is a
consequence of what I have related. Let us consider the degradation that a superstitious people fall into the wide door that
opens to all kinds of meanness and all kinds of crimes. My only
consolation is the idea that even though superstition is unfortunately widely extended, it is not so widespread as some gloomy
people imagine. I will proceed very rapidly through this field of
pain, where corrupt nature shows all its miseries, terrifies with
its corruption and taints the atmosphere with its poisonous
breath.

Who can observe without tears the frivolous, thoughtless,
superficial, juvenile and ridiculous character, in a word, the
monstrous character, that a people acquire when they are dominated by superstition? At the same time that they neglect the
most sacred duties of religion and patriotism, they run after
empty shadows, which always deceive them but never correct
them. It seems that every sneer only paves the way for new
ones. The arts suffer, the sciences moan, literature becomes
depraved, good taste is corrupted, morals are destroyed and in
the end a new order of things is established that is approved by

the applause of an ignorant mob with airs of wisdom. The truly wise become so frightened that the people are left in the hands of the monster superstition and bless it as a real gift from heaven.

Such a deplorable state provokes contempt because it is voluntary, and the same thing happens the general populace—I mean that out of despair they give themselves to indolence when they come to the conclusion that any activity is useless. They take recourse in witticisms in order to cover their ignorance and thus they imitate the irreligious, though in a different style. When the irreligious attack religion they always have some joke to make it more palatable. Thus they prepare the mind to receive the error and avoid the just rebuff that should be found in an upright soul.

THE RELATIONSHIP BETWEEN
IRRELIGIOSITY AND SUPERSTITION

In the same way, the superstitious have their own dictionary of jokes that they use when they do not think gross and blatant insults are expedient. They speak with evil emphasis about philosophy and philosophers, about the *wise of today,* and they use other similar phrases which could be applied to many, but not by the superstitious; for these phrases fit *them* better than they fit those to whom they have the impunity to apply them.

All errors have a certain reciprocity or brotherhood, and no matter how different they may seem they proceed in the same manner and employ the same methods. Superstition, which seems to be so different from irreligiosity, is just as frivolous and vulgar. They are both deprived from the bond of charity, which is the principle of all that is upright and correct, decent and wise. There is no uprightness or wisdom except from heaven, and that is the dwelling place of holy charity. Religion always shines with a torrent of light, of peace and of consolation, which causes no pain other than that of not being able to receive it fully. But superstition, on the other hand, wounds with contempt and with loathsome audacity. Many irreligious, my Elpidio, would like to be believers, but there is not a single one who would like to be superstitious. From this comes debasement, from this comes fanaticism and everything that can make people contemptible.

The good ones, my friend, are not so good that they cease to be mortals and exempt from human weakness. The wearied nature seems to long for a rest before dissolving. Virtue then begins by being complacent and ends by being weak, leaving free reign to superstition. Superstition, having found nourishment throughout all ages and in every climate and in every state, has an infinite number of allies that boldly attack any enemy that begins to give in. Finally it dares to envelope in its own darkness those beings from whom it used to run away in fright. Science and virtue are thus left imprisoned and more than once they compromise with their tyrant and turn themselves into the instruments of superstition, which employs them for wicked designs. This is a very delicate point, Elpidio, which it might be best to touch on lightly. Few people have a character firm unto death. Even though they may not degenerate into wickedness, they do not escape from a reprehensible weakness that gives ammunition to superstition, the very evil they should suppress.

If superstition caused no other evil than this, it would be enough to make it loathsome. It degrades the persons from whom one would expect reform, so that they remain without support and become the toys of anyone who would like to gamble with their ruin. Good judgment is eliminated, and since ignorance is plentiful and passions are unfettered, you may infer that the corruption is general and so is dismay.

We know the force of public opinion, and when this takes the side of a plan or a party, no matter how absurd, if there are not virtuous and wise people to rectify it, it acquires approval with the passage of time and after a while it becomes useless to try to change it. The popular masses become so corrupt that it is difficult to find anyone who can undertake their cure. For instance, those confounding prudence for weakness believe they have prudence to a high degree, when in fact they give into weakness; those who inspire trust on account of their virtue and age come to give approval to the most superstitious

practices. They also pretend that it is impossible to destroy
them.

In this fashion society is like a patient who believes himself
incurable and does not want to be bothered with useless remedies. The loss of very wise people is always the cause of the loss
of many less wise, and the chain of evil acquires new links with
which to imprison the unwary. It is very easy to see when great
minds regretfully fall into irreligiosity; it is not so easy, however, to know when they are the victims of superstition. Sometimes they themselves are not even aware of this and at other
times they try to hide it, and when they are successful they
cause immense damage to people.

When society and particularly those who could have a leading voice in it are debased in this way, religion suffers a tremendous attack because it becomes the toy of both the superstitious
and the irreligious and both boast about a triumph they would
not have obtained if they had fought the true contender. It is
necessary for them to feign an enemy in order to be able to
feign a victory: the irreligious, attacking the *supposed religious,*
and the superstitious, refuting the *supposed irreligious,* indi-
rectly attack holy religion though from different avenues.

The irreligious are filled with joy when they come upon a
catalogue of nonsense with the title of Novena or some *religious foolishness* with a title of pious exercise, anything that
can prove the ignorance and gullibility of the children of the
Church so that the irreligious can unleash over the Church a
storm of satires, mockery, and affronts, making her responsible
for every error and every deceit that is perpetrated against her
will and commandments. They believe themselves to have the
authority to condemn religion in the tribunal of their own understanding, without listening to any defense or at least paying
attention to it. Thus they exile from their souls a heavenly gift
that should make them happy.

Oh, my Elpidio, even without evangelical light we can see
the distortion of these ways of thinking and this thoughtless
conduct. This is how, a long time ago, a gentle author responded
in a most satisfactory manner and with a very proper comparison
to the weak objections of those deluded ones. Plutarch said "we
cure an eye infection if we can, but if we cannot, this is no reason

to pluck out the eyes: in the same way if we cannot destroy superstition, this is no reason to stop believing in gods."² What an interesting lesson for those who despise true religion, mistaking it or pretending to confuse it with the practices that in its name ignorance and wickedness have introduced.

Yes, Elpidio, the irreligious have ample right to deplore the evils produced by superstition and to consider them one of the principal causes of upheaval and disorder in the social body. But, are they the only ones or are they the first ones to raise their voices against the methods of this infernal monster? No, my friend, the Church of God has condemned it a long time ago and the Holy Fathers whose works expressed the true spirit of the Church are full of loving and forceful condemnations against such a horrendous vice.

In other times, superstition introduced opposing gods, but in our time it presents one divinity, but inconsistent and divided. It suggests ridiculous slogans and doctrines that are opposed to each other. I do not know if it is the same idolatry now freed from the names of the ancient gods or if under these gods those idolaters did not consider them different virtues of the same divinity.³

---

2. Si fieri potest lippitudinem auferimus ab oculis: sin id non licet, non tamen eruimus oculum: ita si superstitio tolli prorsus non potest, non tamen protinus credendum nollos esse deos—Plut—vide Anthologia sive Florilogium Langii, 513.

3. There are many people of the opinion, and I tend toward it, that idolatry which we may call *formal*, that is of ideas and actions, has never existed except in the most ignorant parts of the common people. But those who were thoughtful, even without being philosophers, always knew that there could not be many gods. The fact that Seneca was condemned to death for defending the unity of gods leads us to assume that he was the first to believe it. Some believed that the gods were merely *virtues* to which a *personal* name had been given; others believed that they were *real persons*, but not part of the divinity, nor different divinities, but unique beings protected by the only divinity, and entrusted with this or that function. The belief of the latter was very similar to the one we have about the saints, even though there are essential differences between our dogma and those errors. It is, however, necessary to note that the superstitious person who attributes to the saints actions and power that the Church does not recognize really does nothing else but imitate the idolaters of old, and give ammunition to the heretics of

It is vice that by its very nature introduces even more discord than irreligiosity, though such corrupt people may insist on preaching a peace they themselves exclude. The wise observation of St. Augustine about the old idolaters, who in reality were superstitious, since idolatry is one of the classes of superstition, may well be applied to them. "These wretches," said that Holy Father of the Church, "saw themselves forced to look for a way in which to worship their *discordant gods* without mutually offending themselves; for if they wished to imitate the discord in their gods, it would break their bond of union. And consequently, the city would be ruined."[4] The very same thing happens to the superstitious within the fold of true religion. They see the need to disguise their doctrines and even hide them. They have to make great and extremely painful sacrifices just to avoid the discordance of their doctrines being observed in their conduct lest the part be dissolved by the first blow it receives from reason.

They do, however, wish to portray unity because they know that this is a distinctive character of true religion. But they can never convince themselves that they have it. Worship is for them a shallow study given an honest appearance with pious names, the invention of which is not an easy task. Thus little by little these wicked people come to reduce everything to mere formulas without any spirit other than that of the world, no matter how much they pretend to be guided by the divine spirit.

THE IMPACT OF PUBLIC WORSHIP
ON PUBLIC MORALITY

I believe that you may have anticipated my ideas and foreseen that I must say something about the great harm that is

---

the day to attack our holy religion. Religion, however, finds its defense in the very attacker, for if the superstitious and the idolaters have erred in the way they worship, it seems that one as well as the other has recognized almost by an instinct of nature that *God is admirable in his saints* and that the pleas of those fortunate ones are pleasing to him.

4. St. Augustine, *To Marcel*, letter 138, 2:541.

done to society when the true values of religious ceremonies are taken away. You know, Elpidio, that this very point has been the object of many of my meditations because in truth I believe it to be most essential. Perhaps you may remember that in my *Lessons of Philosophy* I pointed out that it is totally useless to ask whether or not there can be public morality without religion, because all nations which are constituted as such must have religion and this should be their norm of conduct. So whether the question is answered in the affirmative or in the negative, in practice we will always end with the fact that religion directs the morality of the people, and the process of investigation is very similar to the investigation of whether the inhabitants of the earth could live on the moon. This being the case, religion will always have such an influence within society that if it is twisted, the people are left without a norm, as is evidenced in the different essays that have been written on this matter in different ages and in different countries.

People never abandon religion unless they do so to give themselves up to vices. I do not need to prove this, for even without referring to history, in our time any one from any class will find proof of my assertion just by looking around. The result is that people start to be dissatisfied with religious practices at the very moment that they begin to suspect the wisdom of those who prescribe them. They confuse all religious ceremonies, both the good ones and the bad ones, to the point of calling themselves the *puritanical irreligious.* Forgive me the use of this name. But so that you may be convinced of the proper application of this name, remember that the Puritans from England started just in this way. All the irreligiosities imaginable were approved for the laudable purpose of purifying worship and abolishing ridiculous and superstitious ceremonies, whose hateful name they gave then and give now to everything which is not in accordance with their ideas. Here you have one of the ravages of superstition.

All ceremonies are rendered suspect and instead of being a sensible means of inspiring sublime ideas that may direct the morality of the people, they are reduced to mere objects of ridicule and contempt. Once ceremonies are held in contempt so is worship and its object, so that little by little people are left submerged in irreligiosity. Then the learned irreligious wish to take up worship on their own in order to enlighten it. They do not, however, wish to be instructed but to give instruction, and the principle that led them to discard religion makes them unable to admit any kind of authority or magisterium. Since all wish to be directors, we are left without people to be directed, and this causes a confusion that result in immorality, for the irreligious believe themselves to be learned without being so.

Under such sad circumstances the superstitious accuse the irreligious and these accuse them in return, making all mutually responsible for the laxity of an ignorant people, as if they themselves were not the most corrupt and the least excusable. I know very well that true speculative belief is rarely found united with immorality. I would dare to point out, as the result of extremely careful observations and almost as a general rule, that every corrupt person is irreligious or superstitious. What then is the value of all their proclamations? These are only useful as symbols of their hypocrisy when they have the audacity to bemoan the evils that they themselves have produced.

In another series of letters I already indicated to you, my Elpidio, the evils that irreligiosity causes, so I will tell you nothing about it here, pausing only to make a few observations about this superstitious hypocrisy. It presents itself with an air of sanctity, but after the mask is shifted a little one can perceive all its deformity. It produces an extreme indignation in the people who consider themselves insidiously deceived. The result is that when these superstitious people wish to cure societal evils, they are not even heard, for fear of a new deceit. It is clear that if the patient refuses to take the medicine the doctor is useless.

What shall we say then about superstitious clergymen who rudely scream from the pulpits against the irreligiosity they themselves have formed or at least have nurtured with their *perverse foolishness*? What shall we say about the bishops who permit them to preach? Let us leave this to the judgment of God, who perhaps may find them innocent because of their lack of light and because of their good though erroneous intentions. From a human point of view, however, they cannot stand but as sinners. When superstition establishes itself as teacher, one can expect that it will find opposition, and since it is so wicked, many will not be too scrupulous in selecting methods to defeat it.

True religion suffers, society suffers and the wicked of every kind triumph, producing effects full of contradiction and corruption. The anxiety it produces is insufferable and the struggle it brings about is deadly. Each attack results in a social upheaval and far from defeating the enemy, it seems to give new strength, or better yet, obstinacy in order to continue the resistance.

Authority, if well used, is a principle of peace and harmony. Because it is abused, authority ends up turning into a means of injustice and degrading oppression. Were it not for the support given by force, authority would never succeed in being obeyed at the level of the heart and the level of the mind, even though it might succeed in directing purely external acts as it sees fit. True religion then disappears and its name is taken by a most despicable farce. Here you have the beauties of superstition.

THE CONSOLATION OF A HAPPY VISION—
A CHRISTIAN SOCIETY

Let us avert our eyes from such a painful scene and console ourselves with the beautiful image of a people who are free from irreligiosity no less than from superstition. They give themselves with pleasure and without reserve to religious sentiments that are in conformity with the divine will, without interference from human passions. True charity disseminated throughout a people sweetens their character and makes them sincere, lovable, firm, constant, humble and elevated, happy and wise—in a word, ready for all that is just and an enemy of all that is wicked.

The loftiness of religion makes distasteful to them the paltriness of the intrigue and meanness that debase the superstitious. The beauty of *Christian nobility* is different from that of the nobility which is only the daughter of human whim and at times of the most shameless iniquity. Such a people would necessarily tend toward liberty, which always exists when laws are observed and are just, and the tyrants are left in ridicule in their wicked designs.

My Elpidio, I already made similar reflections when I treated irreligiosity, but no doubt they have much more force when applied to superstition. I am firmly convinced that superstitious people are enslaved as much as truly Christian people are free. A religious and learned people are superior to all laws and all political systems. Like clothes for the body, these can make it ugly or even uncomfortable but cannot change its nature or the beauty of its form. Christianity is a beautiful and perfect ideal made up of real virtues, the sum of which, when gathered in great number, comes close to the model presented by its divine founder. It is not impossible but it is indeed very rare to find a people who are truly Christian. As is the case with all models, rectifying the one that pleases becomes the norm for the beautiful.

Oh, if unbridled passions would not violate the popular masses with its foul breath. How majestic, noble and pleasing would Christianity march on receiving everywhere the praises of pure and learned reason, the pledge of consoled hearts, the tender embraces of protected innocence, the acclamations of peaceful endeavors, the laurels of victorious wisdom and the smiling olive branch of a permanent and wise peace.

Oh, my Elpidio! I transport myself again to that memorable night to which I alluded in the beginning of this letter, and my soul once again experiences the heightened sentiments which filled me at that time. Once again I see the harmony among the great families that make up the human race and the reestablishment of the empire of reason, usurped for such a long time by those who falsely call themselves its promoters. Once again I see the sudden and amazing cure of all the pains of the human heart, and I see the history of the old calamities of people parade before me, transforming itself into a scene of great delight that becomes visible as the evangelical light dissipates the clouds of unfaithfulness and the darkness of superstition. Once again I see the relationship between heaven and earth as the work of one hand and I recognize the wisdom of an infinite being who could not establish any discord between them, no matter how much miserable mortals may persist in slandering it. Once again I see pure religion in all its beauty bestowing abundant gifts, as thousands of Christians, pleased by its power, fix their gaze on it. Once again I see . . . but enough, Elpidio, I do not wish to take any more advantage of your patience, though I do not offer to reform, because I am preparing to send you another letter to vent my spirit, which always finds great consolation in your correspondence. Horror to superstition. Do not forget me.

THE USE OF SUPERSTITION
BY POLITICS

Politics, which is always looking at the means suitable for its goals, readily makes use of superstitions as the best support for tyranny, which is the idol of almost all rulers.[56] This opening sentence, Elpidio, has perhaps surprised you into confusing me with those restless individuals who do not think they can be free as long as they are governed.

POWER AS AN IDOL AND TEMPTATION

In spite of all the disclaimers that rulers might make, the pleasure to give orders is a misery of human nature from which they cannot free themselves. From this comes the temptation to break the laws and all the shady reasons they find in order to place themselves above them. *Power, then, is made into an idol,* which, as a false deity, does not receive but false honors. The one who exercises it is the first miserable one to be held captive by it. He offers his incense to this titular deity and very soon fear gathers many other sacrificers. They take their part in the governing action, trying to extend the empire of arbitrariness, the necessary consequence of which is tyranny.

This has happened, does happen, and will happen in every nation and in every government no matter what form it takes. Good rulers are, then, just persons, who resist and conquer this very powerful temptation. It is quite evident that they are very

187

rare, to the misfortune of the human race. Generally, these mandarins, when they are not tyrants, wish to be so, and their only hope is to find a pretext to nurture their passion to dominate without laws, or to obstruct these if decorum demands that they be recognized. This is why I have said that tyranny is the idol of almost all rulers, and, if the truth be told, the exceptions are so few that with very little hyperbole I could omit "almost" leaving it as a general premise.

THE ROLE OF RELIGION AND PUBLIC OPINION

IN AFFIRMING JUSTICE

The laws, therefore, are in a struggle with those mandarins. Since it is not expedient to use force against them, we are left with only two protecting principles: *public opinion,* which animates society, and *religion,* which rectifies conscience. Tyrants praise and enthrone superstition in order to destroy one of these principles whose ruin would cause the ruin of the other. They are then left without any restraints to stop their designs.

It is evident that religious ideas give shape to public opinion, and that if pure doctrine is substituted by a confused mixture of superstitions, the people are then left without religion and without rectified opinion. As a result, tyranny finds no obstacle in its way. This is why politics protects superstition and here, then, is the origin of so much perfidy and so much hypocrisy.

You might say that if everyone thought as I do every government would be deformed and all rulers suspect. Oh, my Elpidio, I have never disobeyed an authority, but I am sincere and firm and I would not offer sacrifice at the altar of power. No matter what the result of my efforts might be, these are directed to show things as they are in themselves and not as they hypocritically wish to appear. I wish to give to governments their true support, which is the love of the people, the justice of their laws, and the virtue of the rulers.

To confess the flaws of human nature is not to render suspicious those who have these flaws. An astute and infamous concealment is worst than suspicion. That would make all people suspicious who feel the attacks of vanity! That would mean suspecting of licentiousness all who feel the excitement of a corrupted flesh! The rulers are the fathers of their people and it would be rather strange if a minister of the gospel who has always presented himself as such were to come and preach disobedience and inspire unjust suspicions, which would not be lawful to a particular segment of individuals.

I have always believed that all persons are good as long as it is not evident that they are bad, and that I must be on my guard, as if they were wicked, even though I may know for certain that they are holy. Since you already know the norm which I follow, judge my intentions, and if you judge against me, I have no defense. I have opened my heart—I do not have anymore in it—judge what you see and judge as you please, but also allow me to judge according to the testimony of a conscience which has always been faithful to me and which dictates perseverance in my sentiments.

A ruler who respects the law, even when his errors abound, is always popular. But if he pretends to be the judge of the people's fate, he should expect their curses. The wretches who make themselves so bold as to fate try also to silence the laws, calling superstition, which always finds ways of validating and sanctifying injustices, to their aid. The very same ones who profane religion declare themselves its protectors. They immediately find the beguiled, who in good faith would defend them, as well as the perverse, who would praise them for their speculation. This is the origin of several pernicious axioms that give approval to tyranny while considering the fulfillment of the laws and the preservation of the most sacred rights simply as a favor, or an asset.

LIMITATIONS OF POWER

Among other scandalous doctrines, have you not heard, my Elpidio, the moral and political blasphemy that the *kings are lords of life and property*? They are, no doubt, in reference to delinquents, and then it is the law which is the protector of lives and properties, punishing those unworthy possessors in all justice. To believe that kings may kill anyone they please and take any property they wish is a deadly error that has its origin in the most horrible superstition.

In order to uphold these absurdities, the superstitous have attempted to call kings gods over the earth and, by means of a sacrilegious analogy, have affirmed that it is by virtue of this that they participate in the power of God in heaven; and since life and goods are free gifts of the Infinite Being, the superstitious wish the kings also to be their earthly stewards.

These beguiled take their insanity so far as to think that it is a favor from the kings to let their subjects live, as well as to let them hold property. How different is the doctrine of the Fathers of the Church! I would stop to present it if I had not done so in the letters in which I wrote to you about irreligiosity. Remember that St. Augustine calls *thieves* the kings who would take the property of their subjects without justice.

THE MEANING OF POWER

According to St. Paul all power, my Elpidio, comes from God, as is the case with all paternity. But from this one cannot infer that parents may kill their children or steal from them what they legitimately possess. Still less can we infer that the powerful may proceed crazily or franctically destroying at their pleasure, without any more reason than their will. To believe that God may authorize such despicable persons is not to believe in God but to declare oneself as a *disguised atheist.*

It is true, as the sacred text points out by the wisdom of God: *Monarchs rule and legislators decree just laws* (Prov. 8:15), but to *rule* is not to kill without rhyme or reason, order or design. It is to govern a people in a just way, leading them to happiness according to the principles of divine wisdom. To decree what is just is not to infringe upon the rights of subjects by means of arbitrary decrees.

The superstitious have confused the question of *obedience* with that of *justice.* It is one thing to say that one should obey in order to avoid greater evils and another to legitimize injustice. Let me use ecclesiastical examples and remind you that the very Church approves this doctrine, a doctrine that is also held by all theologians: an unjust action should be obeyed, but the individual over whom it falls should not consider himself censured but rather persecuted.

But what have the superstitious done? They speak constantly and furiously against everyone who dares to indicate the injustices committed by the kings, or rather, the perverse who deceive them. They also treat as seditious and irreligious the true friends of the common good and religion. The mandarins, then, find these athletes of manipulation ready to fight against justice and to sanctify infamy. They offer them plenty of honors, respect, and, at times, money, though in an indirect way.

Once superstition is thus elevated, it fills itself with pride and starts to spread its conquests in a prodigious manner. It immediately attracts to itself a great number of sly ones who go, as the saying goes, to the sun that warms the most. Many beguiled people also run to its flags, for they only perceive the appearance of sanctity with which the great number of monstrous crimes have been disguised.

What do you think is the result? To imprison the kings? Yes, my friend, the kings are the first captives and the first victims of the superstition manipulated by the mandarins, that is to say, the *petty kings*. In order to demonstrate this, let us place ourselves in a necessary dilemma and derive the consequences: the king is either Christian or irreligious. If he is Christian, they make him believe that religion is in danger, that he must give the first example of obedience to its divine mandates, and that these forbid him to do such and such a thing . . . and here enters a catalogue of foolishnesses or wickednesses, supported by vast numbers or reports and authorities, as the fruit of the most profound theological study. A *good king* then believes himself compelled, by Christian humility, not to prefer his judgment over that of so many wise and virtuous advisors as well as the cries of the people who thus try to persuade him. Here, then, is an enslaved king.

But let us suppose the second part of the dilemma, an irreligious king. When he sees himself surrounded by superstition, the king becomes afraid that his irreligiosity will be discovered. Since the king considers that the enemy is already very strong, he does not seek too much to conquer it. In fact he pays no attention to religion. Since what he truly wants is to rule, the king gives in easily and nurtures the sentiments that might keep him on the throne. Here we have another enslaved king.

Who are the friends of king? Will they be the superstitious who try to reduce the rulers to anonymous slavery, or the sincere and truly religious men who would like to give them all the splendor of a supreme, just and rational authority? By whom are they respected: by those who consider them the beneficent fathers of the people, and so that they might be, show them the dangerous cliffs to which a multitude of perfidious and hypocritical people wish to lead them? Who loves them: those who try to degrade them and bring upon them the curses of the human race, which most times they do not deserve because they are very far from knowing the injustices that are committed in their name, or those who, guided by the true religion, never hide the truth from them and always counsel them that by respecting the rights of each and every one of their subjects they assure for themselves the greatest of all the rights, which is to deserve the love of the peoples? But I already see, my Elpidio, that I am digressing from my principal objective and thus, leaving the kings whose kindness or injustice I do not think I will experience, I shall proceed to make a few observations about other means by which politics makes use of superstition.

A DESCRIPTIVE ANALYSIS OF MANIPULATIVE POLITICIANS

When false politicians (for true policy ought to be just) consider that the learned world will not tolerate the praises that governments give to superstition, they take the opposite road and speak against it. These politicians present themselves as the first to be concerned. At the same time, they exaggerate carefully the power superstition has acquired as well as how dangerous it would be to incite its furor. A reform is proposed. They approve it at once and even recommend to its authors that they take any necessary steps to introduce it. With feigned sentiment they then predict that it will be impossible to accomplish it, on account of the superstitious whose number they believe to be almost infinite.

In this fashion they prepare the public not to be too surprised with a result that is contrary to the hope of the good people and to the purported intentions of the government. These perfidious politicians then go on to deceive the superstitious, and to accomplish this they let—even though with precaution—the secret be leaked out. They point out that the government has never been in favor of the proposed dangerous reform. It only condescends to take a few steps in a *tentative* way.

The superstitious conclude that the government either fears them or protects them, though veiledly, or that it wishes to find out if they ought to protect them or if there is reason to fear them. In each of these cases, it is clear that, according to their principles, the superstitious ought to do everything within their power to attain victory, or at least to avoid ruin. Here we have superstition put into practice by clever politicians.

The politicians, then set themselves as simple spectators of the battle waged between the deceived parties and, with great cunning, pull *certain strings* . . . to encourage and discourage . . . *to pull and tug* . . . you already understand me . . . the result is always favorable to them no matter how deadly it may be for the fatherland. If the superstitious win out, the rulers attribute the victory to themselves, indicating that it was due to their prudence. They did not show the means by which they have secretly contained the *enemies of religion,* enemies whom they have always attempted to discourage and who, without a doubt, would have accomplished their perverse ends had they been protected under a less religious government. If the victory is declared in the favor of the opposite party, the rulers also attribute it to their own efforts, without which superstition would have been invincible. They also put on airs of *prudence* for not having confronted it hastily, but in a sensible and more efficacious way, from behind the scenes.

The politicians, then, are always left standing and ready to manipulate the parties at their will. They are very careful to add to the congratulations for their victory the clever insinuation made to the vanquished party that the government operates out of necessity, that all its expressions are *mere formulas* and, as the saying goes, that it *kisses the hands it would like to see burnt.* This is what they call politics, my friend, and it adds up to nothing less than a system of *clever infamy.* Politicians, my friend, have no other rule than to *attain their purpose* or, at least, if it is not successful, to remain in good standing with everyone.

Madame Stael stated accurately, speaking of the sly Talleyrand, "the good Maurice is like the puppets that are made for children to play with—they have feet made of lead and a head made of cork and thus they always land on their feet." Yes, my friend, the politicians are always left *afloat* after the shipwreck of the fatherland. They cohabitate with all the parties shamelessly. They base their glory on this calculation if it is warranted by success. Do not be surprised, then, that even the more unconcerned foster superstition, using it for their own designs.

The politicians go even further for, with utter disregard of nature and religion, they pretend that the evil is inevitable, but at the same time very useful and even necessary, for without superstition it would be impossible to govern the peoples. To this end, they exaggerate the ignorance of the common people and the danger inherent in instructing them. They proclaim the necessity of religion, but at the same time they say that it is a dream to pretend that the barbarous masses may be able to preserve it in all its purity. Similarly, they propose that superstition is much more analogous to the character of the populace and, thus, it is expedient to foster and protect it as a means to manipulate an untamed people.

To cover up they lament the necessity in which they see themselves of having to operate in an abominable and ridiculous manner; they declare publicly that their desires are to destroy superstition. With these and other fables they accomplish their intent, which is to govern without laws while enjoying a good reputation. They play the role of *weepers* and this would be of no consequence if it were not that with their hypocrisy they produce greater evils that are the cause of many justly shed tears.

No matter how unfounded and ridiculous these speeches may be they find many who believe them to be quite correct, and the politicians are left justified in their conduct and applauded for their moderation and prudence. Superstition, then, becomes so rooted that it does not even fear being bothered, since it was already decided that it was not only useful but necessary in order for the rulers to manipulate the people without encountering any opposition from them.

Do you think that the evils end here? No, my Elpidio, another greater calamity follows as a necessary consequence and how I would wish to avoid the pain of telling you. Since I have set out to indicate the ravages of superstition in society, it is necessary that I not omit the deadliest of them all, no matter how much *the soul is horrified as it remembers it and flees in pain.* I shall begin, yes, Elpidio, this sad history of the sufferings inflicted on the Church under the pretext of respecting and protecting Her.

CHURCH AND STATE (THRONE VS. ALTAR)

Superstition is a vice that has been introduced in the Church. Superstitious persons seek or pretend to be believers. The politicians present themselves as defenders of religion, hoping to gain the esteem of the superstitious. In order to really please them, politicians identify the *throne and the altar* as two things that are dependent on each other: both of them come tumbling down if one of them falls.

It is true that public worship started with the conversion of Constantine, but it is also true that religion was already disseminated and that altars had been erected everywhere in spite of all the thrones. Already in the second century Tertullian argued to the Romans concerning the propagation of Christianity: "We are foreigners and we have already filled everything that belongs to you, the cities, the islands, the villages, the municipalities, the councils, the armies themselves, the tribes, the decuries, the palace, the Senate, the forum, and we have only left to you the temples".[1]

The protection of the empires was not the cause for the propagation of Christianity, which then was much more pure and its followers much more fervent, united and powerful. The hypocrites who, faking respect for religion, wished to make her dependent on thrones truly attack and slander religion, making it appear that it is the work of a human power when, quite on the contrary, *God elected the weak to confound the strong.*

On the other hand, the thrones do not depend in any way on the altars, since (omitting other passages of history) even after all the altars were pulled down in powerful England, far from diminishing, the power of the monarch grew. I hope that the beguiled who speak about a union of throne and altar will not declare themselves defenders of a false religion and will not dare to tell me that my argument has no force because England preserves the semblance of a religion, which is what Protestantism amounts to. If they said so, we would be able to unmask them, for it would be clearly known that it is superstition and not religion that they pretend to defend, for a *false cult* is nothing more than a true superstition.

With the same principle, they could defend Islam and every other religious system that could be invented, since all of them can be supported by kings and become friendly with them. The great absurdity would then result of believing that religion is inseparable and depends entirely on the principle that destroys it, or rather, that exists when it is destroyed. A *false religion is void* and it is good only as the unfortunate sign of the loss of a divine gift and the substitution with a work of human pride. It is a cadaver, to make use of the beautiful symbol of St. Augustine, it is a cadaver, my Elpidio, whose features still show us the individual whose spirit has already disappeared.

It is not a throne but a gallows that elevates the occupant

---

1. Hesterni sumus et vuestra omnia implevimus, urbes, insulas, castella, municipia, conciliabula, castra ipsa, tribus, decurias, palatium, senatum, forum, sola vobis reliquimus templa." Tertullian's *Apology,* chapter 37.

only to make him despicable. Nor is a true altar, my Elpidio, that which is erected only to be defiled and, instead of receiving the pure offerings of virtue and peace, receives only the deadly gifts with which crime, always clever, fosters discord. A villified throne and a defiled altar can only go hand in hand in order to spread darkness propagating crime.

Even if we leave wicked intentions out of the question, how many errors have not resulted from this exaggerated alliance of throne and altar? Have there not been popes who have attributed to themselves the empire of the world or, at least, pretended to extend their authority in an indirect way over all the kingdoms of the earth?

Who can ignore the pretensions of Innocent III and Boniface VIII? Who can ignore the ranting of otherwise eminent Italian theologians in order to sustain this indirect power. The renowned Cardinal Bellarmine went to such an extreme that the Apostolic See itself condemned his work on this point, ordering it to be placed on the Index. We know how far French theologians have gone in the opposite direction, especially since the renowned Peter of Marca wrote his concordance of priesthood and empire. Also, the incomparable Bossuet presented himself as defender of the freedoms of the Gallic Church. We see the theologians of modern France, however, become friendly with the Italians, openly rejecting the doctrines of Bossuet, until a renowned writer (not a professional theologian) comes to say that he hopes that God in his mercy may have forgiven Bossuet his errors in recognition of his other famous writings defending the Church.[2] Have there not been in Spain an infinite number of disputes over pontifical privileges and rights, disputes that did so much harm to Melchor Cano and made Campomanes so renowned? What shall we say about our modern Llorente and Villanueva? Superstition has given rise to all these disagreements and they have caused an infinite number of evils to the Church and society.

Yes, my dear Elpidio, there has been a lot of superstition and fanaticism on either side, even though all that has seem-

---

2. Compte Joseph de Maistre, *Du Pape.*

ingly been done is to try to correct these vices. If the contend-
ers had been more sincere, perhaps they would have confessed
the influence that partisan interests exercised on their spirit.
But, ah, others who are really wicked have used these intermi-
nable controversies in order to place throne and altar on a
collision course and have tried to weaken them and exslave the
kings at the same time that they insulted the Church for defending them.

We will always find someone who, reading this letter,
would say that I tried to deprive the Church of the great benefit
of the protection of the throne and to the latter the great support that it can find in the Church. I believe that my answer can
be deduced from what I have already said in this letter, but the
accusation itself would be so outrageous and unpleasant that it
will be well worth taking some time to avoid it, or at least
dismiss it. Let us treat this question in sections: first, considering what the Church ought to expect from the throne and, then,
what the latter can receive from the former.

BENEFITS THE ALTAR RECEIVES FROM THE THRONE

The Church is the whole company of baptized believers
who, guided by the light of faith, united with the bond of
charity, animated by the consoling and well-founded hope and
nourished by the holy sacraments, run along the road of virtue
and peace towards the center of happiness under the Eternal
Shepherd, who is Christ, and his vicar, who is the Pope. This is
the true idea of the Church; this name, however, is usually also
given to the ecclesiastical body or to the whole company of the
ministers of the altar, who have a certain hierarchy and who are
subject to certain laws and with certain civil prerogatives by
way of princely grants.

When the Church is taken in the first sense, it only expects the throne to remove all *civil obstacles* to such lofty
goals; their achievement, however, is not dependent on the
throne; on the contrary, in order to obtain them, the Church
sees itself at times in the hard necessity of opposing the throne
in order to correct its excesses, as was done by St. Ambrose

with Emperor Theodosious and has also been done by many other holy prelates.

I do not wish to deprive the Church from the protection that it should receive, but I do want to take her out of a slavery in which she should not be, being made the plaything of the throne only by reason of supposing that it owes its existence to it. I wish to take this weapon from the cruel, hypocritical and clever hands of politics, which has caused so many ravages.

When the Church is taken in the second sense, that is, as an ecclesiastical body, there is no doubt that it depends on the throne as far as civil prerogatives go; it does not, however, depend on the throne when it comes to the exercise of the sacred ministry. Civil prerogatives should be appreciated when they affect the work and the decorum of the ecclesiastical body; when they only serve the purpose of pleasing vanity, however, they should be considered as one of the many human miseries, and then they depend on the thrones, to be divided as spoils by the kings with their courtesan clerics. If they call this *sorry comedy* the rights of the altar, then I confess that the altar depends on the throne entirely. Yes, my friend, *concedo totum,* and this little scholastic answer would be enough for you to laugh or make fun of me, remembering how much I fought the pat answers of the learned.

The throne rarely grants privileges to the ecclesiastical body in order to honor the Church; as a rule, the throne pretends to enslave her by buying the wicked clerics and deceiving the foolish. I am very far from opposing the demonstration of regard that religious princes have at times given to the Church, and I disapprove even less of civil honors, which at times have been seen fit to grant the ministers of the altars; I repeat, however, that this is a dangerous matter, for sin and not piety is generally the source of these hypocritical honors. In the end, the Church is left oppressed the more it considers itself privileged. Yes, my friend, it is necessary to speak with sincerity and to demonstrate that the politics of those at court produce the evils so as later to bemoan them and justify all the measures to remedy them.

After the court staff lead the princes to grant prerogatives and privileges aplenty to exalt the clerics, they cleverly begin to sow mistrust in the spirit of the very princes, always telling them about the dangers of *forming a state within a state* and of the necessity of guarding themselves against the ambition and *talents* of the clergy. The princes, then, either out of ignorance or misery, become furious after their *worldly clothes* are taken from them, and at times they even commit unheard-of abuses instead of shedding such clothing altogether and throwing it in the face of the perfidious who thought of buying a minister of God with gifts from a mere person. They engage in unpleasant and even scandalous bickering, unleashing the passions; these scenes blemish the ministry, making it extremely hateful, and the princes end up by estimating that the body of the clergy is like a hydra which they themselves have nourished and which it is now necessary to destroy.

When the spirits are disposed in this manner it is only necessary to set them in motion, and then politics coldly calculates what it takes to gain an advantage. Sometimes it exaggerates the *sacrilegious excesses* of the princes (which perhaps consist only of avoiding sacrileges), and thus it compels the body of the clergy boldly to oppose the mandates of the ruler, and other times it leads the prince to take violent measures against the Church. In both cases, there is the most complete theft.

Under the *assumption* that the king is lord of all the goods, *those who are not kings* enrich themselves with ecclesiastical goods under the pretense of *fidelity* or *patriotism* according to which way the wind blows, but, finally . . . with some title, . . . whose holder cares neither for the king nor for the fatherland. What do you say, then, about the alliance between throne and altar? Yes, they have it, but it is a far cry from that made by the henchmen of the former and the defilers of the latter in order to attain their ambitious goals.

BENEFITS THE THRONE RECEIVES FROM THE ALTAR

As far as the throne is concerned, believe me, Elpidio, that they are the enemies of kings who counsel them to follow the false politics of presenting themselves to the people as spokesmen of the Divinity supported by the Church. The

Church teaches that kings are men like everybody else and many times worse than everybody else, and for this reason they are the object of compassion and not envy. This doctrine of the Church, however, is either ignored or the wicked do not wish to remember it, in order to harm the very throne which they perfidiously suppose they are attempting to protect, and thus they manage to make the most just kings hateful to the people, who come to believe that they have no other basis on which to reign.

When the throne loses its true basis, which is the regard and trust of the people, the influence that a few ignorant or disgraced clerics may have over the opinion of the masses can serve them very little: the throne ends up as an object of fear and temptation and it is no longer that high post in which *powerful justice* is seated in order to distribute the riches of virtues and restrain the vices that degrade the human race.

This, then, is the terrible buffeting experienced by the throne because of the machinations of politics availing itself of superstition. Buffeting? No, it is necessary to call things by their true name. It is not a buffeting, it is destruction; for, as I have already observed, the throne, *in its true nature,* does not exist even though its power may exist in all. The throne comes tumbling down and its ruins fall upon the altar, which they dirty and defile.

At other times, politics fakes various attacks against superstition but these are purposely misdirected so as to be unfruitful and frustrate the public. This is one of the most evil machinations of politics: it consists in producing evils while making it look as if it is applying the remedies in order to cure them. This is only a pretense, then, and it even permits superstition to be attacked in an imprudent manner, giving nourishment to ridiculous sarcasm and injustice. The government then takes seemingly *severe measures,* which, in reality, are *void* because they take into account neither moral nor physical force in order to support them.

But you might say, what is the object of a government that places itself in ridicule, appearing weak and imprudent? In these cases, my Elpidio, the object of the government is to prove, by all means, that its circumstances are the most difficult and dangerous and that good people should resign themselves to that which *can be done* (which is nothing) and not demand the impossible. Then superstition becomes a ghost that terrifies now some, now others; it opens the way for the government to continue along the way of despotism, *blindly proffering blows.* And at other times it makes cowardly retreats according to what suits its political ends.

In the meantime, the Church suffers infinite attacks, for it is maliciously blamed for all these evils, and there is no greater proof of its divine origins than when it maintains its position in the midst of so many storms and preserves authority which it would have lost a thousand times if it were of human origin. Yes, my Elpidio, the pretensions of politics, whether *civil or clerical,* have put the Spouse of Christ to the test, and I can do no less than transcribe for you a very notable part of the most eloquent and wise preface of the Abbé Ducreux to his precious and methodical *Ecclesiastical History,* in which the unequivocal protection of heaven is presented as a self-evident sign: "The preservation of a firm center in spite of the never-ending jealousies and mistrust of the priesthood and the empire, in spite of the blows struck by ambitious princes on the legitimate jurisdiction of the pontiffs, and in spite of the abuses that even more ambitious pontiffs have at times made upon the spiritual power, which cannot be useful or respected unless it is contained within just limits; finally, the preservation of true piety in spite of scandals of every kind which have altered doctrine, denaturalized the old rules, consecrated, so to speak, national vices, defiled the holiness of priesthood itself, and at times takes this audacity so far as to install sin itself in the Pontifical Cathedral."

Yes, my Elpidio, human misery, strengthened and embellished with a crown or tiara, many times has used one or the other to weaken the very authority that those symbols indicate, and perhaps kings and popes have been the principal enemies of kingly and pontifical authority. Superstition has found in this a great support, and politics has not overlooked the opportunity to profit as much as possible from this. In such cases, I repeat, my friend, religion is the one that loses the most because it is the most persecuted and slandered, for all the excesses committed by those decorated and fake protectors are attributed to it. How terrible is the persecution that has as its own leaders the very ones who should be leaders of the ranks of the living God!

Without entering into the question (useless from my point of view, though this is not the time to give my reasons), without entering, I repeat, into the question of the infallibility of the Roman Pontiff, we can ascertain that none of them have ever taught an erroneous doctrine no matter the efforts that have been made to present Marcellinus as an idolator, Honorius as a monothelite, and others accused of diverse errors. There have been, however, many popes whose crimes have given nourishment to that superstition which always feigns *holiness* and is always accompanied by pride.

Under the pretext of bemoaning and detesting the miseries of the head of the Church, many hypocrites have allowed themselves to ignore the true principles of religion, mistaking the pontifical dignity with the man who exercises it. Here, then, is another opportunity for politics to achieve its purpose, which is to *debilitate the authority while pretending to strengthen it.* Do not be shocked by what I propose. Politics never wishes authority to be so strong that it cannot be *manipulated,* and it never permits it to show itself to be so weak that it could not serve as an instrument to *manipulate* the people.

PASSIVE OBEDIENCE

From this struggle between religion and superstition has come the dispute over *passive obedience,* which can very well be considered as a play on words of modern invention to make it appear that much is being said when nothing is said and to terrify the people with a ridiculous ghost. So that you may become aware of the basis of my assertion, it is necessary that you remember that I do not now consider superstition in its religious aspect, but only in its relationship with society.

I speak only about politics and within this concept I ask: what is the meaning of *passive obedience?* To obey without thinking? And what right does politics have to manipulate the minds? If it pretends to rule them, its efforts will be void because people will think as they see fit. Is passive obedience *obedience by force*? Then all that needs to be done is to obtain the force, and then obedience would be attained without any need to talk about it. Nothing needs to be done but to take away the mask and say, *I rule because I can,* but then it is clearly not an act of virtue, but a need as a result of force.

All we have left then is the mere name of *obedience,* and here the play on words becomes an equivocal term which no longer means a virtue but a disgrace. Politics, however, knowing its powerlessness in this case, wishes to leave its realm and enter into the field of morality and into the sanctuary of conscience. We could very well, then, repulse politics as an intruder, and so in order to avoid repulsion it allies itself with superstition, which is always ready to protect deceits. Let politics come in, in order to strike a new deathly blow. What are they telling us? That we are compelled to obey, even though the command is an unjust one, in order to avoid greater evils? This we will eventually do, but only to avoid *greater evils,* which we would have a scruple of conscience in producing, only in order not to make a sacrifice of much less *transcendence.* This doctrine is from Saint Thomas who presents it with his usual clarity and precision in the following terms: "We ought to answer the third argument by saying that every man is compelled to obey the secular princes inasmuch as it is required by the order of justice. Therefore, if they do not have a just principality, but an usurped one, or *if they order unjust things,* the subjects are not compelled to *obey* them unless it is in an accidental way in order to avoid scandals or dangers".[3] Saint John Chrysostom had taught the same thing as regards the institution of the princes. "*All power comes from God.* What do you say? Therefore, every prince is established by God. 'I do not say this,' responds the apostle, 'I do not speak about any prince

---

3. *Ad tertium dicendum quod principibus saecularibus in tantum homo obedire tenetur, in quantum ordo institiae requirit. . .Et ideo si non habeant instum principatum sed usurpatum, VER SI INIUSTA PRAECIPIANT non tenentur eis subditi obedire; nisi forte per accidens propter vitandum scandalum vel periculum.* The Great Teacher Thomas, 22 dae q. 104. art. 6 ad 3.

but about the thing in itself. I believe that it is the work of
divine wisdom that there may be principalities in which some
will rule and others will obey and let not things be made simply
and rashly and let not the peoples be battered about like waves
in the sea."' Therefore, Saint John Chrysostom does not say:
"Every prince comes from God," but dealing with the thing
itself he says: "all power comes from God."[4]

We then arrive at the same result in the moral order as in
the political order, which is to say that we give in to force, and,
I repeat, all we have to do is get it and superstition will triumph. If we have the foolishness to believe that anything that a
superior orders is just only because he orders it, then we have a
superstitious obedience, and it goes without saying that a superstitious obedience is not a virtue.

What have politicians done, helped by *accommodating*
theologians who act by pure routine? To suppose that these
ideas are revolutionary and invoked only to disobey their superiors, when they are directed only to render tribute to the true
obedience, which is the only one that gives them honor. The
just princes never fear revolutions that are the effect of desperation, which is always the result of injustice.

Take note, Elpidio, that this distinction between *active*
and *passive* obedience is modern and it was the result of the
degradation of the governments, as was the oath not to defend
regicide or tyrannicide. I have always regarded these precautions as true insults to the kingly authority, supposing that by
the mere fact of being so, it is capable of tyranny. When the
tyrants have died as result of the fury of the people, the people
have not been incited by doctrine but by sufferings, and desperation never stops to think and reflect.

---

4. Nom enim est potestas nisi a Deo. Quid dicis? Omnis ergo princeps a
Deo constitutus est. Istud inquit (Apostolus) non dico. Neque enim de quovis
principum sermo mihi nunc est, sed de ipsa re. Quod enim principatus sunt,
quod hi quidem imperant, isti vero subiecti sunt, quodque non simpliciter aut
temerecuncta feruntur, nec fluctuum instar populi huc atque illuc circum-
aguntur divinae sapientiae opus esse iudico. Propterea non dicit. Non enim
princeps est nisi a Deo, sed de re ipsa disserit, dicens. Non enim est potentas
nisi a Deo. St. John Chrysostom, in Letters to the Romans, chap. 13, 4:223.

Nevertheless, superstition takes great advantage of these *politico-religious subtleties* and politics, for its part, never hesitates to apply them. The lovers of truth are persecuted under the pretext of being *suspects*. This most deadly of terms serves as a code word for the cohorts of tyranny to exterminate and feed upon its innocent victims, while religion and justice bemoan the loss of its defenders.

I am sorry for having spent so much time on this unsavory subject and I am afraid that I may have bothered you with my observations, which may have seemed to you as mere ramblings. I would be happy if they were; but the powerful voice of experience fobids me the consolation of such blissful deceit. I would be happy if I did not see evils that I cannot remedy and at times I envy the "good fortune" of those who have never meditated upon them.

I cannot be indifferent to: my ideas, my feelings, my state of being, my character; everything, yes, everything calls me to the fight for pure religion and against the deadlest miscarriages of hell; and you will know that there is nothing so sensible as to recognize and proclaim the advantages of the enemy.

Yes, I do recognize the advantages that infamous superstition begets and I admit its immense power; but this does not frighten me, and no matter how weak or fruitless my efforts, the mere resistance to sin is a pleasure that I will not be deprived of as long as I live. Wait then for another letter, and in the meantime receive my regard.

THE PREVENTION OF SUPERSTITION

I have always found the role of the whiner to be less than graceful. Since I have had the misfortune of seeing myself play it while indicating the means by which politics takes advantage of superstition, I wish, my dear Elpidio, to avert the pain this causes me by showing the methods of avoiding such deadly evils that I deem effective.

THE VALUE OF PATIENCE AND KNOWLEDGE

The first of these methods is *patience*. You might say that this is taking the air of a sermon. But let us see if, from the perspective of politics, I may be able to give the same advice. Let us test whether this is as useless as it might seem to you.

The desire for an instantaneous, unattainable cure is an obstacle for another cure which is certain though slow. Rashness is the most evident proof of human weakness as much as a measured wait is proof of heroic strength. How many most useful projects have failed because of rashness? Politics should much bemoan, yes much, the daring boldness of those who want to end in one day tasks that by their very nature require many years. We do not wish to leave anything for those who come after us: here is the way of not leaving them anything.

Human vanity always boasts of wisdom and power. But it does not endure in any way the attacks of mistaken or imprudent opinion. No sooner do some thoughtless people begin to call for some reform than the politicians immediately consider it necessary to put a reform *hastily* into effect. They do not want anyone thinking that they have not perceived the evils or that they lack the energy to remedy them. Even posthumous glory has its influence in this unfortunate rashness. Impetuosity destroys everything while wishing to improve everthing in order that history may preserve the names of the reformers with all the honor and veneration that are due to wisdom and energy.

Do no believe, on account of this, that I pretend to justify the criminal apathy with which many who should be opposed to superstition do quite the opposite, letting it be disseminated and run freely. No, my Elpidio, I do not advocate this plan of *quiet destruction* which they see fit to call laudable prudence. I detest it, and I wish that my weak voice could awaken many from their profound lethargy. They could become resolute defenders of the truth, but instead they foster the errors of this mistaken prudence, a discretion that only makes bold an enemy who is by nature fierce and intrepid.

I pray for constant efforts to restrain superstition and that a truce never be declared with it. I also desire that a political fanaticism not destroy the work of sensible patriotism and genuine morality. You might ask, what should be the method to reconcile these extremes? It is well known: one needs only the candid openness to confess that one is not doing it, because it does not please one's vanity and other passions.

In this matter, as is the case in all moral and political matters, the first step should be to place ourselves completely in the place of the persons whom we wish to correct or educate. We then make every rational effort to *feel* and *think* what they would feel and think in such circumstances. We would by then have the *picture of evil,* having *translated to ourselves* the individuals who ought to be the objects of our operations. You can well see that once we know an evil it is easier to find a solution than if we were to flail wildly in the wind in order to destroy it.

I have referred to feeling and thinking because there are many who pretend that they have acted reasonably by merely stating that they know very well that the wicked would be opposed to reform, and that even the good, though beguiled, will grimace as though they were taking a bitter medicine. These, my Elpidio, are popular phrases that, even though they may seem to mean a lot, in fact do not say anything, nor do they serve any purpose. I would like to see in the reformers a *witness* nourished by *meditation* and animated by charity, honesty, and true patriotism.

Once this first step is taken, the cure must begin full force, but with the greatest prudence, and without trying *experiments,* which in politics are even riskier than in medicine. Since the pious, learned and sensible Espiga died and is thus beyond the reach of his enemies, I will be as bold as to relate to you a private conversation that the two of us had in his office. We regretted the rashness of a great number of deputies, who boastfully considered themselves to be patriots while proposing insanities, yet could not keep to themselves this or that knowledge they had about the evils of the fatherland. Espiga told me: "I see much further ahead than these gentlemen, who perhaps have not thought in depth about the matter that they are dealing with, but I am very far from approving a proposal to do, all at once and without preparation, everything that is believed to be correct. Even my friend, who lives far away, writes me letters blaming me of timidity; however, I answered him that if he were in touch with reality he would think differently. Let us use an allegory, which is trivial and simple; if I had to go from one end of this room to the other, and were afraid of stumbling over an obstacle in the middle, I would go around it touching the walls, even though this operation might seem ridiculous and lengthy; for in the end I would arrive safely, and even though I would lose a little bit of time I would not regret this loss in return for my personal safety. I have always proceeded thus in regards to politics and I have the pleasure of saying I have never been disappointed." How many times have I remembered Espiga's statements and almost daily experience has not permitted me to forget this conversation.

If it is pertinent to proceed with such prudence in all political matters, it is much more necessary when dealing with the restraint of superstition. This virtuous action engenders a solidarity with the victims of superstition. At the same time, the superstitious are afflicted by an inexplicable displeasure. It leads the most prudent of persons to lose sense of what is proper and commit great absurdities.

What would a politician do if he were one of those superstitious? According to him, he should devise a strategy of action. It is clear that one will very soon realize one should not act hastily, unless one wishes to lose everything. On the contrary, one will find peace only by taking other steps than those taken by the superstitious.

Achieving this strategy is a great satisfaction to the ruler and to the politician. If, however, he is displeased with these measured steps and has the weakness of hastiness, he will always be starting the task, for it will tumble down time after time. Intellectual evils demand more than any others that healing reach the person through reflection and conviction. It is perhaps believed that in order to destroy superstition it is enough to suppose that it is already destroyed and to remain in an ideal repose like the political quixotics who will later on be compelled to bemoan its continuing afflictions.

ACTING IN THE PRESENT MOMENT

I am the first to wish the accomplishment of projects and perhaps the most impatient in waiting for them. For my ideas about selfishness perhaps differ from those I was taught. I say *perhaps,* because I am convinced that if people did not speak to *deceive* but to *instruct,* they would all agree on this subject as on many other subjects.

I am openly in favor of the proverb, *the early bird catches the worm.*[1] I have always considered it a solemn foolishness not to enjoy immediately the gains of our popular ventures, satisfying ourselves instead with the thought of what others might enjoy when the seeds that we plant produce the desired fruit.

These ideas of mine about selfishness may seem strange and even offensive, but if they are reflected upon, it will be seen that they are just. One is compelled to obtain one's perfection as well as that of the society in which one lives, and when one has fulfilled this duty there will then be good time to think

---

1. "el que viene atrás que arree."

about planting for future generations. I do not learn by what another may know, nor do I feed myself with what somebody else eats. You might say that these principles destroy the sciences and charity, discouraging those who build the foundations upon which the castles of wisdom may be built, and restraining the hand of the one who generously feeds his fellow human being. No, my Elpidio, these ideas are very far from leading to such immoral results, for if I foresaw that this might be the case, I would no doubt be the first to hate them. Listen and you will be persuaded that the contrary is true.

I do not pretend to justify the wicked selfishness of those who do not wish to do anything unless it is for their own advantage. It is a duty to plant, and if the fruit cannot be produced in time for us to harvest, we are not to be less active in our charitable endeavors; but if through abundant risks or alternative ways and efforts we can produce rapidly and without damage, we ought not to omit any effort in order to do so. We thus fulfill the sacred duty of perfecting ourselves and our society.

Even though the society of tomorrow should concern us— for the future of humanity is at stake—we have no right to give up the present for the future. This is only done rationally regarding eternal life, because we all wish to belong to the celestial family there and fulfill the divine will, which is the ultimate norm of morality. When we speak, however *from the roof down* in matters that have nothing to do with morality, and when no rights are infringed upon, the principle ought not to be put off until tomorrow what we can do today.

Slothfulness has always found the support of a *false prudence,* and from here many incalculable evils have originated. Many expect improvements with the passing of time, but these do not come: because *we do not want to work* and must give *some sort of excuse in order not to be accused of laziness.* Briefly, if the state of the matter is such that its correction cannot be hurried without great danger, it is foolhardy, or better said, sinful to hurry it; but if the matter can be accomplished without danger, it would be a deplorable apathy not to provide the means.

Applying these principles to superstition, it clearly follows we must do our best to eliminate it. Those leaving everything to time cannot exonerate themselves. Time is only a succession of existence, and if this is inactive or thoughtless, its prolongation will only serve the purpose of rooting the evils and will lose even the purpose of healing them. It is a horrible and hateful sin to let society be submerged in superstition without making an effort to improve it. But to hazard dangerous remedies is also the deadliest imprudence. Let us correct as much as we can without danger; but let us correct!

Which sensible person would be satisfied with saying: when I am no longer there, perhaps my country will become a rich society, well organized and free from irreligiosity and superstition? It is insane to believe oneself exonerated from doing good, only because others will do it. Furthermore, what would be the basis of such hope if the foundations of such an important building are not established? Some say that the foundations are built when works are established which will appear in the future in all their design and splendor. I agree if they deal with works which could in fact be completed. The extollers of impossibilities usually deceive the people, asserting that the foundations of future prosperity have been established, when in reality nothing has been done. They deceive, with great rhetoric, naive, fostering ambition and all the sins that are the necessary effect of that ambition, which cannot be disguised in any other way. The past and the future, my Elpidio, have at times served the purpose of exercising a vain orator and nourishing the folly of the beguiled, who, living in an ideal world, do not take care of the present.

Taking it for granted, then that we should work incessantly to destroy superstition, proceeding with extreme prudence, being satisfied with what can be accomplished, let us continue exploring all the means that should be used in order to achieve such an important objective.

TACT IN DEALING WITH THE WEAK

Every violent action is useless and wicked. Let us not deal with force, which may be good in order to manipulate beasts but does not promote understanding. There is, however, one very common kind of attack that is equivalent to a true force—political authority and influence. When the superstitious (who consider themselves to be authentic believers) realize that authority looks at them with disdain, they pretend they are called to martyrdom, and here we find the devil in pure battle. They themselves provoke persecution simply to make an acceptable sacrifice to God, since they have read that the martyrs of the true faith and pure religion gloried in the opportunity they had to suffer for Jesus Christ.

Genuine religious politics should use *personal* esteem as a way to hold back the beguiled, whose errors are bemoaned. It must be made clear by every means possible that those wishing martyrdom should start by looking for tyrants, who cannot be found among learned governments and people. We thus put to an end false pretenses and fears, and trust is re-established no matter what the way of thinking of individuals might be.

The same things can be said regarding destinies and honors. If one class of society sees itself deprived of them because of their opinions a formidable reaction ought to be expected, which will always be followed by many others of even greater intensity. So that you may clearly see the basis of these observations, allow me, Elpidio, to remind you about certain passages of the modern history of unfortunate Spain.

THE IMPACT OF SUPERSTITION ON SPANISH CULTURE

On account of the similarities between *political* and religious *superstition*, I will say something about the factions that have afflicted and still do afflict a nation worthy of a better fate. I do not need to tell you that I have never belonged nor do I currently belong to any *party* or *society* other than that of free and religious persons, and if these two categories place me in a party, you may very well place me in it, but you already know (even though I do not believe that you have ever ignored it) who I am and to whom I belong. For my part, I shall never call a part the *true human society,* though there are numerous splintered groups who degrade humankind in one way or another with this delirious nonsense.

The hidden war of political and superstitious fanatics, I mean those gentlemen who are Masons and partisans, has been and will be the ruin of Spain. On points of belief, it ruins Spain more than the public war of superstitious fanatics. When I had the honor and the misfortune of finding myself in the representative body of that illustrious nation, the evidence convinced me of this truth. Mutual contempt, mistrust, *employment depending on who you know and not what you know,*[2] these were the means to arouse all the passions which, once unleashed, could not put an end to the ravages. I do not pretend to write here the history of those moral events, for that will be to depart too much from my principal purpose. I have only made these references in order to deduce from them a proof for my assertion.

Oh! If true tolerance had reigned and if superstition had not been attacked in an imprudent way until it came to be confused with Christian dogmas, if the politicians of the different factions had had more prudence among themselves, how different the fate of Spain would have been! What memorable lessons, my dear Elpidio! I only assure you that one who has been on the inside of the affairs of Spain and does not detest secret societies as much as superstition is either a sly one or a beast. I have to restrain the pen because it keeps going . . . let us just observe that every time avarice and ambition show through in the reforms, things manage to be transformed but can never be maintained once they have tumbled down. Immorality never produces anything but evils, and one who starts by stealing never succeeds in convincing.

In order to attack superstition effectively, it is absolutely necessary that the reformers not be in need of reform themselves but rather that they be able to show themselves to be without any blemish. How can a bunch of sly ones reform their fellow citizens only because their slyness and their motives are of a different order? "As long as you are superstitious, give your money over, and as long as I see *clearly,* I ought to pocket it." "As long as you are superstitious, I deprive you of the employment that you deserve, and as long as I see *clearly,* I

---

2. "la exclusiva de los empleos."

place myself in a job that is not mine." The language of *words* is not as clear as what I have just expressed, but the language of *action* is much clearer and more imprudent.

Is this the way of destroying superstition? Undoubtedly it would root it more firmly, for the wicked do not care about society nor have any other law than their own private interest, for which they sacrifice everything. They really want nothing so much as *tyranny,* which they hypocritically detest. When the intention is to destroy, there is no easier means than injustice, but when the aim is to edify, mutual esteem becomes the necessary basis.

Another absolutely necessary condition for the attack on superstition is that those who try to correct the abuses that are committed under the pretext of fostering religion not present themselves as religious, even when they have the misfortune of being so. I abhor hypocrisy no matter its form, and I believe that it should not be confused with prudence. No one should pretend to be religious, or irreligious, for this would be tantamount to scandal. I know very well that irreligiosity can always be seen, but when it is seen accompanied by respect and moderation it does not offer as much obstacle to reform.

When the superstitious are convinced that the only goal is to destroy religion, every effort to correct and enlighten them is totally useless. But when the superstitious are convinced that regardless of what are the ideas of those who preach reform they ought to respect those whom they themselves respect and oppose those whom they themselves disprove of, some result may be obtained for the reform movement from even the most ignorant.

I have always believed that, other than in a few instances that should be regarded as the exception and not the rule, the superstitious recognize their own extravagance or at least that their whims are not essential to religion, and thus they would help the reform movement, even though reluctantly, if handled with prudence.

My Elpidio, how could anyone who begins stating that he does not believe anything, and that all religion is a farce, correct the superstitious practices? All promises of protection and tolerance would then be in vain; the people would never reach such a degree of stupidity that they would place their religious destiny in the hands of those who openly insult them, denigrating the relationship they hold so dear and with which they have always identified their happiness. I do not wish to make references to the dealings of Spain but I cannot avoid it, and I even believe that it is my duty not to avoid it.

The Constitution of the year 1812 openly protected the Catholic religion and throughout that small but memorable code there is not one single word that shows the slightest irreligiosity. The discussions of the *Cortes* never doubted the dogma, even though on matters of discipline there were at times heated discussions that brought about distasteful expressions. In a word, the political code and the Congress that was ruled by it, always presented to the people the laws and the deputies of a Catholic nation.

However, there were among us a number of insignificant puppets who were loud and imprudent, who in private conversation and even in coffee shops, on boulevards and in theaters spoke irreligiously and indiscreetly. The people who were aware of our activities lost all trust, judging all on account of a few individuals. This is what principally renders useless all the efforts of the *Cortes* to improve public morality, restraining the superstition that harms it so much. These are not theories, these are facts, which regretfully are being repeated in this new age of that unfortunate nation.

Ah, my Elpidio, how well I know most of the fickle ones; I judged the fickleness before it started and regretfully I have not been mistaken. It is undeniable that there is much to reform in Spain regarding religious practices, but it is also undeniable that it shall never be attained through means other than a *learned* and truly *religious frankness*.

The Spanish *character* does not suffer insults and is never dominated. It is beyond me how Spaniards have so mistaken their national character, thinking that they can win by insulting, or hoping that anything can be accomplished, however permanent, against the Spaniards' will. It is necessary to let them do what they want or kill them. There is no alternative. This is an indelible trait of the character of their noble and heroic ancestors, and no matter what the degradation of the people may be, the character is the same.

Do you think such people will stop being superstitious because they are insulted or persecuted? One has to be insane in order to believe this. In fact the imprudent opposition only gave rise to greater evils, rooting the superstitions even deeper. As long as they follow the same road, they will arrive at the same precipice and perish with equal disgrace.

I wish,my Elpidio, that before proceeding on political and ethical matters, one would make practical observations rather than calculations on paper or imitations of ridiculous harangues from *ideal works*. Let us think not about what we wish the people to do but what they themselves would like to do. All the arguments that follow from our mistaken abstract thoughts will inevitably cast us in a more ridiculous light.

If a nation that is religious by conviction, habit and pride—in fact constituted by such—is treated as a group of children who are to be disciplined by school teachers who teach them without engaging in critical questions, the disgusted people will try very soon to let them know that these children are already *grown up,* and to demonstrate the fact they start by *breaking the heads* of their imprudent principals. The orators and the poets then come out with their diatribes against the superstition of the people, but the *heads remain broken,* and the delinquents remain ready to break them again as long as the occasion presents itself.

Do you not think, my Elpidio,that the so-called reformers of Spanish superstitions would be very well placed in the category of fools? I say in the category of fools because not all ought to be placed in the category of the sly, although many do belong in it. They wish in vain to be confused with the genuine liberals, who are good and generous persons. Excuse me, Elpidio, I have tried to suppress these emotions for a long time, to calm my soul, but I deplore the misfortunes of a most noble cause which the most perfidious people have pretended to join.

SUPERSTITION UNDERMINES GOVERNMENT OFFICIALS

When it comes to the people, we should not forget that they are very jealous of their freedom in *all aspects.* Regardless of what their errors might be, they are neither patient nor tolerant when they are forced to do anything, much less when they are offended. They consider themselves as having the right to *social happiness*. This is not reconcilable with violence, even though many times it might be a daughter of whim. When a given people expect to be happy in a certain way, they wish to remain that way. All attempts to perturb their values are perceived as an attack on their happiness, and an infraction of their rights.

When the rulers of a people who are perceived to be superstitious show themselves to be irreligious, these rulers lose all their prestige and authority. As a journalist has written, though he was treating another subject, *ideas are not destroyed with bullets*. I would add: neither are they dispelled by insults. Let us follow the rules of prudence by putting ourselves in the place of those whom we want to correct or educate, and we will immediately recognize the absurdity of such behavior.

The people always consider their rulers and legislators as their representatives, or in another type of government as legal authorities, but never as masters, unless they are infamous and tyrannous. Will the people tolerate it if one of these civil leaders works against their opinion and their laws, or if these are broken even when public trust means nothing? You may then infer how imprudent and ignorant it would be of the representatives of the Catholic people, even if the latter are suspected of being superstitious, if they were to come to the fore to destroy not only superstition but religion itself. The people immediately perceive them as wicked persons who have sold their cause, betrayed their promises and usurped a power they never wished to give them.

The irreligious undoubtedly are pleased to observe that *their own* have been admitted to the legislative body and applaud any measure that propagates irreligiosity, but since they have no right to expect the passage of these measures, their lack of success cannot irritate them, even if it does not please them. When they cast their vote in favor of their representatives they see it as only exercising a *political* right, according to a *political* constitution intended to give their representatives a *merely political power*. From this it follows that they expected only *purely political measures.* It should not be surprising to them, then, to observe that their representatives do not involve themselves in matters that are purely religious, and whether or not the majority of the people have reason to believe what they believe, their representatives only care about insuring civil and political rights, promoting economic prosperity and demanding from the government and the judicial power the observance of the laws.

Religious persons think alike on the powers entrusted to their representatives. When they realize not only that there is a lack of measures protecting religion, which perhaps they were not expecting, but that furthermore there are *positive* acts persecuting them on account of their religious beliefs, their fury knows no bound. The government cannot then compensate for the ravages produced by such a vast number of exasperated people with the cold applause of a small number of thoughtless people.

Let me, my Elpidio, listen to the proverb: *Do not cry over spilled milk,*[3] and especially when I have undergone so much that no matter how big the spill it escapes my sight, which only discovers calm and quite different memories. But I rapidly follow those dear fugitive themes, and I even snatch many lost ones from the hands of death. They are all alive in my memory, causing a *pleasant torment.* This is misery, but it is a noble misery; and since you are in great part the cause, blame yourself and excuse me.

---

3. "con agua pasada no muele el molino."

THE INFLUENCE OF SUPERSTITION
IN RELATION TO NATIONS

Human misery introduces superstition in all nations, making it a part in a certain way of the character of its institutions. Yes, my Elpidio, the monster takes different forms, but it is always the same; its empire is more vast than commonly believed. One can hardly find a society in which it does not have the deadliest influence.

THE MEANING OF AUTHORITY

In the nations where the only and true religion, the Catholic religion, has been established, its divine origin necessarily claims a divine way of acting. The principle of authority is essential to deliver the human mind from its quandary, limitations, and whims. Human pride stirs against authority and puts into action every means at its disposal in order to fight it, but its vain efforts only serve the purpose of demonstrating that it is absolutely necessary. There is no doubt, my friend, about the contradiction, the errors, the ridiculous whims, the uncertainty, the inconstancy, the rage, the unsettling, and even at times the shrewdness, and even the perversity that one observes in the writings and conversations of the enemies of God's authority. These prove more than any other argument that there can be no solid well-being without religion, no true religion without authority.

220

This principle of life, however, has caused death, not by its very nature, but because it has served as a pretext for many beguiled ones and an even greater number of sly ones (for such is their name). They use it to set themselves up as oracles, thus abusing the true authority to the point of even making it ridiculous. In the same way as false prophets, they make pronouncements and perform deeds that divine wisdom detests and condemns.

From this arises the mistrust experienced by wishing to use the power of reasoning to examine the facts and doctrines that are presented as God's works, while the false defender of religion pretends that it is a crime to examine any matters of belief. These beguiled ones confuse the temerity of those who set themselves up as a tribunal, where reason decides the justices or perfection of God's works, with the prudence of those who reflect on the facts and God's will before acceding to believe in spite of lack of understanding. In one word, they confuse Catholics with the superstitious.

Nations, then, go as far as acquiring a tendency to believe everything that seems marvelous, and finding God's presence in all matters. They shield themselves with it, thus committing the greatest offense.[(57)] This is the origin of the vast numbers of miracles that common people believe but the Church has never approved nor can approve. Many beguiled ones have deceived themselves as well as the thoughtless multitude about visions.

There is not a saint to whom a great multitude of unheard-of wonders has not been attributed. One can even find a certain religious vanity and competition, which attempts to portray the saints as rivals and to pit one against the other, finding which one has performed more miracles. This is the name given to as many cock-and-bull stories as they can devise. This results in a *mystical battle* that is not only ridiculous but sacrilegious. It is true sacrilege to treat in such a way the servants of God who eternally delight in his presence and cannot be the leaders of such fools.

As a result, this causes great damage to religion and society, because the true miracles are placed in doubt and confused with the multitude of fictitious ones. If all people were capable of engaging in a critical theological examination of the subject of miracles there would be no danger, as there is no danger that false gold would be sold for true gold to artists, who by means of the touchstone know how to tell the nature of metals.

What does the multitude understand of the rules of critique and theological principles? The multitude labels everyone a heretic who does not believe everything exactly to the letter. As long as they are assured that this or that saint performed a miracle, they find compatible all the visions and dreams, even the most ridiculous.

When people of talent and prudence are intimidated, they sometimes do not dare attack such abuses. Only some buffoons, who may be good and learned believers, enter the joust, but their insults aggravate the evil. Thinking they have scored a victory for irreligiosity, the irreligious take the vain belief of an ignorant multitude as well as the perversity of those who try to deceive it as an argument against religion. The beguilement of the irreligious goes so far that even the most learned commit thousands of errors in their speeches attacking religion based on the defects of those who pretend to or sincerely follow it.

The facts that should legitimate religion are presented as arguments against it, reducing all reasoning to "those who do not have religion are perverse, therefore religion is false." Not just a logical person but even the most ignorant one can recognize the imperfection of this reasoning, or rather, this *nonstatement*. One would do violence to one's capacity of discernment even to consider this combination of words, which is nothing more than a contradiction of ideas.

In my previous letters about irreligiosity, I pointed out this very defect in the writings of the irreligious; take note that they also think alike about superstition. At present, however, my objective is not to examine the exactness of their discourses, but to make some brief observations on how superstition influences the character and the institutions of people.

Observing the nations adhering to the principle of God's authority, there are two great chasms which should be carefully avoided: a stupid fear that admits the greatest absurdity and a licentiousness that denies evidence while invoking the argument of authority.

Even the most sensible people are put off when they see

that the principle of authority has been challenged, and it takes the slightest most insignificant signs to convince them that it has. Once superstition has acquired protectors of this caliber, it spreads the darkness by making the people *afraid to think properly*, leaving them in an ignorant and fierce disposition, for education sweetens customs and manners. This gives rise to cruelty and strong passions, which cannot easily be restrained with the power of reason. They are thus left with an erroneous religious principle, or an antireligious principle, which is what superstition basically is.

We ought not to be amazed that many atrocities are committed, or that the laws are broken with impudence. We should, however, be amazed when we observe meekness and justice from those beings who are led like beasts though they belong to the human race. People think that they are proceeding in a holy way while profaning the altar. They pretend to defend justice when they are really the ministers of the most detestable cruelty. There is hardly any remedy that can be applied to them but to avoid the cause of so many evils that is superstition. This monster sacrifices innumerable victims in cold blood in order to pay homage to God, whose mercy does not destroy the cruel defilers of his holy name, even though they commit so many atrocities in and through his name. How horrible is superstition!

FOLK RELIGION IN AMERICA

In the nations where there is a plurality of cults, the principle of authority is either not permitted or it is pretended that it is not permitted.[58] Superstition makes its influence felt there in quite a different way, which is no less ridiculous and is much more dangerous. It is not possible to give you a complete idea of superstition, with vast numbers of absurdities and disorders; it would be necessary to write a lengthy history. Thus I will limit myself to a few general observations and a particular case or two, which should be enough for you to recognize that the monster always makes its fierce influence felt.

When the foundations of the edifice of true religion are

shaken, and the principle of true authority suppressed, people are taken up by the insatiable desire to innovate. They are pleased when they believe they have made a new discovery in matters of religion, much more so than when they find or believe they have found the truth in a matter of natural science. In this field reason is the *only* guide for the investigative process, which cannot happen when a deciding authority is not admitted. Religion is thus an interesting tool as much for its defenders as for its enemies. The former consider it the source of their happiness and the latter an obstacle to happiness. The victory is as flattering for one as for the other.

I have never been able to accept the position of indifference in matters of religion. Putting important reasons aside, my own experience would be enough to confirm this conviction, precisely because I find myself in a country where I have every opportunity to make a wide variety of observations, which my own ministry obliges me to do. No subject is so much talked about, or disputed, as religion. You can hardly attend a gathering in which, in one way or another, a debate or at least a conversation about points of beliefs is not introduced. Since the subject is so interesting and everyone is concerned about it, it can do no less than arouse the interest about new findings. Here is the way superstition exercises its influence.

Novelty is the prime mover of this great machine, for it is what most pleases the human passions and dallies with the mind, which seems to be quite anxious to obtain a few moments of rest after the great labor of coordinating religious ideas. These ideas are always disquieting, for they do not find a way to appease themselves. When a new system appears, it sort of becomes the fashion, and in the same way that some doctors send a few thousand to the grave while testing a new healing method, these new apostles pervert and ruin a portion of beguiled ones even before they can perceive their illusions, if they ever do perceive them. They then leave them, however, only to give themselves over to new ones, which are even worse, or to fall into a complete unfaithfulness.

The end result is that religion is then offered for sale like a piece of cloth. Each person buys the kind which is most suitable to his taste and social needs. Generally an interesting friendship, a marriage bond, and at times an engagement decide the kind of acceptable religion. Once people get used to this lack of constancy, this lack of reflective process and even, at times, this hypocritical perfidy, society is inevitably left degraded. I truly believe that one cannot expect much constancy from a man who is as ready to change his religion as his shirt.

One does not find in this country, nor in others like it, the multitude of vain believers in false miracles; on the contrary, people may even deny true miracles; neither do Protestants talk about the protection that Christian people receive from saints. On the other hand, at the same time that the protection of the saints is despised, people do believe in all kinds of spells and practice all kinds of perfidious works in order to obtain the protection of the devil. Do not believe that I exaggerate or that I am trying to paint a *grimmer* picture. Everyone who has been in this country could tell you about *fortune-tellers,* that is to say, soothsayers or diviners. They are as common as any other professional who lives off his skill, sometimes earning much more money than the best artist. Those who frequent them are not only the ignorant class (which is not numerous in this country) but even people with a select education. One could not believe that they would be capable of such sinfulness.

ANECDOTES OF RELIGIOUS FOLKLORE

Among other cases, I remember a British lady who about four years ago moved into the house across from us to live with a neighboring family. The members of my household were in the habit of visiting that house as neighbors, and, all of a sudden the woman disappeared. A few days later there was an announcement in the papers stating that the lady offered her services as a fortune-teller. The announcement used a more veiled expression, because she was, after all, ashamed of her absurdity.

She set up office hours from eleven to one in order to help those who sought secrets or knowledge of the future. A few young people who were under my care went to see her without telling me, for they very well feared that I would not allow it.

They found the lady, who had prepared a very pleasant room to welcome money-laden customers (for money was all she wanted). She had a big chair raised as if it were a throne in order to appear more important. The seekers would present their sorrows about lost things, absent persons, etc., etc., as well as their desire to know about their future fate. She gave her answers with a pompous air, after which they would leave either happy or angry, depending on whether her answers pleased or annoyed them.

One of my boys, now in Havana, who was a bit of a scoundrel, did not want to leave without greeting the lady and letting her know that he would not be counted among the fools who believed her. He went close to her and with a sly smile complimented her for her talents which were not apparent when she lived across the street from our house. The poor woman recognized the danger that a group of young people from Havana could cause by making fun of her. She sought a truce, insinuating to him, though with great subtlety and cunning, that one needed a means *to make a living.*

Even though I was saddened by the young people's visit to such an impostor, I was also happy for the important lesson they received. Nothing could so profoundly impress upon them a distaste for superstition as the realization that it does exist in every nation in spite of the quality of its institutions. Unless without this example and others known to the public, it would seem impossible that there should be so much superstition in the most populous and mercantile city in the United States of North America.

Elpidio, I myself witnessed one of these horrible and degrading acts publicly committed in the streets of this city. As I was walking I saw a black man surrounded by a number of persons. Imagine my indignation and grief when I saw him predicting the future and declaring the occult as he read the signs in the palms of his hands?

I proceeded along my way, Elpidio, making the saddest reflections: if a Catholic were to point out the statue of a saint in this street and invite passersby to seek God's mercy through the intercession of one of his servants, that person would at the very least be ridiculed or despised. Possibly they would break the statue over his head and he would have great difficulty in escaping alive. However, surrounded this black man, a minister of the devil, many believing in his nonsense, others looking with indifference but without indignation, as if it were only an innocent game.

Had this charlatan wished to commit any other crime, a policeman would have been there at once, at the very least to prevent him from doing so. When he commits the most transcendental of all sins, perverting not only the heart of the unwary but, what is more, the mind, he does not even fear being bothered.

Seeing young people full of natural curiosity, starting to gather around him, this is what really bothered me and made me sad, I could foresee the effects this would have on those innocent bystanders who are more easily and strongly impressed. Yet I was walking among the most learned people of the world; contrary to other countries where learning is concentrated in universities and in certain social classes, here it is disseminated among all classes. The wise do not appear here as brilliant dots on an obscure surface, but like flowers of extraordinary beauty in a wonderfully bright garden.

Superstition takes different forms according to how it wants to deceive different people. It usurps the rights and the practice of authority among Catholics, while among those of mixed faith it usurps those of reason, which ends up degraded. Even though freedom is the holiest principle, it is turned into a curse when abused in such a fashion. Fanatics believing that they lose their freedom when they prevent this kind of crime, never knew freedom's true nature. Would one expect to find so much fanaticism in this country? Well, I have shown you only a small part of the evidence.

In almost all the bookstores you may find books on how to tell fortunes by guess work, numbers, and other superstitious signs. Following the laws of mathematics, and accurate data, we may reach certain conclusions that surprise the ignorant and entertain the wise.

However, Elpidio, this is not what I am talking about. They do not try to figure out mathematical problems; instead they guess the future by combining one number with another and thus find out if an individual will live a long or short life, if he or she will be married or not, rich or poor, etc., etc., something very much like the occult science that the Jews used to have, and still have today, when they deviate from the doctrine of Moses and the Prophets.

One can also find in all bookstores books about dreams and how to tell the future fate through them, as well as how to make other similar predictions. These books are of course printed in English for exclusive use in this country. They have enough of them in England. In fact, they never send books from this country to England on speculation. Therefore they are manufactured and distributed in the United States in order to bring great profit to their publishers. They would not be able to make a profit at the low price at which they are sold unless they were distributed in great numbers. You may draw your own conclusion on this, Elpidio.

Protestantism is the cause of this superstition, or at least of its unbridled popularity, for it has robbed the basis of religion's authority. Very few Catholics buy these books. An external ecclesiastical forum may not compel Catholics to stay away from this literature, but we have the internal forum. If anyone has the misfortune of buying and using such books, we separate them from the sacraments until they stop such a sin; however, Protestants go to their *communion class* perhaps even with such a book in their pockets.

It is amazing to see the renewal in this country of the most sacrilegious superstition, which was very common in the Middle or Dark Ages. It consists of putting a key between the pages of a Bible, without looking, keeping the key firmly in place so it will not slide from its first position, and then upon opening the Bible one would look for the letter the end of the key is pointing to. This would then be the first letter of the name of a prospective boyfriend, or of the city to which one must travel, or of the business that one must take care of, etc., etc.

In justice to the most sensible of these people, I quickly point out that the above-mentioned books are only found in bookstores, rather than in public libraries or private ones that belong to sensible and educated individuals. Although this happens in all nations, it seems peculiar that this country would not exceed others on such an important point, when it is ahead of them on points of lesser significance.

But what is more, my Elpidio, we are amused from time to time by newspaper announcements about a haunted house, or evil omens. The majority of the people take such announcements as a verified truth. It is then impossible to dissuade them from these cock-and-bull stories. They also have their favorite days; for instance when leaving on a voyage, one is not able to find any sailors to set sail on a Friday, unless certain precautions are taken so that they may not flee. Even the captains are not that free from this superstition!

You may find in this country many other superstitions along the same lines. There are also prophets of doom who announce the death of gravely ill people. If when a salt shaker is spilled on a table one of the guests is bound to be frightened. It seems that *when it rains we all get wet,* especially those who do not have an umbrella to protect them, as is the case with people who do not take such superstitions seriously. Seeing nothing improper with these practices and considering themselves free to accept or set aside anything, these people end up without any moral foundation. The opinion of sensible people is thus all they have to fall back on. How weak is the opinion of sensible people to those who are not compelled to follow it and who even ignore its importance!

With my characteristic frankness, I ought to say that, in my opinion, there are few countries as superstitious as the United States. No sooner have I written these lines than I seem to hear what you might say reading them: A Catholic and foreign clergyman is writing, so let us not pay him any attention; he is not aware that his anger is leading him to make wrong and ridiculous statements which he himself would condemn in others.

No matter how great your friendship is do not think I am wrong in expecting this kind of response from you. Others might answer even more harshly. Before I get to the point, I must confess a weakness I have always had. I have always trusted all causes, political, religious and literary campaigns, so that, far from trying to disarm my enemies, I have always sought to give them new weapons or the opportunity to sharpen their dull ones. The victory gives much greater pleasure when the enemy is fully equipped to defend himself. This is why I place my name on all my writings, and show my profession and way of thinking. But to the point, Elpidio: listen to a series of facts presented by a *foreign Catholic clergyman* writing from a country where the Protestant religion is the most widely spread, even though the state does not designate an *official religion.*

I would like to remove any impression of animosity against this country. I remind you that I have a very high regard for this country. I have resided here for so long, in spite of the dangers to my health at the beginning on account of the weather, and in spite of having suffered so many deprivations because of my lack of knowledge of English. During this time I have had many and highly regarded invitations to move to other countries, yet I have not accepted any of them.

Once the English language became familiar, I have made such good friends that I would be ungrateful to be insensitive to their attentions and favors. In my heart I belong to this country as if I had been born here. I am not a citizen, nor shall I ever be. I made a firm resolution not to become a citizen of any country of the world from the moment I departed from my fatherland, under circumstances well known to you. I do not believe I shall ever return to my fatherland, but I owe it a tribute of love and respect by not incorporating myself to any other. But, my Elpidio, forgive this digression!

No other country welcomes religious impostors as favorably as this one. Anyone wishing to set up a most ridiculous sect can be assured of finding enough followers. All one has to do is begin preaching and assume an air of piety that dazzle one's listeners. If one is able to spend a few hundred dollars in alms, the result is assured and the gamble is certain. This small investment assures the preacher a good life.

I could tell you of several cases, but it would be enough to tell you about an evil man who was here four or six years ago, and was considered by some to be a fool, although there I cannot agree. He had the audacity to say that he *was Christ.* Don José de la Luz, my friend from Havana, came in the company of this "Christ" in a steamer from Philadelphia to this city. He said everybody aboard was listening to him.

By this time the impostor was well known to the point that everyone had come to despise him. The newspapers had informed us a few months before that in a southern city a great number of men had come out to follow this "new Christ." Even some *ministers of the Gospel* (as they are called) followed this impostor, who presented himself with all dignity and pomp. What do you say about these *ministers of the Gospel*?

The impostor caused such an upheaval that some sensible men and women complained to the governor. In spite of the freedom of religion and conscience that exists in this country, they considered that this was an extraordinary case and that such audacity should not be allowed. The governor, who was somewhat timid, saw fit to take adequate action, and he jokingly told the impostor that since he was Christ he could not punish him according to law for there were not any laws against Christ. He expected "Mister Christ" to leave the city, because if he caused anymore disturbance he would be forced to put him in jail for disturbing the peace. The good "Christ" saw fit to follow the suggestion.

Lorenzo Don was another famous impostor who preached everywhere. Don had sincere followers, was well as other henchmen who followed him to entertain themselves. I wonder how sin could entertain them unless these persons were already guilty in their hearts. This peculiar character was well received. At least his prophecy was received without displeasure, for it was against the Catholic Church. Our Church is always attacked as a tool of the supposed Papal domination.

Lorenzo Don predicted that Napoleon's son would come this very year with a *great army* to conquer this country and place it as the Pope's satellite. Napoleon's son died before the year was out, but since Lorenzo also died, he escaped the ridicule of those he had deceived.

There is no doubt that this and other crooks of similar caliber never deceived the sensible elements of this country, but there is also no doubt that they have always found a great number ready to even follow, even as they would masters. I am sure that in other less educated countries the number would have been smaller.

I do not wish to leave out the famous *Matthias,* an impostor who is still alive and has made more noise than any other. Although nobody speaks of him anymore, his cock-and-bull stories are well known; so much so that the presentation and refutation of one of them appeared in a somewhat large volume which quickly sold a great number of copies. This fact shows the extent of his influence, for the people of this country do not spend money for books unless they have real interest in reading them.

This new impostor did not say that he was Christ but showed himself as a similar personage, promising to perform miracles. The newspapers went so far as to tell us that as he was preaching near the city of Troy (because you may know that in this country there are towns with almost all the names of the cities of Greece and Rome) where he ordered a hill to fall and indeed it fell. This impostor deceived many people for a long time, a multitude that is much greater than you can imagine.

Among some of the cases there is the sad one of a poor woman who was one of his followers; one of her sons died but she would not cry; rather she continued to prepare the tea she would share with Matthias when he came. She was certain that once he saw the dead child he would bring him back to life. The prophet came, but the child remained dead and the mother was assailed by horrible despair.

Good Calvin has a similar story, although that case was a bit more serious. It did not concern a child who died as a result of an illness, but a miser who died as punishment from heaven. It is said that Calvin plotted with the miser and his wife in such a way that the husband would pretend to be dead and the wife would play the role of the disconsolate widow until Calvin came to resurrect the presumed corpse. When Calvin arrived however, he found that the man was truly dead and the woman shed real tears throwing all kinds of insults at Calvin.

I cannot prove the truth of this story, neither would I refute it. I have read it in the work of an author who is almost our contemporary. I have not wished to investigate it for I do not care too much to know Calvin's sins and the absurdity of his doctrine.

ON THE QUAKERS

The Quakers are famous in matters of both inspiration and false imputations. Women preach the same as men. At their meetings they remain in silence almost as if asleep, and truly sometimes they are asleep, until the Spirit moves one of them to jump up on the bench and begin preaching.

Several curious Spaniards went to one of these meetings, staying at the door so that it would be evident that they had no other intention than to look in as observers. Once, they were seen by one of those women impostors. Feeling inspired she quickly jumped onto a bench and began to preach against the Spanish Inquisition; she no doubt had recognized them as Spaniards and saw a good opportunity to convert them.

They left outraged but at the same time laughing at the fraud of that truly inspired character, that is to say, inspired by the devil. My friend and companion, Gener, told me with his usual natural jocularity, "this time at least, Varela, the Holy Spirit made a mistake, for there is no inquisition in Spain, nor is it likely that there shall be ever again, and the Spaniards who were at that door, far from being in favor of the inquisition, detested it much more than the preacher lady, so that the inspiration was thus totally useless." My learned and wise friend made many other observations, and we both agreed that fanaticism and superstition did not leave this country with the rise of new institutions, but that they took other forms.

Let us return to the Quakers. They do not swear at all, and thus they disobey the courts and do not give sworn testimony under the pretext that the Gospel, absolutely and without any exception, forbids the taking of any oath. Their rude practice of not doffing their hat for anybody or in any place is the result more of fanaticism and lack of judgment than superstition, even though it has many elements of it, for everything of the kind comes from a false belief.

I remember one time when a Quaker who was decently dressed (in the fashion of a uniform, that is, with dark cloth coat, cut with rounded edges, without lapels, and with a raised collar and wearing a widerimmed white hat) came into my Church. He came in a few minutes before the beginning of

Mass on a feast day. The church was full and all the eyes of the congregation turned to that man who walked around the church with his hat firmly in place. The people immediately tried to show him where he could sit, so that he would be less noticeable (even though he would always be noticed because he did not take off his hat). He declined the invitation, for no doubt he came only to walk around the church and attract attention.

I was able to see him from the sacristy and I was immediately going to send someone to tell him that according to our manners men kept their heads uncovered while women kept theirs covered. Once this was established I would be within my rights, by the laws of this country, to call a policeman to remove him from the church. I did not have to do it, however, because he left once he had achieved his purpose.

Once I saw myself free from that Quaker, I meditated that this man's bearing and ease of movement did show some good social upbringing; nevertheless he came uninvited to a gathering in which he had no business. He did not even want to stop but came only to insult those in attendance, or else his rare fanaticism had blinded him to such an extent that he was not aware of his provocation.

One has only to see that he did not respond to the expressions of welcome, for he showed contempt and shocking rudeness. Such is the power of superstition! That wretch walks through the streets of one of the most learned cities glorying in himself for having given public witness that his doctrine is rooted in the Gospel. Yet all he has shown is that he does not understand the Gospel that he sacrilegiously ridicules. He should really blush with shame at his rudeness and lack of prudence, which are always a sign of ignorance.

Those Quakers have studied well the system according to their own convenience. In spite of some of their genuine good qualities, I have always held that it is the most ridiculous and selfish sect. They do not wish to serve in the military, or to take arms to defend the fatherland, nor do they want to contribute to the payment of those who defend it. It seems that we should expect a miracle from heaven each time we are attacked, and that God will send his angels to defend us while we make no effort on our part; or that we should, in conscience, allow the first tyrant who so wishes to take over our fatherland.

What do you think about this morality and about these *virtuous Quakers*? They are opposed to all kinds of entertainment, and here is another virtue that is as serious as it is ridiculous! Their clothing is very simple, but sometimes it is made of good material that is no less expensive than that of other citizens who are less stoic! The ladies usually wear some coatlike blanket of ample dimensions that are no less expensive than the dresses of the ladies of other sects.

What is more interesting, my Elpidio, is that they have an agreement by which the sect money remains within the sect. If there is only one Quaker shoemaker in a city, he is assured that he will make all the shoes of all the Quakers in that city. They would go to another shoemaker only when the Quaker said *he could not, or would not do it.* The same thing happens with all the professions: the Quaker doctor never lacks patients, etc., etc. Besides these economic considerations, this system gives rise to a hypocrisy and religious speculation, which is the greatest of all evils and the most horrible of all sins. How many would stop being Quakers if they stopped turning a profit, and how many are Quakers because they do make a profit!

I had the occasion to observe the spirit of a sect in a particular case. There is in this city a Baptist doctor who is very zealous about the propagation of his sect, and a good friend of his told me that he had been converted by a Quaker lady. Why, I asked him, did she not convert him to her own sect? And the answer was that among the Baptists there is a smaller number of doctors of his specialty and that sect is very generous. What do you think of this! The good lady, no doubt, believes in her sect and the *pious doctor* has a great belief in the one he has adopted.

ON THE SHAKERS

I cannot leave the topic of the Quakers without telling you about the Shakers, and to do this let me tell you about an interview that I had six or eight years ago with the principal minister of that sect in Lebanon. After I had preached in my church on Pentecost Sunday, an old man, whose dress indicated that he was a Quaker, came to see me in the sacristy. He wanted to talk about the Catholic doctrine, not in order to take it up but to learn about it. We set up an appointment for four o'clock that very afternoon, and he effectively came to my house at that time.

He listened as I expounded the doctrines of the Church for a long time without giving any sign of approval or disgust. Finally he broke the silence: "How do you understand the text of St Paul in which he forbids matrimony?" (Second Letter of Paul to Timothy, 4:3). I brought the Bible and opened it to the place cited, in which the apostle, far from stating what the man was attributing to him, lists its prohibition among the errors and other works of the devil.

I started to read the chapter aloud until I came to the verse he had mentioned, and then turning to him I only said, "thus you can see that the apostle, far from condemning matrimony, lists among the works of the devil the belief of those who separate themselves from the faith by condemning marriage." The matter was so clear that even though my good man saw himself identified with those whom the apostle condemned as heretics and authors of diabolical doctrine, he did not try to defend himself and was content with the ridiculous excuse: "but you cannot deny that virginity is preferable to matrimony." "That is what the apostle teaches," I responded. "However, to prefer one thing is not equivalent to condemning the opposite, and thus the Catholic Church, while praising virginity, respects and counts matrimony among its sacraments."

My Quaker did not respond at all and, turning away from the question he had unwittingly asked, he now inquired if I had any knowledge of his society. I told him yes, but he recognized I did not perceive from his clothing about his special branch of *Quakerism* and even less his distinguished office. He then said, "I am not just a Quaker, but a *Shaking Quaker*. I am also a minister and superior officer."

I confess I would never have thought he was a Shaker, and even less that such an ignorant person was a minister. A minister who had the stupidity of memorizing chapter and verse of an Epistle of Saint Paul which stated the contrary of what he was asserting, only because he had read something about the effect of prohibiting marriage! Like a person wishing to prove that Pontius Pilate is seated at the right hand of God the Father and will come to judge the living and the dead, by reading the words Pontius Pilate in the creed.

Elpidio, I found it quite hard to restrain my laughter imagining that old man in short pants and a wig, if I am not mistaken, giving *small hops,* without a coat, and with his arms raised up bent at the elbow, hands hanging limp as if they were not joined to the body, in such a fashion that, as they hopped, the hands flopped wildly like the wings of a bird. He was, however, visiting me and his grey hair at least commanded my respect. Before departing, he asked for a piece of paper and wrote his name and business, politely suggesting I visit his residence in Lebanon.

The Shakers are made up of numerous persons. One finds those of good faith as well as others joining for commercial schemes. They have left the world and have gone to the country to find a new way of living, where men live apart from women, renouncing the right to marry but without taking the vow of chastity, for they do not wish to be taken for Catholics.

In this fashion, they have no other alternative than to engage in perpetual continence, or in a sinful life. They have scheduled manual labor to provide for their sustenance, as well as time for their prayers. However, if one were to make reference to our monks, it would be the same as if speaking about the devil. They have very strict confessions, yet they become indignant when one mentions the Sacrament of Penance. They entrust themselves to their mother *Anna Lee,* but they do not want to admit the intercession of the Saints.

Who gives them guidance? The ignorant man I just met. I said then to myself, does this not confirm Augustine's wise observation on a *religious cadaver* with the appearance of piety, but without the spirit to give it merit and direct it? Under the guidance of God's Church our monks are not permitted to engage in doctrines or practices of their own; consequently even the most ignorant are wise regarding the science of salvation. Here a most ignorant man gives direction by human whim.

Many nevertheless applaud the society of Lebanon, while the rest look upon it as the gathering of innocent but fanatic people. But let them deal with the Catholic Church, and similar innocent practices are seen as sinful. How true is the saying that while truth is attacked errors always sponsor themselves!

Let me not leave my Quakers just yet, for they truly lend abundant matter for my observations on the impact of superstition when authority is lacking, for it is the only principle that can restrain it.

They have just divided themselves into two great parties that have excommunicated each other. They do not recognize ecclesiastical authority, and they issue excommunications! If by excommunication they mean the separation of the two parties, they are already separated without the need of a formal declaration; if they mean that those split by them are excluded from eternal life, then they admit God's authority exercised through people, that is, ecclesiastical authority, for which they ridicule Catholics a lot.

The same thing happens quite often in this country with other sects. I could prove their ridiculous superstition by running through the *modern history* of each of these rightly called *denominations,* or mere names of Christianity. I only wish to indicate the impact of superstition on free countries. I have given concrete cases to amuse you as well as to avoid giving you the impression that I suffer from hallucination in attacking a nonexistent enemy.

I will now make a few observations about the superstitions in three of the most predominant sects, the Baptists (which should be called Anabaptists), the Methodists and the Presbyterians. The Episcopalians or branches of the Church of England are almost Catholic. No matter how much they want to disguise it, they are returning gradually to the Church which they regret having left.

ON THE BAPTISTS

The Baptists have a very rare type of superstition, apparently consisting of defending the rights of reason and individual freedom. They do not administer baptism except to adults or when they have already received the *spirit,* that is, when they are truly converted. This position is very rational; it would be a sacrilege to baptize someone who is not repentant for his sins. But superstition creeps in in the way they know about such a disposition. Like other sects, they want to *feel that God has forgiven them.* Using various Scriptural texts to prove this doctrine, they interpret them in their own way.

Leaving aside any theological questions, let us consider only political influence. Since there are a great many who are not baptized but belong to this sect only because they want to be *called* Baptists, there *remain* then a number of those not yet converted, which is to say immoral ones. No one can persuade me that there is morality without conversion to God and repentance of sins. The thief who has not repented for stealing will steal at every opportunity.

What results then is a great scandal. Wishing to avoid this serious evil, many take refuge in hypocrisy, the safeguard of rascals, coming to be baptized for they feel the *spirit,* etc., etc. There is no force that compels, there is no authority that will order; everything appears free, but it is not, because superstition, destroying the principle of freedom, compels people to commit these sins. Other scrupulous individuals never receive baptism because they do not *feel* the *spirit.* The deadly consequence is that many times they despair or become indifferent. You may reach your own conclusions about its pernicious effect on society!

I wish, Elpidio, to amuse you with a story about the Baptists, even though it will be a true digression. They baptize in the rivers (even though they already have baptistries large enough for immersion). The minister enters into the water waist deep with the one to be baptized and, placing one hand on the candidate's chest and the other on his back, the minister immerses the person three times, letting the one being baptized fall backwards on the minister's arm.

It happened that in the middle of winter a minister wanted to baptize a small number of new members of his church. It was necessary to break the ice, because the banks of the river were frozen. There was a hole big enough to accommodate the minister and the one to be baptized. During one of the immersions, the minister was unable to hold onto the one being baptized, who apparently fell back with his full weight, and escaping the arm of the minister fell flat under the ice. Without losing his composure, the minister turned to those who were gathered by the river, saying: *God has taken this one to himself, his name be blessed, let another come in.*

Have you ever seen such fanaticism and superstition? Instead of being embarrassed for the deadly result of his superstition and imprudence, which made him think it essential to go into a river for baptism, thus bringing illness to some, and even death to others my good man believed that his only motive was to praise God!

This sect has always been very superstitious, following in the footsteps of their founder Münzer, who played a ridiculous farce in the city of the same name. This story became one of the most notorious in the history of the new sect. Münzer spent three days without speaking, pretending that a supernatural force deprived him of his speech. He then secluded himself for a long time until he burst naked into the street, screaming everywhere and asking for the obedience of all, for God had made him spiritual king. Perhaps he was not too far from desiring a temporal kingdom.

Very soon Münzer had a large number of followers, who forced baptism on everyone *on pain of death,* arguing that infant baptism was not true baptism. They caused great harm, and one can only suppose that many gave in to their threats, committing the horrible sacrilege of allowing themselves to be rebaptized. What can such a fanatic and his followers expect of a forced baptism received under the threat of death? At the same time that the Baptists repudiate the Catholic sacramental confession they practice it very strictly before baptism themselves. I recently had the opportunity to verify this for I have just received into the Church a young man who belonged to that sect. According to him, he found a booklet of written confessions in his home. When he made fun of the person's confession, his mother corrected him immediately with the greatest severity. Now he prudently keeps the secret even though he would not be bound by the seal of the sacrament.

ON THE METHODISTS

Using religion as a mask, the Methodists also show us a poor picture of the human condition. Their preachers take advantage of their drowsy listeners, for their screams are outrageous. If this were an isolated minister, we could attribute it to an effort to exercise the lungs; this happens, however, with all the ministers, Elpidio; so much so that it seems that the ability to scream is a condition for the ministry. The unfortunate ones who do not have a strong voice still try to master their capacity to scream.

Anyone who passes by a church and hears from the street someone screaming outrageously knows that he is in front of a Methodist church. They frighten people with those screams and then think that they have promoted a conversion, for very frequently people get up from their pews and go before the railing that surrounds the pulpit (for the sects do not have an altar). These people had never entered a Methodist church before yet wish to be received in it before knowing anything about its doctrine! Most of them claim they have seen the revealed *glory* as a real material light which they can see shining over something.

One of my lady friends who belonged to the Anglican, or Episcopalian, Church, transferred to the Methodist. I asked her why had she changed. She answered that she had felt deeply moved seeing the *glory* or that material light. I restrained my laughter, and behaving with all prudence I asked her if she knew the doctrine of her new church. She said no. I asked her if she was compelled in conscience to live and die in the Methodist Church. She said no.

With these facts I made her realize that she was not really a Methodist, having a religion based on *feelings* rather than on ideas or dogmas. She asked me, "How do you then explain these feelings?" "Very easily," I answered, "one can understand a virtuous person being moved by eternal truths such as the mercy and love of Jesus Christ suffering for us and our need for conversion. If on top of this we add the feminine frailty and sensitivity, then what you experienced is not a mystery. The heart united itself to Christ and the imagination drew his glory.

The purity of your intentions and the repentance for your faults could have made possible that salutary effect thanks to your lack of knowledge of the Methodist errors; however, there is no excuse for now that you have had the time to reflect."

This case made me aware of the power of superstition. One should fear its effects, even in the most educated society. They are all visions, ridiculous maxims, which form a popular disposition that is very unfavorable to the advancement of true learning. You may then ask, how can one find it in such high degree in Methodism when all the others sects are no less superstitious? There are many other causes that produce it in spite of those inconveniences; however, one could obtain better results if all were removed.

Do not ever think, Elpidio, that I present this country in an unfavorable light, quite on the contrary. My observations are as much proof of the uprightness of its laws and the exemplary manners of the people. These virtues are sufficiently able to counteract and almost nullify such a powerful process which in another country would probably produce complete disorder.

I would like to make a few observations about the Methodist *camp meetings*. It is not my goal and neither do I pretend to enter into a lengthy examination of these meetings. One would need to write volumes to deal properly with the theological principles of these practices.

The Methodists go out to the country every year or during certain periods according to the whim of their ministers. They live in provisional tents for a certain number of days according to the *spiritual needs* of the congregation. Among these one finds many curious onlookers who go for fun and many evil people who go there with other goals in mind. The sincere Methodists allow the attendance of those gawkers only for the sake of converting them.

They scream constantly: the ministers, in order that their listeners may receive the *spirit,* and the listeners when they believe themselves to have received it. The wretches jump and engage in a thousand contortions until they faint from exhaustion and affliction. They are then taken to other tents, where they can rest and recover their senses. Half of these *faints* are feigned, and then there are carriers of the ladies who have *fainted,* and other very "charitable persons" who assist them . . . some, especially women, *faint* from terror and surprise.

There was a young lady who belongs to the Anglican Church and detesting the Methodist doctrine makes fun of its practices. She went with her sister and a gentleman to amuse herself at one of those camp meetings, which perhaps should be called Methodist fairs. When she realized that her sister was lost, she looked for her and found to her great surprise that she had fainted among a group of Methodists who with their ministers were screaming loudly, praising God for the conversion of the young lady.

She tried to tell them that her sister was not a Methodist nor did she want to be one without having had the chance to listen to anything they would convert her as they were claiming. But the minister insisted that it was the work of the Lord and they were determined to take her to one of the tents of recovery. The gentleman, however, told them boldly that he should take her to her parents. He was determined to do so by force if they would not listen to his reasons. They promptly left the poor young lady alone and she was immediately taken to the carriage.

She did not come to herself until after half an hour on the road. When her sister and the gentleman asked her why she had fainted, she thanked them for having taken her away from the hands of the Methodist ministers, explaining that all had been due to a sudden terror when she found herself by chance (or because she was pushed) in the midst of one of the circles of screamers, who confused her. They had insisted that she play the *role of a Methodist,* and since she could not see her sister nor the gentleman, she believed herself defenseless and, filled with fear, she fainted. What good conversions, Elpidio!

I wish to tell you, however, about another case that is even more amusing. This was a joker's trick played on the Methodists to demonstrate how easy it was to deceive them. A student of theology from the College of . . . , which is one of the best Catholic centers of learning of this country, went with one of his classmates to amuse himself at one of these *camp meetings.* After they had observed all the contortions of those *converted,* the spirituals, he turned to his companion and told him: "I am going to be a Methodist for fifteen minutes." His friend said, "Don't you know that it is not licit, even in jest, to feign that one gives up the true religion to admit a false one?" "I am only going to mock these fools," responded the malicious student. "Let me know when the fifteen minutes are up." And he jumped into the middle of one of the circles of screamers, screaming more than any of them and making a lot of contortions. The ministers came immediately to encourage the young man who had received the spirit (truly, he was a mischievous and cunning spirit), giving thanks for such a sudden conversion.

In the meantime, the converted one kept eyeing his companion, and when this one brought out a watch to let him know that the fifteen minutes were up, he immediately returned to his natural composure and started to leave the circle. The ministers were dumbfounded and asked him the cause of such a sudden halt of the spirit, to which the joker student answered: "I have offered to be a Methodist for fifteen minutes and since that time has elapsed I now leave, free from my commitment."

The joker student's actions are reprehensible; I must confess, however, that it was a terrible warning to those beguiled ministers. They were able to see clearly that at times feelings are the result of circumstances and that others are mere fiction. It is easy to get confused in the absence of norms that distinguish the works of God from those of the devil. Regretfully, however, common opinion holds that it is very easy to make that distinction. All the sects thus talk about the *spirit* whose presence or absence they are able to determine and decide according to their whims.

Note the difference, Elpidio. A hypocrite can be as pretentious in the true religion as much as in a false one, but in the latter norms are not followed. When we are only guided by diverse and opposite feelings, our judgment is not certain but rather it is risky. When feelings are the only guiding norm, one does not need faith. But this reasoning is a complete contradiction. It would amount to receiving an unbeliever into a body of believers. He was right in saying he had made a promise to be a fifteen-minute Methodist, but he was quite wrong in even considering this game.

The Methodists go out to their *camp meetings* and run around aimlessly pointing to different places and saying: "look at him, look at him there." "Yes, there is Christ." The wretches fail to remember that in the same gospel they pride themselves on reading with so much frequency, Christ openly prohibited searching for him in the desert or in hidden mansions. However, let us not enter into theological blame but restrict our reflection to how such *camp meetings* influence society.

When people are either not aware of superstition or they glory in it, the popular masses become rapidly contaminated. It is almost impossible to prevent it on account of vanity in some and stupidity in others. A multitude of both sexes attend a *camp meeting,* openly sharing their ridiculous religious ideas and extravagant feelings. Another multitude of onlookers increase the evil by encouraging their zeal and pretending to be disciples of Jesus. Without realizing it, both groups cause great harm to society.

Superstition is then rooted in such a way that it is much more difficult to uproot. There is no norm other than the *spirit,* which is reduced to a mere name, impiously used for all kinds of human emotions. The inescapable effect is the perversion of all religious principles and a superficial and ridiculous popular character. However, these effects are not as noticeable because of the constraints of admirable institutions and laws.

The fanaticism and superstition of Methodists have reached such proportions that no care is taken over their ministers' education, and thus almost all of them are most ignorant, although one may find among them a few men of reputable learning. One cannot help but laugh at the foolishness they preach. The people are so much convinced of this that the true or fictitious stories about ridiculous preachers are, among Methodist, almost always taken for granted. These sectarians believe that it is the *spirit* that directs them and that a good person, zealous for the glory of God, is a good *minister,* regardless of the degree of instruction. It is strange, Elpidio, that those who deny the presence of spirit in the

Church would grant it so easily to any person. Even though they do not believe in their ministers' infallibility, they behave as if they did, without taking care to assess their knowledge or prove their ignorance, always counting on divine assistance.

My observations will help you realize that when the religious dimension, which is the most influential in the education of the people, is entrusted to ignorant ministers, one can expect little of religion's beneficial influence among the people. They should rather fear the progress of superstition and all its evils. These sectarians have an incorrect idea about ministry, even though they talk so much about preaching, which is their favorite theme. Ignorant preachers are equivalent to false teachers, or at least, uncertain ones, and since they do not take care of the ignorance of their ministers, it becomes clear that nor do they take care of the rightfulness or certainty of their doctrine. If one tells a minister: "Preach and I will laugh or applaud you at my whim," is the same thing as saying to him: "Call yourself a minister even though in reality you are a ridiculous impostor." This sect, however, enjoys a most prominent place, as if it were the center of renewal and piety. Can there be a greater superstition?

ON THE PRESBYTERIANS

It is time, Elpidio, to make a few observations about the Presbyterians, somewhat less ridiculous but no less superstitious. They are not as noisy, as the Methodists, but certainly they exceed them in terms of *silent peculiarities.* Superstition has found two wide doors through which to come into this sect, the idea of liberty and simplicity. They are analogous and they both have a great influence in the human heart, but they have both been abused by the Presbyterians, who have used the gifts of religion to support error and the most ridiculous hypocrisy. They want a Church not only without head or principal leader, but without any director or intermediate heads, as if they were an army without generals or any other officers. In this Church all are seen as soldiers of the same rank with the freedom to do as they please. Can there be any greater ignorance and superstition or any greater abuse of the expression "religious freedom"?

Attempting to show piety (which they know full well is not reconcilable with the principle of pride on which this sect is founded), they take things to an extreme, that is, they are rigorous in all *matters that do no require them to conquer their pride* by means of obedience, a word unknown to them. They are well aware that without showing great piety they cannot beguile anyone with such an unchristian system that is opposed to the history of the primitive Church, and, what is more, to the same Scriptures they boast as their norm.

The Presbyterians do not have Church precepts compelling them through conscience; there are no mortifications, fast or abstinence. They marry or divorce when they please, without impediment of any sort. Besides all these liberties, they add the incentive that other sects do not have: they are more respected and they have more influence than Methodists and Baptists, who in reality are Presbyterians insofar as they do not recognize bishops. Truly, there is a small and insignificant number of Episcopal Methodists.

ON THE NEW ENGLAND PURITANS

The Puritans in England went to ridiculous extremes such as banning all ceremonies, music, and ornaments and replacing them with a *pious pride* in appearing simple. The same thing can be observed in that kingdom as well as in these republican states. One can see, Elpidio, that the churches, benches and everything that belongs to the congregation are luxurious, but God's sanctuary is very simple, even offensively so. They are partly correct in confessing publically that their churches are only a stopping point for human gatherings. Let us now observe their superstition by beginning with some paragraphs of *Anquetil's Universal History Abridged* on the New England Puritans, which today is the bulwark of Presbyterians, as well as of the deists.

"It does not surprise me that the fanatics would at the same time be believers; what surprises me is that the very

fanatics have believed in witches. But among the persecutors
we see a governor, some Puritan ministers and some magistrates, in whose presence the most cruel torments were performed in order that luckless women would confess that they
had bewitched others. In order to get rid of *the spirits* they sent
many to the gallows. There was a judge who got so tired of
presiding over these bloody execution, he did not want to continue in his job. The judge was accused of being an accomplice
and had to flee in order to save himself. They then accused one
of his brothers of having flown on his dog in order to attend
witchcraft rituals: he was in fact already condemned. It was
very hard for him to avoid death, but they killed his dog. The
news of such barbarous insanity could be left unmentioned, but
it is important for people to find in history examples that inspire horror about persecution. Let it be known then that almost 200 people were accused, 150 were imprisoned, 20 were
sent to execution."[1]

The superstitions of the New England Puritans are evi-
dently manifested in the *blue laws,* which are so called because
they were printed on blue paper. Maybe I shall have the opportunity to discuss them in more detail in the course of our correspondence, but for the time being I will limit myself to present
a few that show how ridiculous human misery is when it wishes
to cover itself with the veil of piety. In a strict sense, such laws
should be called articles of a single law; however, following
common usage, I will consider them distinct laws, and I shall
jot them down with the same number that they have in the
printed volumes in which they appear.

18. "No one is permitted to run on Sunday, to take a
stroll in their garden or any other place, and one
is only permitted to walk reverently to and from
Church."
19. "No one is permitted to travel, cook, make beds,
sweep the house, cut hair, or shave on Sunday."

---

1. Anquetil's Abridged, 17:295.

20. "No mother shall kiss her child on Sunday or on a fast day."

31. "Anyone who would adorn their clothing with gold or silver or liner-lace worth more than two shillings a yard shall be brought before a grand jury, which will make them pay a fine of three hundred pounds." (750 *pesos*).

35. "No one shall read the Book of Common Prayer nor shall keep Christmas as a holiday nor any other one; no one shall make meat pies, dance, play cards or play any musical instrument, with exception of the trumpet, the drum and the *Jew's harp.* (This is a small instrument commonly played by children and called a *mouth harp,* and it consists of an iron arch that ends in two parallel bars between which you find a steel protrusion that is soldered to the middle of the arch and is free to vibrate at the touch of a finger, producing a sound in the mouth that is controlled by breath.)

36. "No minister of the gospel may perform marriages. The only ones suited are magistrates, who can do so with the *least possible scandal for the church of Christ."*

46. "All men shall cut their hair in conformity with the shape of their hat." (That is with bangs all around the head.)

I want to quote you another of these laws, even though it cannot properly be said that it indicates superstition or fanaticism, because it does demonstrate that, as far as demanding it as a duty that the faithful support their ministers, the Presbyterians are no less rigorous than other sects, while all of them are much more demanding than the true church. The law, then, states: "Anyone who refuses to pay his quota to support the parish minister shall be fined 62 pounds (156 *pesos*), paying 4 pounds each trimester until the sum is paid."

Have you seen greater superstition than among the Puritans? Few observations would be necessary to convince you that this infernal monster introduces itself in every sort of gov-

ernment and in all peoples. Superstition is always as unjust as it
is cruel and ridiculous. No one can perform a marriage but
magistrates who do it without *scandal to the Church of Christ.*
Is there any greater insult to Christ, who sanctioned marriage,
elevating it to the dignity of a sacrament? But let us suppose
that, according to the Protestant doctrine, marriage is not held
as a sacrament, could these Puritans deny that Christ approved
of them by attending marriages? If they were afraid of scandal
on the part of the contracting parties, it would be even worse,
for the same law presupposes that the *Puritan saints* could not
be married without profaning the nuptials. Today all their ministers perform marriages because they have recognized their
insanity; however, the *spirit is the same,* and as far as my goal is
concerned, it is enough to present this undeniable and interesting fact from their history in order to demonstrate the influence
of superstition on even the freest of people.

What would constitute a more direct attack on the freedom of people than to forbid them to bake pies and eat them in
their homes; or to forbid a mother to kiss her child on Sunday,
as if an expression of natural affection could offend God, when
in reality it should be considered as a gesture of thanksgiving
for the grace of having received a child from the hands of divine
providence and a sign of respect by loving a creature of God
whom he himself orders to love?

After so many observations and many others which I will
not present here, for I may be accused of quite different motives than are my true intentions, how could you wish, Elpidio,
that I would not bemoan the blindness of those who make the
true religion responsible for the superstitions that afflict society
and who have also the naivety to believe that heretics are free
of these evils? How much harm has this inconsiderate belief
done to religion!

If irreligiosity ought to be avoided, some say, and it is
necessary to have some religion, at least let us select the one
that would be free of superstition, which degrades the human
species; let us select the one that is in accord with wisdom and
freedom. However, in fifteen years of ministry in this country,
I came to know of only one young person who became a Presbyterian in order to get married. The Spaniards, Elpidio, are

either Catholics or nothing. I am proud of the fact that Spaniards as well as their descendants show ample evidence of this.

Returning to the mistaken language of the enemies of religion, who attempt to substitute it with some false beliefs under the pretext of avoiding superstition, it is enough to say that it is illusory to pretend to avoid an evil by approving it, that is, to avoid superstition by establishing it. A false belief is really a true superstition. As such, it produces and fosters as many *religious foolishnesses* as can be invented by the human mind and motivated by a false zeal, which is the fruit of true pride, which has always been the origin of all heresies. The modern light with which they wish to enlighten scenes that will be always gloomy, and which, if they were shown in their proper perspective, would be seen as horrible monsters; the true modern light, my dear Elpidio, far from guiding people to so much crazy nonsense, points out the cliff in order that it may be avoided. They all speak about modern lights, but half of them are blind people who do not see them and wish them to be as they imagined them. Antiquity is always burdened with slanders and the present age approves of them, so that the former cannot defend itself against injustice and the latter cannot avoid its being committed in its name.

It is about time to end this letter, which I may find to my sorrow displeases you. This would cause me great pain, and I hope you will not doubt my sincerity and honesty; but I also assure you frankly that even if you disapprove of everything I have written I consider myself repaid with the pleasure of telling the truth without any human misgivings. But I realize that I do a great injustice to your wisdom and sound judgment by suspecting a displeasure that I should not fear.

Even common people with a philosophical streak can be beguiled by the appearances of piety and religious novelty; they can follow the *fad* or admiring or pretending to admire everything that the Church condemns. Those who, like you, have meditated about the deviations of the mind and the deadly effects that these religious *insanities* produce on society cannot take offense if a friend has made a few observations about them and has dared to present them freely.

I have shown by reasoning, and verified with facts, that

superstition influences in different ways according to the nature of the popular institutions and the prevailing religious ideas. Where true religion flourishes, superstition takes the principle of authority in order to abuse it, and in countries where *religious disorder* or, what is the same, a multitude of religions, rages rampant, it uses reason in order to abuse it. Forgive this most burdensome letter, but take note that it is such because it is filled with truths that oppress and attack human pride and weakness.

ADDITION TO LETTER IV

After the publication of Letter IV, there came into my possession a business card that proves with certainty how easily superstition enters such an educated country as this; I have considered it necessary to publish such an important document, which is given out in the streets by boys who are paid to find clients for an *Astronomy/Astrologer*!!! The shameful card states: *J. Nelson who resides in Webster Street No. 202, offers his services to make calculations on births, to answer questions on how to win disputes, on love, on marriage, speculations, trades, travel, etc., etc.* I am sure that Mr. J. Nelson will make a better living from his profession of Astronomer/Astrologer than a real astronomer, and this in the great city of New York.

RELIGIOUS TOLERANCE

Finally, dear Elpidio, the sequence of our correspondence requires that I write to you about religious tolerance, which has been the object of so many discussions and has caused so much displeasure. But the matter is simple and the confusion is the fruit of either ignorance or malice, and I shall try to present the basis of my opinion as clearly as possible.

I believe that we must distinguish three kinds of tolerance: *theological, social,* and *legal* or civil. *Theological tolerance* refers to dogmas, and thus it is equivalent to admitting all of them or, at the very least, being indifferent towards them. *Religious/ social* tolerance consists in not bothering anyone on account of their religion; and *legal tolerance* subjects its transgressors to punishment. Of these three kinds of tolerance, only *legal tolerance* can exist in all perfection; *social tolerance* is very difficult, and *theological tolerance* is impossible.[59] Before demonstrating it, let us define the question so as not to waste our time, as almost all of those who have worked on this matter have done.

We are not dealing with the question of the existence of religion; that is already a given. We are not dealing with feigned belief, but with sincere belief in what one professes; that is, with *theological tolerance* as it appears to the human mind, or as we perceive it. If we consider it in itself, the question is reduced to whether some theological principles can admit the existence of their opposite.

As regards *social tolerance,* it is not a matter of questioning whether a large portion of society can observe it, but whether such perfection can be attained and whether its transgressors can be so few that they would not be noticeable or produce displeasure in the community.

Let us then approach the subject by starting with dogmatic or theological tolerance, considering it first of all as it exists *in the mind*. If someone tells me that not believing in any religion, he is indifferent to whether others believe in it, and that laughing at all believers, he does not find any difficulty in tolerating them, and even goes as far as to associate himself to one religion in order to live peacefully and advantageously, I can indeed understand it. There would be no reason to argue: but if he tells me that he is a true believer of one of the religions, and that he nonetheless approves or accepts other religions as true, religions that would be contrary or opposite to the one he professes, that I cannot understand at all. I shall speak more clearly: I do not believe anyone who uses such language, unless through various means I establish that he is a *complete fool* or a beguiled person who is so absolutely hopeless in his religious madness that he does not realize the meaning of his words when he takes up the theme of tolerance, for what really matters to him is that he not be taken as an intolerant person. This truth seems so clear that it is not necessary to demonstrate it. and, on the other hand, one cannot expect to convince those who cannot perceive it because they are stupid or those who do not wish to percieve it because they are beguiled.

Considering theological *tolerance in itself,* its impossibility is even more certain. I demonstrated it in my first letter when I made a few observations about the nature of religion. Who could concede that a dogma contains within itself the approval of its opposite, which is to say the proclamation of its falsehood? It would be necessary that the dogma not be a dogma and that we only repeat words without understanding them. The enemies of religion know this truth full well, even though they pretend to hold the opposite. If not, where does the spirit of proselytism that exists in all the sects come from? If a true theological tolerance existed, there would not be so much effort invested in bothering others with argumentations and many times with satire and invectives only for the sake of making them change their minds about their way of thinking in religious matters. I know full well that vanity and at times the interests of politics are the cause for proselytism; but I am also fully aware that these are not the only causes and that many times they may not even be present in any way, as is the case when proselytism is the result of a charitable though erroneous concern for the salvation of souls.

No matter how one may regard proselytism, it is an infraction of theological tolerance, or better yet, a proof that it does not exist. It clearly presupposes the wish to remove and destroy a dogma in order to substitute it with another, leading everyone to the particular sect that is being advanced by means of an *intellectual and moral force*. It is clear, however, that all the sects have this spirit of proselytism and that each spares no effort in order to convert the entire human race to its beliefs. Where then is theological or dogmatic tolerance? Irreligiosity itself is intolerant, for it cannot stand the existence of believers.

My ministry in this country provides many occasions to verify the exactness of this judgment. I have known the irreligious for a long time, but here I have come to know the Protestants. Both accuse the Church of being intolerant, and both exceed her in intolerance. The Catholic Church, as the work of God, openly says: "I do not wish to please anyone, but to save everyone; and convinced that the way that I show them is the only one that can lead them to eternal life, I cannot condone following any other way; and anyone who follows another by that very fact has separated himself from me, and does not belong to me." Here then we have a theological intolerance firmly rooted in justice and charity, and espressed with a noble frankness proper and characteristic of the spouse of Jesus Christ.

I point out, Elpidio, that I am speaking about theological intolerance and not about legal intolerance, which does not pertain to the nature of religion but to a purely civil power that may or may not establish it. It is abolutely necessary not to confuse these two lines of thinking or orders of things, if we wish to judge accurately and avoid groundless scandals. With a heavenly voice, religion absolutely compels people to follow it in order to achieve eternal life, but it does not compel their deaths if they do not wish to be saved.

Superstition, wishing to please the people, to whom it owes its existence, speaks to them about tolerance, in this way letting them demolish themselves if they so choose, as long as it is applauded for its *charitable condescension;* rather like the person who, knowing that the road being followed by a friend would lead him to a cliff, over which the friend would unwittingly fall, would say to him nevertheless, "you are on the right track, go along your way," at the same time whispering to himself, "that poor devil is going to be destroyed."

Elpidio, you may perhaps say that all of this may be an assumption on my part, for they believe that everyone who follows a correct road arrives at the desired goal, letting divine mercy take over for the defects of human weakness. If this language were just naive and by explaining themselves further they told the truth, maybe somewhat unclearly, without embelishment or digressions, as they perceive it, then the argument would end there and all of us would agree, as I shall soon demonstrate; but their aim is to make the Catholic Church hateful and to cater to the corrupted world and thus to pretend that it is the *exclusive* doctrine of the Catholic Church that there is no salvation outside of it.

The Protestants, my Elpidio, hold as we do the necessity of belonging to the Church to attain salvation and they excuse those who through an *invincible* ignorance do not belong to their number, as we excuse those who under the same circumstances do not belong to ours. The only difference is that they believe, or appear to believe, that their Church is the true one and we say that the true one is ours; but in the end they do believe as we do that outside the true Church there is no salvation. It is a *worldly hypocrisy* to pretend that their doctrine is different from ours on this point and to seem to be scandalized when they hear what they themselves teach.

THE MEANING OF SALVATION OUTSIDE THE CHURCH

I recognize that this subject is very delicate and thus I deem it necessary to explain the Catholic doctrine regarding the need of belonging to the Church in order to be saved. It is our belief that Christ is God made man and Redeemer of the world. One should clearly admit that as our Lord he can make any conditions that he wishes on the use of his merits or the reception of the *gratuitous benefits* of redemption. As a matter of fact, we read in the Gospel that he did make such conditions; among others there is the one about receiving baptism and believing the doctrine of the apostles: "Go," he told them, "and preach the gospel to every creature: he who would believe and be baptized will be saved, but he who does not believe will be condemned."

He thus established only *one baptism.* The apostles preached one doctrine, and this and not another is the doctrine that we are told to believe under pain of condemnation. It is thus clear that the will of Jesus Christ was to gather all peoples in only *one belief,* to bring them through only *one door* into only one temple, and thus form only one *religious family,* in which eternal salvation is obtained, and outside of which one cannot expect salvation. Here then we have conclusive proof of the unity of the church and that outside of her there is no salvation.

On the other hand, it is true that since God is essentially just he never punishes the innocent, and consequently those who suffer from an *invincible* ignorance of the Catholic doctrine are not punished for that ignorance, and having received baptism (which is valid and is only one, whatever the belief of the one who administers it) they are members of the one church which is the Catholic, even though common usage speaks of belonging to one or another sect. My Elpidio, many live and die within the fold of the Roman Church who never knew about her. There is one Lord, one Faith and one Baptism, as Saint Paul teaches, and consequently there is *one Church.* Once a child is validly baptized, he receives the application of the merits of Jesus Christ, he is cleansed from original sin; and if he dies, he is saved as the Lord's child, and it is clear that this happens with all children baptized by heretics. But none can be saved outside of the true Church, which is no other than the Catholic, Apostolic and Roman Church; thus it is clear that they enter into the Catholic, Apostolic and Roman Church by means of the baptism that they received at the hands of the heretics. This is why the incomparable Augustine, with his usual wisdom, said that the Church begets some children in her womb, and others in the wombs of her *maidservants*. Therefore all baptized children remain in the Roman Church until they reach adulthood, when they may wish to leave her voluntarily, and then, and not before, they become heretics. To be a heretic, it is not enough that someone be educated in a different religion and that he voluntarily call himself a member; in addition, it is necessary that he persist in his error, aware that he is leaving the Church and that he is voluntarily doing so. I include a copy of many authorities[1] on this point, so that you may not think that it is my personal opinion. The ideas may perhaps upset those who have not meditated enough about it or repeat vague assertions, whose far-reaching effects they themselves do not perceive.

In this country, the Catholic congregation is made up of those who come to our temples and of many who go to the heretical temples without knowing where they are going or why they go. But, who are these? Who are the truly innocent, who in spite of believing heresies are not heretics? This is a point which is better left to divine justice, following the counsel of the Apostle: "Far from passing judgment on each other, therefore, you should make up your mind never to be the cause of your brother tripping or falling." That is true tolerance. We do not condemn anyone, on the contrary, we consider all as innocent until they give evidence that they are not. When we say that the heretics do not have any part with Christ we merely hold the doctrine of the gospel, but then we do not try to find out who the heretics are; as if we were to condemn thievery without finding out who are the thieves.

SALVATION OUTSIDE THE CHURCH
ACCORDING TO THE PROTESTANTS

This is not a doctrine peculiar to the Catholic Church, no matter how much her enemies try to prove the contrary. The

---

1. Authorities on these and many other matters discussed in these letters will be found in the appendix to this volume.

Protestants, my Elpidio, believe the same thing, as is evident from the previously cited authorities as well as from daily experience; for no matter how much they try to disguise it, one clearly sees that they believe what we Catholics believe, with the difference that each one wishes to be Jesus Christ's Church. Since I deal with them quite frequently and I have experienced their attacks almost at every turn, it has been necessary for me to observe them, and by now I believe that I know them in depth. I have made it a practice to respond to them with another question when they pretend that they want to know why the Catholic Church believes that there is no salvation outside her womb. I ask them, "What is the belief of Protestants who thought that they could not be saved in the Catholic Church and left her in order not to be condemned?"

PUBLIC DEBATE ON SALVATION OUTSIDE THE CHURCH

Allow me to tell you about one of my encounters with this particular family, for even though it is a personal case, I hope to be able to disguise it in this letter to a friend. About seven years ago a Protestant minister came to my residence to tell me that one of their societies, which had been established in order to attack the Roman Church in public debate, was to have a meeting in a few days. He was in disagreement with his fellow members about the theme of the debate, which was to prove that the Roman Church was the prostitute of whom St. John speaks in the Apocalypse, and thus that persecution and cruelty were inseparable from Roman Catholicism. He insinuated that he did not want to go alone but wanted someone to help him and invited me to be part of the discussion. He repeated several times that his intentions were pure, that he did not wish to deceive me and that even though he did not agree with me on points of dogma, he could also not agree with his fellows on the absurd interpretation that they wished to give to the Apocalypse. I found myself so harassed by his insistence, and it seemed so wrong to me that he should believe that I could not or would not defend the cause of the Catholic Church, that I finally consented to go with him.

The day arrived and I went at the appointed time to their Church, in which the discussion was to take place, and the presiding minister of that church introduced me, as they say here, saying: "Ladies and gentlemen, Mister Varela, of the Catholic Church." Even though I already knew the little respect they have for their temples (because it seems that they know that these are not temples), I could not but be puzzled by that introduction as if we were at a party, and by this I surmised how the rest of the meeting would go. It is not necessary to tell you all the details of the discussion, so I will only point out those that relate to the point we have been dealing with. After one of the Protestant ministers had spoken against the Catholic Church, the president gave me the floor to answer him. I tried to keep in mind the arguments, or rather, the errors of the speaker, among which, you can already guess, was the one of attributing to the Catholic Church, as *exclusively* hers, the doctrine that there is no salvation outside her fold. I began to answer the doubts in the order in which they had been presented, and as soon as I had spoken two minutes, the president, breaking all the rules of the discussion, one of which was that each speaker would have fifteen minutes without being interrupted, and breaking all the rules of good manners and diplomacy, interrupted me saying: "let us get to the point of salvation outside the Roman Church."

He used this scheme to alert those present or to signal his own people so that they would behave in the less than decent way in which they went on to behave. He wanted to let them know with this interruption that I was trying to avoid the difficulty by ignoring it. The result was a general applause by the more than six hundred people in the audience to celebrate the ingenuity and perspicacity of the president, who, according to their belief, had bewildered me by exposing my scheme. Such applause, a sign of respect for him, was a sign of scorn and insult to me, but taking the entire matter in stride, I crossed my arms and remained silent until they were tired of making fun of me, and then addressing myself to the president of the discussion, I said: "I have been answering the arguments in the order in which they were presented, and the one that you have just mentioned was one of the last. I have not spoken more than two or three minutes and I have hardly had time to remove the first doubt. I do not think, then, that I have given any reason for you to suspect that I am trying to avoid the difficulty to which you refer. If you had had the kindness to wait a few more minutes we could have avoided this interruption; since you seem to be very anxious to deal with the matter about salvation outside the Church, I shall deal with it right away, anticipating it as I invert the order which my speech should have followed." Turning then towards the audience and to the other Protestant ministers I continued, saying: "I expect that my answer will please you, for it will be your own, and your conduct will be the norm for mine. This is a point on which we do not agree. I can see your surprise, but I repeat, we do not disagree. In order to demonstrate this I wish to grant you what all accusers desire, and that is to set them as judges. You know that I am a Catholic priest and you have me here as if before a tribunal: judge me according to your religious principles. I ask you: Can I be saved? If you answer yes, you have already denied your doctrine; if you answer no, you have already professed mine. I leave the choice up to you. According to your principles, I am only an idolatrous imposter; I preach idolatry with malice and ostentation, for in spite of your charitable efforts and bright dissertations, I continue to be a minister of the prostitute of which St. John speaks, and I come to this place to defend its unworthy cause against your Christian and pious intentions; I am obstinate in continuing to pervert the people and separate them from Jesus Christ; in a word, I am a most perverse man and have no excuse whatsoever. Let us suppose that I die (as I expect to die) firmly standing on these principles, without changing my conduct and detesting what you call the Church unto the last breath of my life. I again ask you: Can I be saved? If you answer yes, I tell you again that you believe not one word of your doctrine, for if you believed it you could not say that a perverse man who is obstinate in his perversity, an enemy of Christ who dies unrepentant, would enter his kingdom; and if you answer no, then it follows that my belief separates me from the kingdom of heaven, only because I am not in your Church. Here you have my doctrine professed by you yourselves, that is, that outside the Church there is no salvation;

and the difference is only that you believe that the Protestant Church is the Church of Christ, and I firmly believe that this divine Lord has no other than the Catholic, Apostolic and Roman Church. I repeat that as far as the need to be in the fold of the Church in order to be saved, all of us agree, and the question then becomes which is the true Church and who are inside or outside of her."

"Allow me," I continued, "allow me to continue asking you: are all Catholics to be condemned? Shall all perish? Who remain in that Babylon? It seems to me that I am following your answer. Without a doubt you will tell me that the God of innocence shall never punish but those who are guilty and that the persons of righteous heart, who without malice and obstinacy find themselves by mistake in the fold of the Catholic Church, seduced by me and by other similar imposters, shall be considered a sinful people but ignorant, not heretic; thus they shall be saved, not by virtue of the Roman Church but by the application of the merits of Christ, which can be applied in spite of error, on account of their innocence. You will tell me the same thing about the children who belong to Catholic families. This, no doubt, would be your answer, unless you would like to condemn to eternal flames all Catholics without distinction, and then you would fall in the same error that you want to fight. Now then, change the name of the Catholic Church and put in its place *Protestant Church* and answer yourselves. I judge you as you would judge me: I excuse the righteous and simple souls who by mistake find themselves among you, as you would excuse the Catholics who find themselves in the Roman Church by mistake. What is your complaint then? What right do you have to complain ? Why do you criticize in the Roman Church what you applaud in yours? Why do you disguise your belief and do not speak like we do, firmly and frankly?"

The president of the discussion was Dr. Brownlee,[60] minister of the Reformed Dutch Church, which is one of several classes of Presbyterians, a clever man who knows very well the keys he should play in order to stir up his own people and escape the attacks of others. Brownlee has, above all, a great talent to generate laughter while seeming to preserve his dignity. Never has he proven his character better than on that occasion. At the moment that he became aware, from the silence of the audience, that my reasons had given them something to think about, that the laughter, gestures and insults had stopped, he took a different road, which was to applaud me, presenting me as an exception among Catholic priests.

Dr. Brownlee stood up and started his speech, that is, his string of jokes, congratulating himself for having heard such *liberal* language from the lips of a priest of the Roman Church; but then he immediately said: "But Mr. Varela expresses his feelings, however, not the doctrine of the Roman Church, and if Rome got hold of him, they would burn him alive. He speaks like this because he is in America." He said all this with so many gestures and so much chicanery that he made the whole audience burst into laughter, and I confess that even I myself could not contain it.

Another one of the ministers spoke immediately, and said quite heatedly: "I am sure that this gentleman (he was referring to me) would not last twenty-four hours in his ministry without being suspended by his Bishop."

After I saw them proffer such insult I recognized their wickedness. Their only object was to avoid the very question into which they had entered and to obtain, on the other hand, their original intention, which was to portray me as a very clever man who, not being capable of sustaining my doctrine, or that of my Church, had taken the way out of disguising it; that is, they were accusing me of the crime they they themselves were committing. I requested the floor and said: "I am very pleased that the matter of *principles* has turned into a question of fact. It is no longer denied that my doctrine is exact, but it is pretended that it is not the doctrine of the Catholic Church. A passage of modern ecclesiastical history leads me to predict a happy resolution to this discussion. When the famous Bossuet wrote his incomparable *Exposition of the Catholic Doctrine,* the Calvinist minister Claude, who read the manuscript, said that Bossuet was not writing the doctrine of the Roman Church and that he was like the dove, which, not finding a place to land during the flood, returned to the ark; in a word, that Bossuet already was coming to the Church of

Christ, that is, the Protestant Church. The book was published and there was not a single Catholic who was not able to read in it the doctrine of his Church. This is what will happen with this discussion: you will print it, Catholics will read it, and if my doctrine is not their own they will express their indignation; my Bishop will suspend me and maybe we will even have someone who will accuse me to the Holy Father himself, and His Holiness will not look upon my errors with indifference. The facts shall speak and our discussion about this point is finished. But I am certain," I said turning towards the audience, "that your ministers have only tried to find a refuge and that I shall remain in my Church with no one bothering me".

Such or similar were my expressions in that discussion, which I could not preserve word for word because the secretaries (no doubt in agreement with the Protestant ministers) hardly made any notes, and since I had spoken two or three times they made a mixture of all the brief speeches, taking one idea from one and another from elsewhere in such fashion that the notes that they presented did not make any sense. They were sent to me in such state three or four days after the discussion by one of the ministers who had spoken and who was the editor of the paper in which it was to be published. To this insult he added another by attaching to the notes a *seemingly* political message in which he requested that I make whatever correction I deemed necessary, giving me a *deadline of three hours*. It was the afternoon of Good Friday and I believe that they took this circumstance into account to see if the ministry in my Church would permit me to correct the notes or make me hurry the correction, in order either not to publish my speech on account of my delay, or to publish it with mistakes in *their own way*.

Since I know these people very well, they were not able to deceive me. I left the Church in the hands of my associate, I called a clerk, and I started to write what I had said in the discussion as best as I could remember. Within the three hours they had granted me I finished my work and sent it with an open letter so that the carrier could be a witness and would be able to testify to its content. In this letter I answered that my speech should be printed in its entirety and without alterations, the same way I was sending it, or that it should be omitted completely.

The editor answered that he would print everything. However, he did not keep his word, because he only printed the introduction up to the point in which I was interrupted, but without saying that I was interrupted, and much less what I had continued to say. Since then, they have not brought any more secretaries to the discussions. Have you seen a greater fraud? Sometime after the conclusion of the discussions, the Protestant ministers took up the subject again, and in a newspaper published by some of them, once again they began to censure the Catholic Church for the doctrine that there is no salvation outside the Church. I thought that the explanations that we had about this matter had been enough and that we would understand each other, but the experience has convinced me that the method of these people is to continue to repeat what they have said without paying any attention to explanations. I do not know how I saw myself in the need to answer and to do it in their own paper, and in this way a small written controversy was started, which served the purpose of showing even more that I had not been mistaken in telling them that, as regards the point of salvation outside the Church, they believe in the same way as Catholics do, and therefore they want to convert us so that we will abandon our errors and be saved.

Listen, Elpidio, to the words with which they finished an article in answer to one of mine: "Speaking about Catholics, as a Christian society we are sad to say that because of the *errors and heresies that they defend we completely despair of their salvation,* unless they would convert and abandon their errors. We sincerely desire and fervently pray for the conversion of the Roman Catholics; and our hearts would be filled with joy to know that the God of grace and truth has brought Mr. Varela to such enlightenment and belief in the truth, so that he would be able to accomplish the salvation of his inmortal soul."

They wish me to be converted, so that I would know the truth, so that I would stop being Catholic, and what for? So that I would be saved! After these facts, what can one say? We are not dealing here with a particular individual who would have expressed himself as a fanatic, but about a meeting of Protestant ministers who with due reflection tried to answer their adversary in an article, which no doubt they discussed and premeditated.

After its publication there was not a single minister who would oppose it, as it was their duty, if the article attributed to the Protestants a doctrine that was not truly theirs. All newspapermen kept silence in spite of the fact that religious papers are quite numerous in this country and that they watch and attack each other and never forgive each other. What this really proves is that Protestant doctrine holds that there is no salvation outside their Church, and consequently, that there is none for me, for I have no excuse to remain in the Catholic Church and much less to be a priest in her. How easy it is to unmask this family, and how simplistic are they who believe only because they are masked!

You would tell me, my Elpidio, that I have abused your patience taking so much of your time and attention with stories about my amusements with the Protestants, but friendhip is forebearing and it should be no less so than when it is asked to endure the nonsense of friends. Returning then to the principal question, we should conclude that theological tolerance only *appears* to exist, but in reality it neither does nor can exist. It is equally evident that this is a *general* doctrine, admitted not only by the true Church but by *all the sects*, even though their henchmen try to pretend the opposite. Be aware, my Elpidio, that this is also the doctrine of *all the irreligious*, even though they pretend to be horrified when they listen to it; but really, not admitting the theological existence, so to speak, of any religion, they can ill admit the true tolerance, which necessarily presupposes the existence of the things that are tolerated. No one would have disputed so much about it if there had been a true tolerance of feelings; I mean, if there had been more charity and less pride. Believe me, Elpidio, that the strongest argument against tolerance is the very fact that so much is disputed about it. This evil also suffers from a *lack of logic* at the same time that almost all arguers believe themselves to be full of such science. Let us go on to consider religious tolerance, civil or social.

SOCIAL TOLERANCE

This type of tolerance is nothing more than a political consideration and as such it is only window dressing, and it is kept for no other purpose than to avoid upsetting the peace or making society unpleasant. People ridicule one another at the same time that they bestow a thousand courtesies on one another, and at times they declare vehemently that they see fit that each shall proceed as he may wish regarding religion and that everything practiced is good as long as the intention is good. There is no such thing, Elpidio; let us speak clearly: generally this is a lie more detestable than any other, because it is the fruit of the most refined hypocrisy. Very few people indeed think this way because they have meditated on the subject or because they have a true indifference in matters of religion, which is equivalent to having no religion at all. Social religious tolerance never goes beyond being a measure of prudence, indicated by necessity and accompanied by compassion, and at times, by contempt towards those who profess another belief. Very few hold this attitude to the letter and most keep it only when they cannot transgress it. Take a look at the facts, which is what is important.

History proves to us that nations, far from looking with kindness upon the enemies of their particular brand of worship, have persecuted them with more or less rage and cruelty, but always with much determination. Paganism shed the blood of Christians; heretics, for their part, have not been less cruel, and irreligiosity has far exceeded all of them. Overlooking many other eras, it would be enough for us to remember the times of Nero and Diocletian: the horrors and cruelties that the Arians committed in the fourth century; the iconoclasts (or enemies of sacred images) in the eighth century under the protection of the emperors Leo the *Isauro* and his son Constantine *Copronimo*, and in the ninth century under the emperors Leo *Armenius*, Michael the *Beodus* and Teophilus; the excesses of the Lutherans because of the same hatred of images at the beginning of the sixteenth century, excesses that Luther himself condemned, spreading further the fanaticism of the new iconoclasts; the cruelties of the Anabaptists, not only against

Catholics but against all the sects; the ravages caused by the Calvinists, who also burned people alive, and let Servet serve as an example; the cruel persecutions indulged by the English people under the reigns of Henry VIII and the bloody Elizabeth; the atrocities of the Puritans and of the abominable Cromwell, and of the Puritans themselves in New England, which is to say, in the most educated part of this country, where the famous *Blue Laws* came to light, a copy of which I include.

In order to prove intolerance of irreligiosity it is enough to remember that in the French Revolution to be recognized as a believer was enough to lose one's life. History offers us subsequent facts which confirm this assertion, but as you well know, Elpidio, it is not prudent to touch upon them. Let it be enough to observe that when the heretics or the irreligious cry out against the Inquisition, which never left Spain, Portugal and Italy, and when they remind us of the history of France with its memorable *St. Bartholomew* or its cruel and treacherous massacre of Huguenots under the reign of Charles IX, they do so with the precise ignorance of their own history or with an unforgiveable hypocrisy. It would be enough for them to observe that wise England has been the most infamous country as far as persecutions are concerned, for all others have given in to the struggles of the century, while that nation has given in only *to a point* simply because of the fear that has been inspired by the man of the century, the truly great man who, *without the aid of secret societies,* intrigue, or any weapon other than his tongue and his pen, has made the British power tremble. You are no doubt aware that I am talking about the modern Demosthenes, the incomparable O'Connell.

ANECDOTES SHOWING THE LACK OF
SOCIAL TOLERANCE TOWARD CATHOLICS

As for this country, it is painful for me to admit that there is a legal but not social tolerance, at least as far as Catholics are concerned, for the sects keep each other in high regard. Let the facts speak for themselves, and since they are innumerable, let us consider a few of the more public ones. About four years ago a convent of Ursuline sisters was burnt down in Charles-town, a town near Boston, almost a suburb. The circumstances of this action are noteworthy. This convent, according to the nature of the institution, was a house of education, located on a beautiful hill, and it was inhabited not only by the sisters but by a great number of girls, most of them of Protestant, universalist and unitarian parents. The sisters took great pains not to cate-chize their students nor to touch on points of religion that could compromise the good harmony they had with the parents, who were quite satisfied about the conduct of the nuns, and as proof of this kept their daughters in this establishment. However, the hatred towards Catholics in New England was such that at midnight a great multitude of people came over and set the convent on fire, causing sickness and even death among the sisters and the innocent girls, who were peacefully sleeping. Two days before the newspapers had announced that this would be done, but it was regarded as unthinkable and no precautions were taken to avoid it.

The next day, articles started appearing in almost all the Protestant papers, condemning the cruel arsonists, and this *reshuffling in the papers* lasted for many months, reaching all parts of the United States. Many Catholics were beguiled, be-lieving that Protestants *truly* felt that way and that they de-tested what had happened, but I have the pleasure of never having been taken in, for I abhor playing the role of the de-ceived one. I did not look behind the scenes and I only read the newspapers. I told a friend of mine, "these people bestowing compliments on us in the newspapers so that we may become careless, as well as to avoid the opprobrium that their actions would cause them, but they shall repeat it very soon." I did not deceive myself, Elpidio; time has proven that it was not a mere suspicion of mine. Now they say that the sisters are returning to Boston and that they expect that the public treasury will com-pensate the losses they suffered, for there is a new law that provides for such cases, but I suspect that their case will be declared an exception for being a Catholic institution.

This experience proves, my Elpidio, that the public opin-ion in the city of Boston was against the Catholic religion. The city is very far from the tolerance that is spoken about so much, but practiced so little. A fire always evokes compassion, and especially when it is accompanied by such circumstances as I have just related; but the Bostonians limited themselves to the *lamentations they published in the newspapers* and they did not believe that they should do anything for an educational institution that was reduced to ashes on account of religious hatred. This very fact proved the extent of this hate. Even the few who truly desired to build the academy again so that their daughters could receive a select education did not dare take up a public collection, for they knew full well what the public opinion towards Catholics was.

This is a country in which each one is free to believe and to do as one wishes on religious matters; it is thus even more noteworthy that public opinion, and public opinion alone, should close the doors to charity, justice and the common good. I shall say even more: not even Catholics were exhorted to proceed without fear in rebuilding their academy, and everything was limited to charges against the arsonists, as it was in earlier times against the thieves of the *Sierra Morena;* but without making sure that the unfortunate one who dared to go through would not be taking too many risks. If the Bostonians truly had the spirit of universal tolerance, when they saw that this philanthropic principle was attacked by such an unpleasant public gesture, they would have taken the opportunity to consolidate their doctrine, extending a charitable hand to those Catholics who had so unjustly been persecuted; but undoubtedly the religious principle that directs their conscience was stronger and they were not able to bring themselves to protect a few nuns from a Catholic institution. Do you think that I blame them? No, my friend. I shall always bemoan their blind obstinacy, but as long as they are blind, I am not amazed that they should behave in such a manner, and even though they do evil when they burn and destroy, they act rightly for following their conscience and thus not supporting the extension of a religion that in fact they detest. My dear Elpidio, I detest only their abominable hypocrisy in feigning that they have a tolerance when in reality they do not.

The funniest thing about all of this was the judicial process undertaken against the arsonists. In a country like this, in which everything is thoroughly investigated and a criminal never escapes, no one was able to find out anything whatsoever about this fire. Only a thirteen or fourteen-year-old boy was found guilty. They really knew that because of his young age he would come out all right. Even the Catholics themselves took steps so that he would be set free. All others who had been arrested *were found innocent.*

I was in Boston when the news arrived that those who had taken part in the burning of the convent had been set free, and the rejoicing in Charlestown (which as I have already mentioned is almost a continuation of the city of Boston) was such that they fired shotguns and cannons on the streets as they do on great feasts. If they had done this merely out of that pleasure that every loving person experiences when those who had been considered criminals are found innocent, one could accept it, even though it would appear as an excessive demonstration of joy; but the purpose was only to show that they had obtained a victory against Catholics, and thus from happiness they went on to frenzy and shouted: "the heads of Catholic priests." I was having dinner with the Bishop of Boston and some of his illustrious clerics when we heard the shots, whose purpose we could not figure out until one of clerics came in and gave us the good news. Everyone remained calm and I had the pleasure of observing so much firmness. We only said: "Here you have religious tolerance!" They then told me about several incidents, which confirmed the idea we already had about the animosity with which we are regarded by the Protestants.

Among other cases, they told me that when the Sunday school girls were coming to church in procession, led by the Sisters of Charity and a few ladies, a few barbarians had the cruelty to step on their feet and blow cigar smoke in their faces, to see if those innocents would disband in terror. On another occasion, they poured red wine from a window under which they were passing; they stained the dress of one of the young ladies, whose father took matters into his hands, as he should, and went to find out who was the aggressor, and presented himself against him. But he did not go as a Catholic, on account of the affront to his daugher's religion, but as the father of a girl who had been insulted and as owner of the dress that she was wearing. The tribunal ordered the accused to pay two hundred dollars.

While I was staying in Boston there was another case which could have had deadly consequences had the Bishop not proceeded with his usual prudence. On the feast of Pentecost, just before the principal Mass, a good number of people were in and around the doors of the church waiting for the festivities to begin, when someone in the house across the street threw a cross tied with a rope out of a window and jingled it up and down in various ways. When the Catholics became aware of the mockery, they went in and asked the Bishop what they should do; he told them, "venerate that cross that they throw out of a window no matter how they try to profane it, and beg them to use all of their influence so that a cross may be placed in every door of every house in Boston." Thanks to this prudent advice the Catholics were peaceful, who had been ready to enter that house and scare the sacrilegious jokers out of their wits.

Two or three years after the fire at the Ursuline convent in Charlestown, when the enemies of the Catholic religion realized how well they had fared in their scandalous deed, they wished to perpetrate another in this city of New York by burning our cathedral church. In order to prepare the people for such an attempt Protestant ministers began to preach almost daily that Catholics would like to submit this country to the Pope and that we had set up the Inquisition, whose dungeons were ready under our cathedral church. No matter how absurd their assertions were, they were believed, because of the Protestants' desire to find a motive to attack us. The burning of our church was certainly agreed upon; and since projects of this nature require purely executing hands, which can always be found among those of limited education, it seems that they made use of the butchers, among whom I do not know if there is a single Catholic. They were not too careful and they had a conversation in public at the market, which was overheard by one of the merchants who was a Catholic and who immediately came to tell me, for she belonged to our congregation. Under other circumstances I would not have paid any attention, but as I remembered what had happened in Boston and knowing how public opinion was being stirred up against Catholics as a result of the *charitable* sermons of their ministers, I put the *trustees* or administrators of the cathedral church on guard. They informed our people very soon by word of mouth because being lay people they were in touch with our people.

On the night we feared that the attack would take place more than five hundred Catholics gathered around the cathedral church. The Governor of the city immediately came over, either because he was told what was going on or because the unexpected large number of Catholics around a closed church caught his attention. Two or three hundred would-be arsonists came at the appointed time. But imagine their surprise when they turned the corner and saw our church surrounded by so many people! The Catholics immediately sent someone to tell the attackers they should leave, because for their part they were determined to defend their property. This information, or the news that the Governor of the city would take whatever measure was necessary against them, made them retreat and go away. The Catholics were afraid that they would come back and they were determined to spend the entire night around the cathedral. The Governor of the city then told Reverend Thomas Levins, a Catholic priest (who was a curate of the very cathedral), that he should address the Catholics in a high spot assuring them that the government would be responsible for paying for anything that was destroyed by the people, but that they should not be afraid of this taking place because the police would break up any disorder. Reverend Levins did as requested and the Catholics went away immediately.

Last year in the city of Baltimore they made another attempt to attack a convent of the Carmelite sisters (which, if I am not mistaken, is the only one of that order in this country), but it did not have any serious consequences, although they had the barbaric pleasure of upsetting those poor sisters. It must be said, however, that in the states of the south there is not as much animosity against us as in those of the north; and especially in Maryland they are very kind towards us, perhaps because of the memory of Lord Baltimore, who was a Catholic and from whom the principal city takes its name, and of the illustrious Carroll, who was one of the signers of the Declaration of Independence of this country and the last of the signers to die. His family is quite revered and respected and has great influence in that state. Bishop Carroll, the first Archbishop of Baltimore, also belongs to this family.

Another noteworthy case concerns a school that the Bishop of this Diocese was building, and I shall even say was built, in Nyack, which is about thirty miles from this city of New York. From the time he bought the land, the Protestants, especially the Presbyterians, started to cause trouble. One of the ministers, Dr. Brownlee, was so zealous that he even traveled there to preach to the people that they should not permit the Catholics to establish themselves there under any circumstances, for they would corrupt the entire area.

Brownlee and his friends even went to the state legislature to prevent the granting of the *charter*[61] to the Catholic Bishop. The *charter* is a government title that sets up an organization as a moral body with all due civil rights. Brownlee wanted to delay the building; no one would wish to donate any money for a school knowing that there was opposition to and difficulties in its establishment. The Presbyterians' delegation was insane, but it could not be dismissed and had to be heard when its turn came up; and since there were many other matters that took precedence at the legislature, the school *charter* could not be considered until the following session, which is to say, the following year.

The Bishop continued building the school, for he did not need anybody's permission. The worst that could happen was the denial of the *charter;* but when the Presbyterians saw his determination they once again began to attack the new school almost openly. Some trustworthy information was received that they intended to burn it, for it was almost finished. The Bishop had to appeal to the state Governor, who was most cooperative, saying that he would order the police to guard it and to avoid any attempt against it.

At first nothing happened and I would not dare to say positively that the unfortunate occurrence that took place later on was the work of the Presbyterians, but the school started to burn between noon and one o'clock one day, and nobody came to put the fire out, with the result that everything was reduced to ashes. They said that the fire was the result of an unwary carpenter who lit a fire to boil some eggs in a place where there were a lot of woodshavings, but the carpenter said sometimes that he was boiling water to cook the eggs, and at other times that he was heating glue. These two items are so different that one cannot help but be suspicious . . . There is no doubt that the Protestants wanted to destroy the school to prove their *tolerance*. The Bishop sold the land to avoid new persecution, and the Presbyterians succeeded insofar as there is no Catholic school in Nyack.

Even though you may say that I always tell you personal things, I wish to dedicate to you two anecdotes that took place at a hospital in this city. About eight years ago I was giving communion to a patient when a Protestant took it upon himself to make fun of me, tapping the potbelly stove (for it was winter) with the tongs as one would ring the bells in our church at the time of distributing communion. A Catholic lady who went with me to visit the patient noticed the insult as I did, and we both felt sorry for such a rude wretch. On another occasion I went to the Navy Hospital to visit a patient who had called me, and as soon as I entered the room I was followed by a gentleman, whom at first I could not recognize as a member of the ministry. I begged him to leave the room so that I could speak with the patient, but he started in with a string of nasty arguments, to which I answered that this was not the time to discuss the points of my religion and that the patient, who belonged to my Church, had called for me. In order to insult me anyway, he then told me that he did not believe a word I was saying and addressing the patient asked him if it was true that he had called for me. The poor dying man answered affirmatively, and with this answer he had no right whatsoever, according to the rules of the hospital, to remain there, for it was clear that the patient wanted to talk to me in private and he did not have any business listening to what the patient wanted to say. I recognized his embarrassment and even though I could have said many other things, I was satisfied with begging him once again to leave the room. Then, with an air of arrogance, he told me that he did not know why he should leave and that he would not leave. "We shall see," I told him, "if my religion is protected here or if it should be subjected to your whim." "Your religion," he answered, "shall be respected, but neither your superstition nor your romanism." "We shall see," I told him, leaving the room where I could not do anything because of that dimwit, and turning towards the office of the Hospital director. But when I realized that he had also left the room, for he had really come to bother me, I turned back, heard the confession and annointed the patient (for you might know that here we always carry in our pocket a silver box with the oils), and then I immediately went to the Church for the sacrament. However, even though it took a brief time, when I returned the patient had died. I then reflected about the evil that would have occurred had that dimwit not come out of the room or had I persisted in disputing the point before the director of the hospital.

However, talking with the Rev. Dr. Power, an educated churchman, we agreed that we should not let this matter go on and we went to the hospital at the same time that they had the *trustees'* meeting. They allowed us in, and treated us quite politely and with a lot of consideration. Once our grievance was heard, they expressed how sorry they were that the incident had occurred and immediately proceeded to find out who had bothered me. It turned out to be one of the officials of the Baptist Church. He was told that ministers of whatever religion were not to be bothered at the hospital, and that if he should break that rule again he would not be welcome at the hospital. Notice, Elpidio, that where laws and rules are concerned everything proceeds all right, but there is no tolerance regarding attitudes.

A similar event had happened in the same hospital to Rev. Malou, who is a respected churchman. Malou had left a crucifix in the hands of a patient. When the patient died, one of the servant girls started to make a mockery of the image, joking about it in a thousand ways. They told Rev. Malou what was going on at the hospital and he immediately went there. He rebuked the irreligious profaner and all those who had made a mockery of the image of the Redeemer. He then complained to her superiors and obtained complete satisfaction. Another churchman had been treated as an imposter at the same hospital by a lady who was the wife of one of the officials of that institution. Well, the cases are not as rare as some people might think.

A little over a month ago a poor woman asked me for a letter of reference so that she could get back her children, who had been placed in an orphanage without her consent. She presented the document, and the elderman, Palmer, who apparently was the head of the commission in charge of that place, after seeing my signature, said in a loud voice with scorn and laughter: "Do you believe that I am going to pay attention to the signature of a Catholic clergyman? I would pay more attention to that of a garbage collector. The man who has signed this would forgive you all your sins for a few dollars, and you want me to believe anything he might say?"

We are dealing with a public servant, in a country that is *legally* tolerant, and his reason for scorning me was precisely my religion and my ministry, which was the equivalent of scorning all Catholics; and so that there would be no doubt, he continued to express his feelings by telling the woman that even if all Romanists came there to recommend her he would not pay attention to anyone.

Since we are presenting anecdotes, the following is a noteworthy one even though it is not mine. Two officers of Bonaparte's army who left the service after he fell dead came to live in this city, where they began one of our better schools. There was a parcel of land put up for sale and they wished to purchase it for their building, but when one of them went to the owner, this one answered absolutely that he would not sell it to *any Catholic*. Undoubtedly he was trying to avoid the building of the school, in spite of the assurance that such gentlemen would welcome students from all sects and would not bother anyone's belief. You can imagine the fury of a French soldier from Napoleon's troops when he received such an insult. Fortunately he is talented and thus sought a rational means of punishing such audacity. He asked the help of a friend, who bought it, and after the papers were signed, he told the seller, "now your land is in the hands of a Catholic."

These particular cases could easily fill volumes. I wish now to present a fact which I can call universal, for it sums up an infinite number of undeniable ones, which are so notorious they cannot be ignored by any informed person who has had to intervene in family matters in this country. The custom here is to marry Protestants and Catholics, leaving the impediment of *disparity of cult* reduced, as theologians universally teach, to the baptized with the nonbaptized, and not putting into practice (for it is impossible) other canonical dispositions that make heresy a truly obstructing impediment. A dispensation is thus never requested for these marriages, and the only thing that is asked is whether the Protestant has been baptized in his sect. Such marriages are quite frequent, and I can assure you that they are much more frequent than one could expect when one sees the attitudes against Catholics. In spite of all the promises that the Protestants make not to oppose the Catholic party in the free exercise of its religion, you will find only one out of a hundred who will keep his word and many times not even fifteen days go by before it is broken. At least one can say that the first child sets off the scandal, for the dispute begins immediately as to which Church the child is to be baptized in, the one to which the father belongs or the one to which the mother belongs, and there are children who live a long time without baptism because the parties cannot agree.

I am tired of listening almost daily to the complaints of women who are persecuted by their Protestant husbands, bemoaning that they do not stop ridiculing the Catholic Church, and that many of them absolutely forbid them even to enter our temples. There have been some poor ones who have died from the pain of not having been able to receive the sacraments because the husbands have opposed it, and, regretfully, those visiting these persons were not aware of the rights given by the laws of this country, by which, in spite of the opposition of the husband, any minister of any religion called by the patient is allowed to enter.

In my congregation there are similar cases and among others there is a lady who converted to the Catholic Church. She was one of the most fervently faithful, and unfortunately she was naive to trust a Protestant and married him based on the promise that she would not be bothered in matters of religion. She entered this unfortunate marriage about four or five years ago and since then she has been forbidden to come to Church even though she assures me that her faith has not changed.

There is not a servant, nor an apprentice, nor a seamstress who can live in peace, having to suffer at every turn the mockeries, insults and abuse of the persons on whom he or she is dependent. At every turn they are called fanatics, superstitious, they hear that the Catholic clergy are nothing but rascals and that our doctrine is a detestable idolatry and apostasy; in a word, anything that can be said to torment simple people without education. What do you say about tolerance?

Finally, my Elpidio, Protestants have used the theater to persecute and ridicule us. Who would believe that in a country that presents itself as the norm for tolerance the theater would become a tool to ridicule the religion of thousands of its inhabitants and that the public would applaud such insults! Our solemn high masses, vestments and all, are represented in a comical way; and to give credibility and disseminate their slanders, the jesters use exclamations that purport to express the doctrines they attribute to us, and they say, for example, "we adore you most holy Mary," and other blasphemies like it. I ask you, Elpidio, what do you say about this tolerance? I anticipate your answer: that there is none for Catholics, and consequently it is not as universal nor as perfect as they pretend it is; and if it were not for the laws that protect us, the people would persecute us with as much or more fury as their English ancestors.

LEGAL TOLERANCE

As far as legal tolerance is concerned, one cannot deny that it is most perfect in this country, for aside from an extraordinary case, which could be seen as a phenomenon, one can never find a judge that would not proceed with impartiality and firmness where the freedom of conscience sanctioned by the constitution is at stake; and on this regard we Catholics cannot complain. I do not believe that there is any other country in which this point is observed so strictly, and this is the basis of its peacefulness. It is clear, then, that perfect legal tolerance is not an illusion.[62]

I must warn you, however, that they are also intolerant among themselves, although not with as much fury as when they deal with Catholics. The Presbyterians are the least tolerant and the ones more prone to do what they condemn in Catholics. They have a great desire to see that their religion is the *predominant* religion in this country, even though they try to disguise it. About eight years ago one of the Presbyterian ministers dared to express from the pulpit the intentions of his sect, stating that in a short while his religion would be the predominant religion, the state religion. He caused great alarm among the other sects, who attacked the naive and imprudent minister. On account of this incident there were several private meetings, and among others, I remember hearing a gentleman who belongs to the Anglican or Episcopal Church say that a very rich Presbyterian, seeing himself pinned against the wall by the argumentation placed before him, finally answered in anger: "so it will be in spite of our enemies, and we have many millions of dollars to achieve it." Shortly afterwards one of the newspapermen from the same sect printed an answer to their accusers and in it he clearly stated without any beating about the bush that the Presbyterian Church would be officially established even if it required *flooding the country in waves of blood.* You can infer that at once the rest of the newspaper people came out like furies, which served the purpose of making this incident more public. I brought this up to the Presbyterians in some of our discussions and in their articles answering me they avoided this subject, as if I had written nothing about it, which is their favorite tactic.

I am already aware, Elpidio, that this letter about tolerance is turning out to be so long that I risk losing yours and thus I should bring my observations to an end with one that is most interesting. The touchstone of truth is the opposition of errors, and errors cannot tolerate truth because they cannot be melded with it. I have presented facts that are true, notorious, undeniable, and my inferences about them have been so few, so natural and evident, that I think I have *demonstrated them.* However, my experiences about the human heart lead me to anticipate that my proofs shall be regarded as the folly of a religious interest, for my language is different from that found in the books of mere *political calculations;* and from the language used by many who believe they know this country after only having strolled along the streets of some of its cities or attended some meeting or other.

I trust from your good judgment that if this letter leads you to believe that I am intolerant that you will give me a lesson about tolerance, disguising my honesty. Tolerate me, Elpidio, for I have only attempted to unmask the *nominally tolerant,* call the attention of the thoughtless and establish the true *evangelical tolerance,* which, without allowing error, is never lacking in charity, the soul of Christianity. If people hate me for telling the truth, I have here a new encouragement to continue to proclaim it; and thus you can expect another series of letters, in which I do not know what I shall write, but I already sense that they are not going to be inconsequential things, for I hope to deal with fanaticism.

I then finish my reflections about the deadly influence of superstition in society, asserting that it has lost the divine worship and imprisoned men who can only be truly free when they are animated by the true evangelical spirit; for as the Apostle tells the Corinthians, "where the Spirit of the Lord is, there is freedom."[2] How well the energetic, frank and apostolic St. Ambrose understood the divine text when he wrote, "neither is it proper for an emperor to deny the freedom to speak, nor for a priest not to say what he feels. The difference between the good and the bad princes is that the good ones love freedom and the evil ones love servitude."[3] Did St. Ambrose need to take lessons about liberalism or could he give them to the beguiled who think that freedom and religion are incompatible? But I am already entering into another matter, for the soul is stirred and the pen glides. I conclude, then, with a "goodbye, my Elpidio."

---

2. Ubi autem spiritus Domini, ubis libertas (2 Corinthians 3:17).

3. Neque imperiale est libertatem dicendi denegare, neque sacerdotale quod sentiat non dicere. Hoc interest inter bonos et malos principes quod boni LIBERTATEM amant, SERVITUTEM improbi. Ambrose, letter 40, also 29.

Appendices

I. Authorities which prove that the Protestants admit the necessity of being in the bosom of the Church in order to obtain salvation.

II. Experts who prove it is Catholic docrine that many are saved without being united to the visible body of the Church, when this separation is not culpable and when in other ways they find themselves united to the soul of the Church.

III. Some of the *Blue Laws* of the State of Connecticut.

IV. Extracts from the Acts of the Scottish Assembly.

V. Extracts from the Penal Code of England.

VI. Abolition of Catholicism in the European Continent.

VII. Intolerance taught by Voltaire.

VIII. Tolerance taught by St. Thomas.

IX. Calvinists persecution of Catholics in France.

APPENDICES

Authorities which prove that the Protestants admit the necessity of being in the bosom of the Church in order to obtain salvation.

I
LUTHER

"I know that in these last fifteen years many have thought that anyone can be saved *in his belief;* strange is the audacity and imprudence of the Zwinglians, who dare to advance similar doctrine and to cover it with my authority and example."[1]

MELANCHTHON

"We do not speak of the Church as if it were a platonic idea, but rather we demonstrate it in the meaning of the words: *refer it to the Church.* We must understand the visible Church." Later he is asked if it is necessary to be united to this Church to be saved, and he answers: *"It is absolutely necessary."*[2] It is known that Melanchthon was the most famous of Luther's disciples.

---

1. Luther, Com. 47.
2. Melanet, Examination to the Ordained on the Church.

CALVIN

"Outside the communion of the Church there is no hope for forgiveness of sins nor for salvation; such that separation from the Church always produces death."[3]

BEZA

"There has always been and there always will be a Church outside of which there is no salvation."[4]

CASAUBON

"Those who are separated from the Catholic Church or from its communion have no hope of salvation."[5] It should be noted that Casaubon, being Protestant, did not mean by Catholic Church, the Roman Church.

CATECHISM OF THE HUGUENOTS

"No one obtains forgiveness of sins without first being incorporated into the people of God and without persevering in the unity and communion of the Body of Christ as a member of his Church."[6]

PEARSON, PROTESTANT BISHOP

"The necessity to believe in the Holy Catholic Church is demonstrated primarily because Christ has established it as the only way to eternal life."[7]

---

3. Calvin, book 3, Inst. chapter 1, lesson 4.
4. Confession of Faith, chapter 5.
5. Response to Cardinal du Perron.
6. Art. 10.
7. Exposition to the Creed, art. 9.

HOBART, PROTESTANT BISHOP

"Union with the church is the means marked out (by Christ) to save us."[8] It must be noted that Hobart was Bishop of New York and died almost two years ago, so that he wrote according to the actual doctrine of the American Episcopal Church.

BICKERSTETH

It is our duty to announce the wrath of God against those who are united to the Roman Church."[9] The preacher continues denouncing the modern spirit of unfaithfulness inappropriately called liberalism, which considers it a lack of charity to condemn so many millions of souls. One might infer, then, that according to the preacher all Catholics are condemned.[10]

CONFESSION OF FAITH OF THE SCOTTISH CHURCH

"We highly detest the blasphemies of those who say that all men who act with equity and justice will be saved regardless of whatever religion they may happen to be."

THE CHURCH OF ENGLAND

We can say that the whole Church of England or the Episcopal Church expresses its opinion in Europe as in America (The American Episcopal Church is a branch of the European) when in its ritual or book of public prayer it explicitly states: "Oh Merciful God! have pity on the Jews, the Turks, the pagans and heretics; take away from them all ignorance, hardness

---

8. Candidate for Confirmation, 36.
9. Sermon preached October 4, 1836.
10. See Dublin Review, December, 1836.

of heart and contempt for your word and *bring them back to your flock so that they may be saved."*[11]

Would the Protestant still tell us that only the Catholics teach that outside the Church there is no salvation?

II

Experts who prove it is Catholic doctrine that many are saved without being united to the visible body of the Church, when this separation is not culpable and when in other ways they find themselves united in spirit or to the soul of the Church.

ST. AUGUSTINE

"If I thought, Honoratus, that a heretic is the same as a man who believes heretics, I would cease speaking and writing on this subject. But since a great difference exists between these two things, then in my opinion a heretic is he who starts or follows false and new opinions for some temporal advantage, mainly glory and superiority; but whoever believes these men is only deceived by a certain imagination of truth and piety," etc. etc.[12]

"Those who do not defend their false and perverse opinion for a pertinent animosity, especially when they have not originated them by their presumptious audacity but rather received them from their fathers (who were seduced and enticed to error), yet search truth with determination and are ready to

---

11. Book of Common Prayer, Collect for Good Friday.

12. Si mihi Honorate, unum atque idem videretur esse haereticus, et credens haereticis homo, tam lingua, quam stilo in hac caussa conquiescendum esse arbitrarer. Nunca vero cum inter haec duo plurimum intersit: quando quidem haereticus est, ut mea fert opinio, qui alienius temporalis commodi, et maxime gloriae et principatus sui gratia, falsas ac novas opiniones vel gignit vel sequitur; ille autem qui hujusmodi hominibus credit, homo est imaginatione quadam veritatis ac pietatis illusus, etc., etc., Augustine, *On the Utility of Beliefs,* chapter 1.

correct themselves having found the truth: they cannot at all be counted among the heretics."[13]

"The same (that is the Church) conceives in her womb, and in the womb of her servants (any one in attendance) by means of the same sacraments . . . But if some among those who are born become haughty and refuse to be with their legitimate mother, then they are like Ismael, about whom it was said dismiss the maid and her son."[14]

It would seem that it is enough to let St. Augustine speak and that it is unnecessary to quote anyone else. But to demonstrate that contemporary theologians are devoted to the doctrine of that glory of the Church, let us see what some experts say.

PATUZZI

"If he were able to ignore without fault all the mysteries of the Catholic faith, if he really did ignore them blamelessly, he would not be condemned because he did not believe but because of the original sin or for other sins, unless God in his mercy converts him."[15]

DELAHOGUE

"It is one thing to say that there is no hope of salvation outside the Church, and another that those who did not live in

---

13. Qui sententiam suam falsam atque perversam nulla pertinaci animositate defendunt, praesertim quam non audatia praesumptionis suae pepererunt, sed a seductis et in errorem ductis parentihus acceperunt, quaerunt autem cuneta socitudine veritatem, corrigi parati cum invenerint; nequnquam sunt inter haereticos reputandi. St. Augustine, letter 43, also 162.

14. "Ipsa" (Ecclesia) "generat, et per uterum suum, et par uteros ancillarum ex eisdem sacramentis . . . Sed qui superbiunt, ei legitimae matri non adiunguntur, similes sunt ismaëli, de que dictum est ejice ancillam et filium ejus," etc., etc. St. Augustine, book I, cont. dont., chapter 10; see 12:114.

15. Cum omnia fidei misteria inculpabiliter ignorari possint si ita reapse ab aliquo inculpabiliter ignorentur, damnabitur quidem non propterea quod non crediderit, sed nici misericordia Dei illum praevenit, atque converterit damnabitur propter originale peccatum te propter alia. Patuzzi, 6:51.

the visible bosom of the true Church or did not belong to her body are condemned. All the theologians count as members of heretic and schismatic societies, many of whom partake of the inner communion of the true Church; and this applies not only to children but also to adults who because of invincible ignorance belong to a heretic or schismatic society, and who will be saved in heresy or as schismatic, unless guilty of another crime . . . This even includes those who seem inexcusable in their adherence to a heretic or schismatic society, and who die in it; since no one knows what is their internal mental affliction or the disposition of their hearts in their last moments we cannot count them, with certitude, among the reprobates."[16]

NICOLE

"It is certain, *according to every Catholic theologian,* that there are a great number of living and true children of the Church among the believing communities separated from her; it is taken for granted that they include many children, and perhaps some adults, even if they are not noticed because they are not known."[17]

THE UNIVERSITY OF PARIS

"Children and ignorant ones are incapable of falling in heresy or of becoming schismatic; they are excused because of

---

16. Aliud est dicere extra veram ecclesiam nullam sperandum esse salutem, aliud dicere eos omnes qui dum in vivis essent non fuerunt in sinu visibili verae ecclesiae, vel de ejus corpore esse damnandos. Namque omnes teologos numerant in societatibus haereticis, et schismaticis, qui ad animan ecclesiae pertinent, quod quidem non tantum accipiendum est de pueris, sed etiam de adultis, qui haereticae aut schismaticae societati ex invincibili ignorantia adhaerent, qui proinde in haeresi si vel schismate salvabuntur, nisi alia obstent corum deluta . . . Quo ad illos etiam quorum ahaesio haereticae aut schimaticae societati vedetur excusari non posse, qui in illa moriuntur, cum nemo in terris cognoscere posit quis fuerit illorum internus mentis affectus, quaenam interna cordis dispositio in ultimo instanti, quo extremum spiritum reddiderunt, certo dicere non possumus eos esse e reproborum numero. Delahogue, *Treatise On Ecclesiology,* 41–42.

17. Nicole, *On Unity,* vol. 1, chapter 3.

invincible ignorance. God does not impute them their errors to which they adhere on account of invincible ignorance. Thus they can be in communion with the Church through faith, hope and charity."[18]

DU CLOT

"To show disdain for the axiom (that there is no salvation outside the Church) unbelievers and other enemies of the Catholic Church presume that, according to our doctrine, salvation is denied to those who are heretics or schismatic, by reason of their birth, or because of invincible ignorance, for which they are not to be blamed. This is totally false. *All those who have not participated in heresy or schism by their own will and will full knowledge belong to the true Church.* That is the teaching of St. Augustine, St. Fulgence,[19] and St. Salviano.[20] If some theologians have said otherwise, their *own opinions prove nothing.*"[21]

ST. THOMAS

"If one who has always lived in a jungle is guided by that natural reasoning that searches for good and avoids evil, I most certainly believe that God would either reveal through inspiration the things necessary for salvation or send to him a preacher as he sent Peter to Cornelius."[22]

---

18. Censure of l'Emile.
19. On Peter's Faith, chapter 39.
20. On God's Government, book 5, chapter 2.
21. Du Clot, *The Vengeance of the Holy Bible,* vol. 3 (Paris, 1837), 487.
22. Si aliquis in sylvis vel inter bruta nutritus ductum naturalis rationis sequeretur in appetitu boni et fuga mali, certissime est tenendum quod ei Deus vel per internam inspirationem revelaret ea, quae sunt ad salutem necessaria, vel aliquem fidei praedicatorem ad eum dirigeret sicut missit Petrum ad Cornelium. Thomas, *Truth,* 9, 14, art. 11; see Cellet Insti. Theology, 2:10.

III

Some of the Blue Laws of the State of Connecticut (so called because they were first published on blue paper):

Law 10. No one will be a *free person* or will have the right to vote unless he converts and becomes a member in good standing in one of the Churches permitted in these dominions.

Law 12. No Quaker or person who dissents with the Church established in these dominions will vote in the election of judges or other office.

Law 13. No food or lodging will be offered to Quakers, Adamites or any other heretic.

Law 14. Whoever becomes a Quaker will be exiled, and if he returns to this country, he will be condemned to die.

Law 15. Catholic priests are forbidden to live in these dominions; they will be exiled, and if they return they will be condemned to die.

Law 16. Every Catholic priest can be apprehended without the express command of a magistrate.

Law 18. No one is allowed to run on Sunday, to take a stroll in his garden or any other place, and one is only allowed to walk reverently to and from Church.

Law 19. No one is allowed to travel, cook, make beds, sweep the house, cut hair, or shave on Sunday.

Law 20. No mother shall kiss her son on Sunday.

Law 28. No minister (of the cult) will be teacher in a school.

Law 29. Anyone who refuses to pay his quota to support the minister of his city or parish shall be fined 62 pounds, and in addition he is bound to pay 4 pounds every quarter until he pays what he must contribute to the minister.

Law 31. Anyone who adorns his attire with gold, silver, or lace worth more than two silver coins a yard will be brought before the Grand Jury and its members will make him pay 300 pounds.

Law 31. No one will have in his possession common prayer books, nor will he observe either Christmas or any other determinated date as a festive day; no person is allowed to bake meat pies, dance, play cards, or play any musical instrument except the drum, the trumpet and the Jew's harp.

Law 36. It is forbidden to any minister of the Gospel to go hunting. Only the magistrates have the authority to hunt, since they can do so with less scandal to the Church.

Law 46. Every man will style his hair like his cap (that is to say, his hair will form a ring).

IV
EXTRACTS FROM THE ACTS OF THE SCOTTISH ASSEMBLY, A.D. 1643

"When they are crowned, the monarchs of Scotland must swear among other things to *abolish all false religions* (the ones opposed to the Presbyterian religion), *to rule the people according to the true religion* (Presbyterian), *and to eliminate every heresy.*"

They also have to take an oath that they will try to eradicate popism (that is to say, Roman Catholicism, for they derived the word "popism" from "pope"), every prelacy, superstition, schism, heresy, and profanation.

"Using the authority that *God has granted to us,* we will defend and conserve all the reforms that have been carried out and we will protect peace by opposing every heresy, *sect* (belonging to one of them; what tolerance!), and schism that could possibly arise."

"The assembly, considering the propagation of errors due to the independence and separation of the Kingdom of England, our neighbor, and knowing that this could be like gangrene for us, because the same errors, heresies, schisms and blasphemies that are present in their erronious books, works and letters will be introduced here, has determined that all precautions be taken in order to prevent their propagation and in virtue of the present act all the Presbyterians and synods are directed to judge and take action against the transgressors of these laws or of any of them. The assembly seriously recommends to the civil magistrates that they help the ministers and Presbyteries in the execution of this act."

The civil magistrates should control those who disseminate heresies or foster schisms by means of corporal punishment."

V
EXTRACTS FROM THE PENAL CODE OF ENGLAND

It is forbidden, under penalty of incapacitation and the denial of all civil rights, to send someone outside the realm to study in the papist religion, whether this be in public seminaries or in a private family, and *to send anything for that person's sustenance.*

It is forbidden to send any person under 21 years of age outside the realm, unless it be as a sailor, apprentice, or artist; and the judges will force the parents and the tutors to present the fugitive, and if they do not do this in a period of six months they will be punished according to the laws.

The Protestants who have converted from Papism will educate their children under fourteen years of age in the established religion, or they will lose all their rights.

When one of the parents is Protestant, the Chancellor will assure that the children be educated in the Protestant religion, determining how they shall be educated as well as the person who shall educate them, and the father shall pay for the costs.

The Chancellor may separate children from a Catholic father or mother.

No papist may be a public teacher or a private one, except in the case of his own family, under penalty of fine or prison.

Any Papist who dares to teach publicly or privately, even as an assistant to a Protestant teacher, will be considered as convicted papist clergy and will suffer the penalties accordingly; that is: 1. will be imprisoned; 2. transported; 3. if he returns he will be considered as a traitor, that is, arrested and hanged, and he will be decapitated and quartered, his remains left to the disposition of the Queen.

If a Protestant woman marries without first having certified that the husband is Protestant, she will lose all her inheritance; and in the same way all Papist heirs will be considered dead. The husband will be arrested and he will pay ten pounds.

If a Protestant marries a woman who cannot prove that she is Protestant, he will lose all rights and he will become incapacitated for all civil and military offices.

If a Papist presbyter administers matrimony knowing that one of the parties is Protestant, he will receive the punishment that a regular or established Papist minister is subject to; that is, he will be jailed, expelled from the land and if he were to return, hanged, etc.[23] By the laws of George I and George II, these penalties will be extended to all those cases where a Catholic presbyter marries a couple, even if the couple were Protestants.

If a convert is a judge and behaves as such, as long as his wife is Romanist or his sons educated in that religion, he will pay 100 pounds and become incapacitated.

Any courtier who marries a Catholic and fails to convert her in a year and present a certificate of this action to the chancery will be incapacitated.

Any woman who converts while her husband is alive will receive a third of the property of her husband even if he does not wish it.

Any son who wishes to be converted to the Protestant religion can do so against the opposition of his father, and his father will have to maintain and give a part of his possessions to his son. The son can also oblige his father to declare his goods under judgment *toties quoties* (by this it is meant that he can rob his father and brothers whenever he wishes).

If the eldest son is converted he can take away all his father's feudals, leaving him with only the profit made by them, and after his father dies he is obliged to maintain the younger

---

23. This law, as well as the previous ones, is not totally abrogated, although out of shame it is not executed. Yet, an excellent Irish Catholic curate, using this custom, married a Protestant gentleman to a Catholic lady a little over a year ago and the husband's relatives tried to punish him according to this law. He had no choice but to escape and come to this city of New York; but being a man of great merit, and having good friends in Ireland, they succeeded in getting the complainers to drop charges and then he returned to Ireland.

sons with an amount that should not exceed a third of the produce.

If the sons of the papist educated in the Protestant faith until the age of twelve assist the morning or evening prayer, they will be treated as converts who are apostatizing

VI
ABOLITION OF CATHOLICISM
IN THE EUROPEAN CONTINENT

Zwingli prohibited the practice of the Catholic Religion in Zurich in 1523.

The Catholic Religion was also abolished in Bern in 1528 and in Geneva in 1535.

VII
INTOLERANCE TAUGHT BY VOLTAIRE

"Will each one be permitted to believe what his reason is telling him whether it be true or erroneous? Without a doubt, as long as order is not disturbed, because it does not depend on the individual to believe but it does depend on him to respect the customs of his country."[24] Prescinding from the dogmatic errors that these lines contain, it is clear that Voltaire was not defending civil tolerance when it is opposed to the customs of his country. And, when does it not oppose them!

Let us say, then, that Voltaire openly defends civil intolerance, allowing only an intellectual freedom. The following text is much clearer: "In order for a government not to have the right to punish human errors it is necessary that these errors not be crimes; they are so when they disturb society, and in fact they disturb it when they provoke fanaticism. It is therefore necessary that men begin by not being fanatics if they want to deserve tolerance."[25]

---

24. Voltaire, Mel., 24:102.
25. Voltaire, Mel., vol. 29.

We hold, thus, that the government must chastise the fanatics for an intellectual crime, and if these ask that in fairness the irreligious such as Voltaire be chastised on account of another intellectual crime, though of a different nature, we will end up by having abundant punishments and an absence of tolerance; the irreligious would accuse the fanatics of disturbing order and these would accuse the irreligious in return. Let us speak frankly: Voltaire and those like him want, as some funny Spaniards say, to establish the *law of the funnel, wide for me, and narrow for you and let it be executed without discussion.*

VIII
TOLERANCE TAUGHT BY ST. THOMAS

St. Thomas asks if the pagan rites ought to be tolerated[26] and he answers affirmatively, beginning his reasoning on St. Gregory's statement on the Jews[27] It says: *May they have freedom to observe and celebrate all their feasts as they and their ancestors have had up to the past for such a long time.* After-

---

26. Thomas, Q. Q. cf. 10, art, 2.

27. Sed contra est quod in decret, dist XIV cap. qui sincera, dicit Gregorius de judoeis. Omnes festivitates suas, sicut hactenus ipsi et patres eorum per longa colentes tempora tenuerunt, liberant habeant observandi celebrandique licentiam. Respondeo dicendum, quod humanum regimen derivatur a divino regimem, & ipsum debet imitare. Deus autem quamois sit omnipotens & summe bonus permittit tamen aliqua mala fieri in universo, quae prohibere posset; ne eis sublatis majora bona tollerentur, vel etiam majora mala sequeruntur. Sic ergo & in regimine humano illi qui praesunt, recte aliqua mala tolerant, ne qliqua bona impediantur, vel etiam ne aliquia mala pejora incurrantur . . . Sic ergo quamvis infideles in suis ritibus peccent, tolerari possunt vel propter aliquod bonun quod ex eis provenit, vel propter aliquod malum quod vitatur.

Alliorum infidelium ritus qui nihil veritatis aut utilitatis afferunt non sunt aliqualiter tolerandi, nisi forte ad aliquod malum vitandum, scilicet ad vitandum scandalum, vel disidium, quod ex hoc posset provenire, vel impedimentum salutis corum, qui paulatim sic tolerati convertuntur ad fidem. Propter hoc enim haerctieorum et paganorum ritus aliquando ecclesia toleravit, quando erat magna infidelium multitudo. St. Gregory, Decret., dist. chapter 45, *Qui Sincera.*

ward, St. Thomas continues his article: "My answer is that human government is derived from the divine and must imitate it. But God, in spite of being all powerful and genuinely good, allows certain evils in the universe that he could prohibit, in order to prevent greater goods being destroyed, or greater evils coming about. In the same way those who govern human beings tolerate with justice some evils in order not to prohibit other goods or in order not to cause greater evils. . . . Thus, even though the pagans sin through their rites, it can be tolerated for some good that may result from them or to avoid some evil.

"The pagan rites that do not contain any truth or usefulness, should not be tolerated except to avoid evil, that is, scandal and dissension, or to remove an obstacle to the salvation of the pagans themselves, who, tolerating them, in this way are converted gradually to the faith. For this reason, the Church has sometimes tolerated pagan and heretical rites whenever there was a large multitude of them."

IX
CALVINISTS' PERSECUTION OF CATHOLICS IN FRANCE

In order to form an impartial judgment on persecutions and not to talk only about the Catholics' persecution of Protestants, we will present some of the countless ones that Catholics have suffered from the Calvinists.

In 1559 they destroyed St. Leger's Abbey in the Diocese of Saintes, and in 1560 they destroyed St. Cyprian of Poitiers' Abbey and that of Bellevaux in the Diocese of Nerves, where all the religious were killed and the building destroyed to the last stone. They expelled all the clerics and the most important Catholics from Montauban; they ousted the churches and monasteries prohibiting totally any manifestation of Catholic worship. In Pamiers, they destroyed both the cathedral and the episcopal residence as well as the canons' residence and two hospitals and many more buildings. On December 18 of the same year, they entered the Amiens Cathedral by force and made the blood of

Catholics flow. In Maux they destroyed images, profaned the Blessed Sacrament and robbed the churches.

In 1562, when Admiral Coligny took the city of Montagne, he killed almost all Catholic priests. Arnold Ronald, governor of the city of Angely, looted St. John's Abbey and expelled all the religious. The Calvinists destroyed all the Catholic churches in Maxene, stealing as much as they could, trampling on saints' relics and images. They burned the Abbey of Etroile in Poitiers. On March 16 of the same year, the Calvinists took Beziers, plundered the Cathedral, profaned the sepulchres and made a stable out of the temple. They destroyed St. Gilles's churches and convents along with their libraries, which had precious manuscripts. They converted the city of Usus into a bloody theater, for they massacred the city while the Baron of Adretz destroyed Holy Spirit Convent. They profaned the Cathedral of Montpellier and killed several canons. The Calvinists destroyed forty-six churches in this city and its environs.

Admiral Coligny entered Orleans promising religious freedom, but after receiving military reinforcements he took off his mask and abolished the Catholic religion, destroyed the churches and committed the same cruelties as in Montagne. Coligny passed through the entire Diocese of Orleans plundering and destroying whatever belonged to Catholic worship. The Abbeys of Isar and Hairitirelliers were looted and destroyed. As if plundering and profaning churches were not enough, the Calvinists demonstrated their hate for the episcopacy in Coutances by taking the Bishop through the streets riding on a mule with his face toward the animal's tail. In the same province, they destroyed the Abbeys of the Valais of St. Stephen, Trinity, Autunay Savigni, Ivry, St. Martin, St. Peter and many other churches. In Castres they destroyed not only the churches but also three hospitals.

A terrible massacre took place at Candom in 1569. They went to excess in Angouleme and in Seintes. A few years later they pillaged Piregueux Cathedral; they also entered the city of Salart and killed many ecclesiastics. Many were Baron Albretzs's cruelties in Laguedoc, Delfin and Provence. But they were rivalled by those committed by Monthrun, Mirabel, and Montgomery. Among his many other atrocities, Montgomery killed three thousand Catholics in *cold blood* in Orthies.

In 1562 the Calvinists made a treaty with Elizabeth of England and as a result gave the city of Havre, which is like the key to France's. What nice fellows![28]

---

28. These data has been taken from M. Ficet's *Historical Essay on the Influence of Religion in the Seventeenth Century in France*, 1824. See also Dr. Heylin's *History of Presbyterianism* and Laing's *Account of the Episcopalian Persecutions in Scotland*. See also *Catholic Diary of New York*, October 8, 1835.

NOTES TO THE LETTERS TO ELPIDIO

1. José de la Luz y Caballero (1800–1862) was one of Varela's beloved students in Havana. He also succeeded Varela in the chair of Philosophy at *San Carlos* and later founded his own college, *El Salvador*. Luz was a prolific writer, his *Aforismos* is considered his best work. Examining Jose I. Rodriguez's papers, who is Varela's first biographer, one realized Jose M. Casal, lawyer, editor and writer, was very close to Varela and kept contact with him through an active correspondence.

2. Varela, *Lecciones de Filosofía,* 5th ed., 283–307.

3. St. Thomas Aquinas, *Summa Theologiae,* 2a, 2ae, qq. 92–100.

4. John Tracy Ellis, *American Catholicism* (Chicago: University of Chicago Press, 1969), 41–86; J. P. Dolan, *Catholic Revivalism: the American Experience* (Notre Dame: University Press, 1978), 8ss.

5. J. P. Dolan, *The Immigrant Church* (Notre Dame: University Press, 1975), 9, 167.

6. Ray Allen Billington, *The Protestant Crusade, 1800–1860* (New York: Macmillan, 1938).

7. *Encyclopedia of Theology: The Concise Scaramentum Mundi* (1975), s.v. "Theology" by Karl Rahner.

8. G. de Bertier de Sauvigny, *La Restauration,* vol. 4 of *Nouvelle Histoire de L'Eglise,* 5 vols., ed. L. J. Rogier, R. Aubert, and M. D. Knowles (Paris: Ed. du Seiul, 1966), 409–11.

9. Roger Aubert, *La Chiesa dei Nostri Gorni,* vol. 10 of *Storia della Chiesa,* 10 vols., ed. Hubert Jedin (Milan: Edizioni Jaca Books, 1977), 14–16; Jimenez Duque, *La Iglesia en la España Contemporanea,* 406.

10. Roger Aubert, *Le Pontificat de Pie IX, 1846–1878,* vol. 21 of

300

Historie de l'Eglise Depuis les Origines jusqu'à nos Jours, 21 vols., ed. Agustin Fliche et Victor Martin (Paris: Bloud & Gay, 1952), 225.

11. Manuel Revuelta González, *La Iglesia en la España Contemporanea,* vol. 5 of *Historia de la Iglesia en España,* 5 vols., ed. Ricardo Gracia Villoslada (Madrid: Biblioteca de Autores Cristianos, 1979), 95–100.

12. *Ibid.,* 95.

13. *The New Catholic Encyclopedia* (1967), s.v. "Spain" by J. Fernandez-Alonso.

14. Ricardo Garcia Villoslada, gen. ed. *Historia de la Iglesia.*

15. Jose M. de la Guardia, "Filósofos Españoles de Cuba: Felix Varela y Jose de la Luz," *Revista Cubana* 15 (1982): 233–47, 412–27, 493–502.

16. *Dictionnaire de Spiritualité* (1964), s.v. "Feijoo y Montenegro" by Robert Picard.

17. G. Andres Mendoza Sadaba, "Cuba y su Revolución, *Informes de Pro Mundi Vita* 8 (1977): 4–5.

18. Joseph McCadden, "The New York-to-Cuba-Axis of Father Varela." *The Americas* (April 1964): 388.

19. See p. 104.

20. See p. 136.

21. Felix Varela, *Institutiones Philosophiae Ecclecticae Ad Usum Studiosae Iuventutis,* translated into Spanish by Antonio Regalado y Gonzáles (Habana: Cultural, 1945), 22–24.

22. Manuel F. Gran, "Varela y la Ciencia," *Cuadernos del Historeador de la Habana* (1945): 149–70.

23. It is important to take note of Varela's strong adherence to Thomistic thought. While in New York, in the fifth edition of the eighteenth lecture of his *Lecciones,* Varela made the following statement: "I only have taken St. Thomas's thoughts, because his language is charged of scholastic elements, which makes it a little obscure for those who are not well versed in his work. I wish his writings were available to everybody. I, who perhaps have had an inclination to *modernize,* have never done it with regard to St. Thomas on *theological matters,* I well loathe *modernism* when it is applied to them. If my advice can help those students who are studying by *Lecciones de Filosofia,* and later on will study sacred science, I would dare to beg them not to abandon the *Summa Theologica.* One is burdened by the worthless discourse found in it, but this task is recompensed by the discovery of a very precious diamond" (Felix Varela, *Lecciones de Filosofía,* 286).

24. See pp. 26, 160.

28. Letter, Varela to Luz y Caballero, August 23, 1839, in Gonzalez del Valle, "Cartas Ineditas del Padre Varela," *Rev. Bimestre Cubana* 50 (1942): 69.

29. Alejandro A. Gurudi, "Dos Entrevistas con el Pbro. D. Felix Varela," *El Figaro* 28 (1904): 350.

30. Dictionnaire de spiritualite (1964), s.v. "Fuga Mundi" by Zoltan Alzaghy.

31. Nuovo Dizionario di Spiritualita, s.v. "Mondo" by T. Goffi.

32. *Ibid.*

33. J. I. Rodriguez, *Vida del Presbitero Don Felix Varela* (New York: O Novo Mondo, 1878), 297–300.

34. Humberto Pinera, "Introduction," *Cartas a Elpidio sobre la Impiedad, la Supersticion y el Fanatismo en sus Relaciones con la Sociedad,* 1:i-xiv.

35. Raimundo Lazo, "Epilogo, *Cartas a Elpidio* 2:i–XIV.

36. Sociedad Cubana de Filosofia (Exilio), *Homenaje a Felix Varela* (Miami: Ediciones Universal, 1979), 20–29.

37. *Ibid,* 57–72.

38. Gurudi, "Dos Entrevistas," 350.

39. Ronald A. Knox, *Enthusiasm* (New York: Oxford University Press, 1950); St. Thomas, *Summa* I–II, q. 28, a.4, ad 2 and II–II, q. 36, a. 2–3.

40. Varela, "Essay on the Doctrine of Kant," *The Catholic Expositor and Literary Magazine,* August 1842, 200.

41. Varela, *Lecciones de Filosofia,* 5th. ed., 304.

42. Varela, "Editorial Notes," *New York Catholic Register,* October 8, 1840, 98.

43. Varela, "Specimen of Fanaticism," *New York Catholic Register,* July 23, 1840, 12.

44. Varela begins his first letter on irreligiosity with a profound meditation of the problem of evil; he starts out his first letter on superstition with a remarkably happy dream.

45. This is a vital idea in Varela spirituality: a freedom that respects the laws and affirms legitimate authority. He considered the United States "the classical land of freedom." In 1924, Varela published in Philadelphia a newspaper, *El Habanero,* considered by Foix "the first Spanish Catholic magazine published in the United States". This paper called for the Cuban independence from Spain in order "to prevent bloodshed." Varela ends his last *Letter* with the theme of liberation, affirming the human right of free speech, and quoting 2 Cor. 3:17: "Where the spirit of the Lord is, there is freedom." As

Joseph A. Fahy has recently pointed out, Varela had a serious impact upon the antislavery thought, especially of the *Cortes,* 1822 (Joseph Augustine Fahy, *The Antislavery Thought of Jose Agustin Caballero, Juan Jose Diaz de Espada, and Felix Varela, in Cuba, 1791–1823,* Ph. D. diss., Harvard University, 1983, 361).

46. Varela frequently uses the genre of satire which suits his purpose of "unmasking" wickedness, for the three monsters had been "the constant object of [his] observations".

47. Varela had a personal inclination for the new emerging sciences. Two of his three tomes of *Lecciones de Filosofia* are totally concerned with the physical sciences. He was the first to introduce in Cuba tools for establishing an experimental laboratory. In Philadelphia, Varela also translated into Spanish Humphrey Davy's *Elements of Chemistry Applied to Agriculture.* A review of the articles he wrote in the seven issues of *El Habanero* would show his abilities in explaining and making accessible the new advances of technology.

48. Influence of 1 Cor. 12:10 on the gift of recognizing the spirits, and 1 John 4:1; Gal. 5:14–22 and refined by Ignatius of Loyola with the experiences of "consolations and desolations."

49. Varela's letter on *Religious Tolerance* expands on this theme.

50. Cf. *Lecciones de Filosofia,* 305. ss and *Miscelaneas Filoficas,* 134–148, where Varela explains his educational principles at length.

51. Varela was an accomplished violinist. As pastor, Varela promoted the presentation of concerts and cultivation of sacred music. See F. J. Estevez, *Spirituality of Felix Varela* (Rome: P.U.G., 1980), 35–37.

52. Varela's work with the poor, and especially his detachment, was the most remembered feature of his life in New York. Most of his own money was spent to acquire the two churches in which he was pastor. He was so burdened by the bankruptcy of one of his parishes that he even had to beg from door to door and did not receive his own salary for an entire year. See Estevez, *Spirituality of Felix Varela,* 69–73.

53. In the Biblical tradition, dreams, visions and ectasies are vehicles by which the believers gain a deeper knowledge of God's providence. See Gen 20:3, 31:24, 37:5, 41:1, 5, Ps. 73:20; Mat. 1:20, 2:12. Was this happy dream of an unforgettable night a factual religious experience or was it a literary device that the author used to introduce the theme of superstition? The editor is inclined to think Varela was describing an actual event. This text stands out remarkably from Varela's usual writing style, a style which was sober, precise, analytical and argumentative. Moreover, there is no other in-

stance where Varela used this genre. In fact, he makes another reference to the event of that special "night and dream," which shows that it was not just a mere device to introduce a subject.

54. These principles constitute the essence of Ignatius of Loyola's *Exercises*.

55. The Spanish for theologians is *teologos,* hence Varela's reference to the three *o*'s in the name.

56. The second letter on Irreligiosity dealt with the roots of despotism. This one also deals with the political community; both letters show the danger of manipulating religion for the aggrandizement of a few.

57. The huge immigration of slaves from Africa was bound to have a deep impact in the practice of the faith. On the other hand, the discussion of the black intensive religious manifestation was a well-kept secret in Cuban literature, and some even think that there were strict and explicit orders from the government not to discuss this subject publicly. (Lydia Cabrera, *El Monte* (Miami: Chichereku, 1983), 149–95.

58. Varela had many friends among Protestants. To Joseph and Helen McCadden, "in an era of blinding religious animosities, Varela was the pioneer ecumenist, able to conduct dialogue without violence, astonishing his opponents by his learning, his patient exposition, his liberalism" (Joseph and Helen McCadden, *Father Varela— Torch Bearer from Cuba* [New York: U.S. Catholic Historical Society, 1969], 87). Varela respected the social and legal tolerance existing among denominations. In fact he even lectured on the participation of all the baptized in the same Church. He stood for the need of one Church. He also belonged to an epoch of rhetorical debates on the tenets of the faith, which attempted to show the truth of one's position vis-à-vis the others' false positions. His observations in the *Letters* are more in the genre of an observer and social critic of an explosive religious time.

59. Echoes of this analysis are found in the greatest English theologian of the nineteenth century, John Henry Newman, the *biglietto* speech, on the occasion of his installation as a Cardinal: "And I rejoice to say, to one great mischief I have from the first opposed myself. For thirty, forty, fifty years I have resisted to the best of my powers the spirit of Liberalism in religion. Never did Holy Church need champions against it more sorely than now when, alas! it is an error overspreading, as a snare, the whole earth. . . . Liberalism in religion is the doctrine that there is no positive truth in religion, but that one creed is as good as another, and this is the teaching which is

gaining substance and force daily. It is inconsistent with any recognition of any religion as true. It teaches that all are to be tolerated, for all are matters of opinion. Revealed religion is not a truth, but a sentiment and a taste; not an objective fact, not miraculous; and it is the right of each individual to make it say just what strikes his fancy. . . . Religion is so personal a peculiarity and so private a possession we must of necessity ignore it in the intercourse of man with man. If a man puts on a new religion every morning, what is that to you? It is as impertinent to think about a man's religion as about his sources of income or his management of his family. Religion is in no sense the bond of society. . . . The general nature of this great apostasia is one and the same everywhere." Edited in Marvin R. O'Connell, "Newman: The Victorian Intellectual as Pastor," *Theological Studies* (June 1985): 332.

60. W. C. Brownlee, D.D. of the Collegiate Protestant Reformed Dutch Church, New York was a brilliant controversialist. *The Religious Controversy between Rev. Dr. W. C. Brownlee . . . Rev. Drs. John Power, Thos. C. Levins, and Felix Varela* (Philadelphia: Boyle & Benedict, 1833) 21ss. Also, W. C. Brownlee, *Letters in the Roman Catholic Controversy* (Philadelphia: J. Whetham, 1834). Varela wrote at least nine letters during this controversy.

61. Varela employed the English word "charter," which he underlined.

62. Varela always admitted the United States' respect for law, and as his second letters on irreligiosity and superstition point out, he upheld that governments are servants of the law, and that the laws are sources of peace and order in society, avoiding any type of absolutism of individual powers.

SELECTED BIBLIOGRAPHY

PRIMARY SOURCES

Archives and Collections

American Antiquarian Society, Worcester, Massachusetts. All issues of *The Catholic Observer.*
American Catholic Historical Society of Philadelphia, Philadelphia, Pennsylvania.
Archdiocese of Baltimore Archives, Baltimore, Maryland. Two letters relating to Varela.
Archdiocese of Havana Archives, Havana, Cuba. Varela's baptismal and priesthood certificates; Varela's English catechism (recently discovered).
Archdiocese of New York Archives, Dunwoodie Seminary, Yonkers, New York. Archbishop J. Hughes Papers; financial statements of Transfiguration Church; partial collections of *Truth Teller, New York Weekly Register and Catholic Diary,* and *New York Freeman's Journal and Catholic Register.*
Archivo Histórico Nacional, Madrid, Spain. Information on secret societies in Cuba.
Archivio Segreto Vaticano, Vatican City State. Data on Bishop Espada.
Beato Private Collection. Three letters from Varela to José M. Casal and a bound manuscript annotated by Varela.
Biblioteca Nacional de la Habana, Havana, Cuba. The *Revista Biblioteca Nacional* (July–Sept., 1953), which is itself in-

cluded in this collection, provides a complete list of the Varela works located here.

Boston Public Library, Rare Books Collection, Boston, Massachusetts. Varela's translation of Humphrey Davy's book and Jefferson's *Manual.*

British Museum, London, England. Good collection of Latin-American rare books; first editions of Varela's philosophy books.

Butler Library, Rare Books Collection, Columbia University, New York City, New York. *The Children's Catholic Magazine* and *The Young Catholic Magazine.*

Catholic University of America, Washington, D.C. Excellent collection of catechisms and pamphlets.

Center for the Study of American Catholicism, Notre Dame, Indiana.

Diocese of St. Augustine Archives, St. Augustine, Florida. Information regarding the transferral of the remains of Varela to Cuba.

Florida Historical Society, St. Augustine, Florida. Literature related to Varela's obituary.

Hispanic Society of America Library, New York City, New York. Spanish first edition of *Cartas a Elpidio.*

Historical Society of Pennsylvania, Philadelphia, Pennsylvania. Poinsett Papers.

Library of Congress, Manuscript Division, Washington, D.C. Delmonte Papers; Rodríguez Papers.

Loyola Historical Library, Fordham University, New York City, New York. Partial collection of nineteenth-century New York Catholic newspapers and many issues of *Catholic Expositor and Literary Magazine.*

National Collection of fine Arts, Smithsonian Institution, Washington, D.C. Its inventory of American paintings reveals Daniel Huntington as painter of one of Varela's portraits.

National Library of Paris, Paris, France. Excellent collection of nineteenth-century Cuban magazines.

New York City Library, New York City, New York. Partial collection of Catholic newspapers of the nineteenth century.

New York Historical Society, New York City, New York. Only

place where issues of *New York Catholic Register,* 1839–40, are found; complementing issues of the *Catholic Expositor* missing in other collections.

Propaganda Fide Archives, Rome, Italy. A number of Varela's letters; vast number of sources on the American Church during the last century.

St. John's Seminary, Brighton, Boston. Massachusetts. All the issues of *The Protestant Abridger and Annotator.*

Transfiguration Church, New York City, New York. Sacramental records. (Minutes of meetings of the trustees used by Del Ducca and Dolan are lost.)

Vatican Library, Vatican City State.

Woodstock Theological Center, Georgetown University, Washington, D.C. Only place known where beginning issues of *New York Catholic Register* are to be found.

WRITINGS OF VARELA

Correspondence

(These entries are in chronological order and arranged in the following way: the person to whom Varela wrote, the date, and where the letter can be found today.)

José A. Saco. 1823. José A. Fernández Castro, *Medio Siglo,* 25.

Editor of *Revisor Político y Literario.* April 16, 1823. *Rodríguez Papers,* Box 16, "Correspondence Mo-Mu."

Joel Poinsett. January 27, 1825. Historical Society of Pennsylvania.

Joel Poinsett. January 28, 1825. *Ibid.*

Archbishop Eccleston. September 23, 1829. Archdiocese of Baltimore Archives.

Bishop Dubois. October 8, 1829. Propaganda Fide Archives.

Propaganda Fide. 1830. *Ibid.*

José A. Saco. January 2, 1830. Fernández Castro, *Medio Siglo,* 31.

Editor. January 31, 1832. *Truth Teller*, February 2, 1833, 38.

Editor of *Revista Cubana*. February 28, 1832. *Rodríguez*, 289–91.

Luz y Caballero. March 7, 1832. *Ibid.*, 292–93.

"Inquire." November 17, 1832. *Truth Teller*, November 17, 1832, 375.

"Inquire." December 1, 1832. *Ibid.*, December 8, 1832, 399.

"Inquire." December 15, 1832. *Ibid.*, December 15, 1832, 407.

"Inquire." December 21, 1832. *Ibid.*, December 22, 1832, 414.

W. C. Brownlee. February 23, 1833. W. C. Brownlee, *Letters in the Roman Catholic Controversy*, 12.

W. C. Brownlee. March 16, 1833. *Truth Teller*, March 16, 1833, 83.

W. C. Brownlee. April 6, 1833. *Ibid.*, April 6, 1833, 106.

W. C. Brownlee. June 8, 1833. *Ibid.*, June 8, 1833, 180.

W. C. Brownlee. July 20, 1833. W. C. Brownlee, *Letters in the Roman Catholic Controversy*, 116.

Editor. August 17, 1833. *Truth Teller*, August 17, 1833, 262.

Editor. November 23, 1833. *Ibid.*, November 23, 1833, 369.

Tomás Gener. June 2, 1835. González del Valle, "Cartas Inéditas," 65.

Luz y Caballero. June 2, 1835. *Ibid.*, 64–65.

Guadalupe Junco de Gener. September 3, 1835. *Ibid.*, 66.

Editor. October 24, 1835. *New York Weekly Register and Catholic Diary*, October 24, 1835, 39.

Editor. October 31, 1835. *Ibid.*, October 31, 1835, 55.

Editor. November 7, 1835, *Ibid.*, November 7, 1835, 70.

María J. Varela. April 12, 1836. González del Valle, "Cartas Inéditas," 66.

John Dubois. April 23, 1837. Archdiocese of New York Archives.

John Dubois. May 18, 1837. Propaganda Fide Archives.

María J. Varela. January 20, 1839. González del Valle, "Cartas Inéditas," 67.

José de la Luz. June 5, 1839. *Ibid.*

José de la Luz. August 23, 1839. *Ibid.*, 68–69.

José de la Luz. November 12, 1839. *Ibid.*, 70.

A. P. Halsey. April 8, 1840. William O. Bourne, *History of the Public School Society*, 327–28, 346–47.

Anastasio [*sic*]. October 22, 1840. González del Valle, "Cartas Inéditas," 70.

Manuel González del Valle. October 22, 1840. *Rodríguez,* 337–42.

Propaganda Fide. July 28, 1842. Propaganda Fide Archives.

Propaganda Fide. October 1, 1842. *Ibid.*

María J. Varela. December 30, 1842. González del Valle, "Cartas Inéditas," 70.

Propaganda Fide. January 15, 1844. *Ibid.*

María J. Varela. July 26, 1844. González del Valle, "Cartas Inéditas," 71.

Editor. February 15, 1845. *Freeman's Journal and Catholic Register,* February 15, 1845, 260.

Editor. March 1, 1845. *Ibid.,* March 1, 1845, 277.

María J. Varela. March 12, 1845. *Ibid.,* 72.

María J. Varela. July 20, 1848. González del Valle, "Cartas Inéditas," 72.

Archbishop Hughes. April 24, 1850. Archdiocese of New York Archives.

Cristóbal Madan. July 11, 1850. *Rodríguez Papers,* Box 148.

Editor. October 10, 1850. *Freeman's Journal and Catholic Register,* November 9, 1850, 5.

Published Writings

Books

Apuntes Filosóficos sobre la Dirección del Espíritu Humano. Habana: Fraternal, 1824.

Cartas a Elpidio sobre la Impiedad, la Superstición y el Fanatismo en sus Relaciones con la Sociedad, 2 vols. Habana: Editorial de la Universidad, 1944–45.

El Habanero: Papel Político, Científico y Literario Redactado . . . Seguido do las Apuntaciones sobre el Habanero. Habana: Editorial de la Universidad, 1945.

Institutiones Philosophiae Eclecticae Ad Usum Studiosae Iuventutis. Translanted into Spanish by Antonio Regolodo y González. Habana: Cultural, 1952.

Lecciones de Filosofía. 5th ed. 3 vols. Habana: Editorial de la Universidad, 1961–62.

Miscelanea Filosófica . . . Seguida del Ensayo sobre el Origen de Nuestras Ideas, Carta de un Italiano a un Francés sobre las Doctrinas de Lamennais y Ensayo sobre las Doctrinas de Kant. Habana: editorial de la Universidad, 1944.

Observaciones sobre la Constitución Política de la Monarquía Española, Seguida de otros Trabajos Políticos. Habana: Editorial de la Universidad, 1944.

Poesías del Coronel Don Manuel de Zequeira y Arango, Natural de la Habana, Publicadas por un Paisano Suyo. New York: n. p. 1829.

The Protestant's Abridger and Annotator, 3 vols. New York: G. F. Bunce, 1830.

Translations

Elementos de Química Aplicada a la Agricultura en un Curso de Lecciones en el Instituto de Agricultura, by Humphrey Davy. New York: Gray, 1826.

Manual de Práctica Parlamentaria para el Uso del Senado de los Estados Unidos, by Thomas Jefferson. Annotated. New York: Newton, 1826.

Articles

"Absolution." *The New York Catholic Register,* July 30, 1840.

"Abuse of the Scriptures and Spicemen of Fanaticism." *Ibid.,* April 2, 1840.

"Address to Protestants." *The Catholic Observer,* December 15, December 22, and December 29, 1836; January 12, 1837.

"Anniversary of the New York Catholic Temperance Association." *Truth Teller,* 1841.

"Antiquity of the Catholic Doctrine." *The Catholic Expositor and Literary Magazine* May 1844, 124–33; June 1844, 203–11; July 1844, 299–307; August 1844, 354–56.

"Authority in Religion." *Ibid.,* April 1841, 10–16.

"Beauties of Luther on Matrimony." *Truth Teller,* August 10, 1833.

"Beauties of the Reformers." *The Catholic Expositor and Literary Magazine,* May 1842, 72–74.

"Bishop England." *New York Catholic Register,* February 27, 1840.

"Bishop Kenrick of Philadelphia and the Protestant Bishop of Vermont." *The Catholic Expositor and Literary Magazine,* March 1843, 343–45.

"Bishops of the Church of England."*New York Catholic Register,* December 12, 1839.

"The Book of Common Prayer of the Church of England." *Ibid.,* October 3, 1839.

"Breve Exposición de los Acontecimientos Políticos de España, desde el 11 de Junio hasta el 3 de Octubre de Octubre de 1823 en que de Hecho se Disolvieron las Cortes." Quoted in *Rodríguez,* 264–69.

"Candles in the Church." *New York Catholic Register,* September 21, 1839.

"The Catholic Church and the Scriptures." *The Catholic Expositor and Literary Magazine,* May 1841, 60–65.

"The Catholic Church Bears the Stamp of Divine While the Protestant Bears that of Human Institution." *New York Catholic Register,* October 24, 1839.

"The Catholic Miscellany." *New York Catholic Register,* April 30, 1840.

"Caution Against Dr. Brownlee's Logic and Quotations." *New York Weekly Register and Catholic Diary,* August 23, September 6, September 13, September 27, October 4, October 25, November 1, and November 15, 1834.

"A Charitable Proposal." *Freeman's Journal and Catholic Register,* August 22, 1846.

"Children Temperance Memorandum." *New York Catholic Register,* August 6, 1840.

"Christmas Day." *Ibid.,* December 26, 1839.

"The Churchman." *Ibid.,* June 4, 1840.

"The Churchman and the Common School Fund." *Ibid.,* August 27, 1840.

"Comments to Rt. Rev. Bishop Hughes' Letters." *Ibid.*, June 25, 1840.

"Contempt of the Calumnies Against the Catholic Church." *Ibid.*, April 9, 1840.

"The Debt of Transfiguration Church." *Freeman's Journal and Catholic Register,* November 21, 1849.

"A Demonstration of Truth of the Catholic Doctrine from the Very Nature of the Scripture." *New York Catholic Register,* November 28, 1839.

"Despedida." Quoted in *Observaciones sobre la Constitución,* 256.

"Discurso Inaugural." *Ibid.*, 1–5.

"A Dissertation on the antiquity of the Catholic Doctrine." *New York Weekly Register and Catholic Diary,* September 1834.

"The Divisions of the Church of England." *Ibid.*, January 19, 1850.

"Doctrinas de Lógica, Metáfisica y Moral, Enseñadas en el Real Colegio de San Carlos de la Habana." Quoted in Antonio Ballicher y Morales, *Apuntes,* 157–76.

"Dr. Brownlee, Nestorian Presbyterian Preacher." *Truth Teller,* June 29, 1833.

"Editorial." New York Catholic Register, October 10, 1839.

"Editorial." *Ibid.*, November 28, 1839.

"Editorial." *Ibid.*, December 5, 1839.

"Editorial Observations." *The Catholic Expositor and Literary Magazine,* February 1844, 363–65.

"Editorial Observations on a Review of the Religious Press in Spain." *Ibid.*, December 1843, 213.

"Editorial on a Letter from Veritatis Vindex." *New York Catholic Register,* August 20, 1840.

"Education of Catholic Children in Our Public Schools." *Ibid.*, February 20, February 27, and March 5, 1840.

"Elogio de Don José P. Valiente y Bravo." Quoted in *Rodríguez,* 81–96.

"Elogio de S. M. el Señor Don Fernando VII." *Ibid.*, 70–81.

"Essay on the Doctrine of Kant." *The Catholic Expositor and Literary Magazine,* August 1842, 294–300.

"Essay on the Origin of our Ideas." *Ibid.*, January 1842, 383–86; February 1842, 420–22.

"Examples from History." *New York Catholic Register*, October 3, 1839.

"Extract from the Roman Ritual Relative to the Blessing of Images." *New York Catholic Register*, October 3, 1839.

"Fictitious Anecdotes Produced as Arguments Against the Catholic Church." *Ibid.*, May 7, 1840.

"The Five Different Bibles, Distributed and Sold by the American Bible Society." *The Catholic Expositor and Literary Magazine*, September 1841, 236–40; December 1841, 338–42; March 1842, 447–48.

"From the Churchman." *New York Catholic Register*, June 18, 1840.

"A Glance at the Catholic Question." *The Catholic Observer*, February 16, February 23, and March 2, 1837.

"Gramática de Salvá." *Revista Bimestre Cubana*, February 1832.

"Inconsistency of the Doctrine of the Church of England with its Own Liturgy." *New York Catholic Register*, May 14, 1840.

"Influencia de la Idiología en la Sociedad, y Medios de Perfeccionar este Ramo." Quoted in *Rodríguez*. 57–64.

"An Instance of the Judicious Piety of Bossuet." *New York Catholic Register*, January 9, 1840.

"Instrucción Pública." *El Mensagero Semanal*, June 1829, 313–16.

"Intercession of the Saints." *The Catholic Observer*, January 26, 1837.

"Intercession of the Saints and Prayers to Them." *New York Catholic Register*, October 31, 1839.

"Letter of an Italian á un Francais, sur les Doctrines de M. Lamennais." *The Catholic Expositor and Literary Magazine*, July 1842, 224–28.

"Letters of Dr. Cway, a Minister of the Church of England to the Archbishop of Bohemia." *Ibid.*, September 1842, 330–38.

"A Letter to a Friend, on the Tract Entitled, 'Roman Fallacies and Catholic Truths' Published by the Protestant Episcopal

Tract Society." *The Catholic Expositor and Literary Magazine,* July 18, 1843, 331–41; September 1843, 407–19.

"Letter to an Infidel." *New York Catholic Register,* September 21, 1839.

"A Literary Notice on Father Oswald, A Genuine Catholic Story." *Ibid.,* May 1843, 129–39.

"Liturgy of the Church of England." *Ibid.,* June 11, 1840.

"The Mass." *Ibid.,* November 7, 1839.

"Meeting of Catholics for the Enlargement of the New York Catholic Register." *Ibid.,* July 2 and July 9, 1840.

"A Middle State." *Ibid.,* November 1844, 81–89.

"Modern Pantheism." *Ibid.,* September 3, 1840.

"The Mother of St. Augustine—A Tract." *The Catholic Expositor and Literary Magazine,* March 1843, 364–66.

"New Church in Southwark, Philadelphia." *New York Catholic Register,* August 13, 1840.

"New Church in Williamsburgh, L. I.," *Ibid.,* July 2, 1840.

"New York Catholic Temperance Association." *Ibid.,* February 13, 1840.

"Notes on an Extract from a Letter of the Honorable F. H. F. Berkeley to the Wesleyan Ministers of Bristol." *Ibid.,* September 21, 1839.

"Notes on an Extract from the Last Number of the London Quarterly Review on the Study of the Evidences of Christian Revelation by Phillip S. Dodd." *Ibid.,* October 3, 1839.

"The Novena of Saint Theresa, Revised and Approved." Quoted in Alban Butler, *The Life of Saint Theresa,* 153–80.

"Observations on the Proceedings of the American Bible Society." *The Catholic Expositor and Literary Magazine,* April 1843, 57–61.

"Observations to Protestants." *Ibid.,* December 1842, 143–54.

"On Merits." *The Catholic Observer,* January 19, 1837.

"On the Prohibition of Eating Meat on Certain Days." *New York Catholic Register,* September 21, 1839.

"Oración Fúnebre a Carlos IV." Extracts quoted in *Rodríguez,* 97–100.

"Oratorio at St. Peter's Church." *New York Catholic Register,* June 18, 1840.

"Original Translation." *Ibid.,* June 18, 1840.

"Our Views in Publishing this Paper." *Ibid.,* September 21, 1839.

"Paraphrase of Some Passages of Dr. Brownlee's Address to the Roman Catholics." *Truth Teller,* September 6 and September 21, 1833.

"The Petition for a Part of the School Fund." *New York Catholic Register.* May 28, 1840.

"Popular Prejudices - Rites of Burial." *Ibid.,* May 21, 1840.

"Prospectus of the New York Catholic Register." *Ibid.,* September 21, 1839.

"Protestant Argument Retorted." *New York Weekly Register and Catholic Diary,* August 9, 1834.

"The Protestant Doctrine Compared with the Scriptures - An Essay." *The Catholic Expositor and Literary Magazine,* April 1842, 35–42.

"Protestant Spy in the Catholic Church, Ann-Street." *New York Weekly Register and Catholic Diary,* January 24, 1835.

"Protestants and Tradition." *The Catholic Expositor and Literary Magazine,* May 1842, 100–102.

"Proyecto que Demuestra la Necesidad de Extinguir la Esclavitud de los Negros en la Isla de Cuba, Atendiendo a los Intereses de sus Propietarios." Quoted in *Observaciones sobre la Constitución,* 157–79.

"Proyecto de Gobierno Autónomo." Published in Chacon y Calvo, "El Padre Varela y la Autonomía," 451–71.

"Public Meeting of the Catholics." *New York Catholic Register,* March 26, 1840.

"The Public School Funds." *Ibid.,* March 12, 1840.

"Purgatory." *The Catholic Observer,* March 23, March 30, and April 6, 1837.

"Reflections on 'Vantage Ground of Popery.' " *New York Weekly Register and Catholic Diary,* July 18, 1835.

"Reflections Which Could be Made by a Person Who May be About to Embrace the Protestant Religion." *The Catholic Observer,* January 12, 1837. Same article published in *The Catholic Expositor,* October 1844, 1–5.

"The Reformation Examined, According to the Protestant Principles, and to the Reasons Assigned by the Reformers for that Separation from the Catholic Church." *The Catholic Expositor and Literary Magazine,* June 1842, 151–54.

"The Religious Controversy Between Dr. F. Varela and Dr. W. C. Brownlee." Quoted in *The Religious Controversy Between the Rev. Dr. W. C. Brownlee and the Rev. Drs. John Power, Thos. C. Levins, and Félix Varela.* Philadelphia: Boyle and Benedict, 1833, 17–21.

"Religious Courtesy." *New York Catholic Register,* July 16, 1840.

"Remarks on the Book Entitled 'Six Months in a Convent' - Attributed to Miss Reed." *New York Weekly Register and Catholic Diary,* May 23, 1835.

"A Reply to the Assertion that Catholics are Forbidden to Read the Scriptures." *The Catholic Expositor and the Literary Magazine,* October 1844, 45–47.

"Review of Alethia, or Letters on the Truth of Catholic Doctrines. By the Rev. Charles Constantine Pise, D.D." *Ibid.,* June 1843, 208–11.

"A Review of the Bible in Spain or the Journies and Imprisonments of an Englishman in an Attempt to Circulate the Scriptures." *Ibid.,* June 1843, 197–208.

"A Review of 'Hints on Catholic Union by a Presbyter of the Protestant Episcopal Church.' " *The Catholic Observer,* March 9, 1837.

"A Review of 'No Union with Rome—An Address to the Members of the Protestant Episcopal Church. by Reverend Samuel Farmar Jarvis." *The Catholic Expositor and Literary Magazine,* January 1844, pp. 284–86.

"A Review of the Report on the Subject of Appropriating a Portion of the School Money to Religious Societies for the Support of the Schools." *The New York Catholic Register,* May 21, 1840.

"A Review of the Rev. S. B. Smith's Renunciation of Popery." *New York Weekly Register and Catholic Diary,* January 31, February 7, March 7, March 14, March 26, and April 11, 1835.

"Reviews of 'Our Protestant Forefathers' by W. L. Gilley, D. D." *The Catholic Expositor and Literary Magazine,* January 1844, 241–58.

"The Right Rev. Dr. Loras." *The New York Catholic Register,* June 11, 1840.

"The Saints." *Ibid.,* January 9, 1840.

"St. Peter's Church." *Ibid.,* December 19, 1839.

"St. Thomas Christians." *Ibid.,* January 2, and January 9, 1840.

"St. Vincent de Paul." *Ibid.,* January 9, 1840.

"Specimen of Fanaticism." *Ibid.,* July 23, 1840.

"Speech at the Meeting of the Protestant Association." *Truth Teller,* May 5, 1832.

"Temperance." *The New York Catholic Register,* January 16, 1840.

"Tenets Attributed to the Catholics by the Protestants." *Ibid.,* September 21, 1839.

"Theologia Dogmatica, etc. by the Rt. Rev. Francis P. Kenrick." *Ibid.,* February 6, 1840.

"The Time for Writing." *Ibid.,* January 2, 1840.

"Translation of the Bible." *Truth Teller,* February 8, 1834.

"There Cannot Be a Church Without a Bishop." *The Catholic Expositor and Literary Magazine,* February 1844, 356–58.

"Treatise on the Church." *New York Catholic Register,* August 6, 1840.

"Veneration of Images." *The Catholic Expositor and Literary Magazine,* September 1844, 450–56.

"Which Is the Right Interpretation of the Scriptures as to the Making of Images." *New York Catholic Register,* October 3, 1839.

"Young Catholics' Magazine." *Ibid.,* March 19, 1840.

SECONDARY SOURCES

Writings About Varela

Books

Amigó Jansen, Gustavo, S.J. *La Posición Filosófica del Padre Varela.* Unpublished Ph. D. dissertation. Havana: Havana University, 1947.

Bachiller y Morales, Antonio. *Apuntes para la Historia de las Letras y de la Instrucción Pública en la Isla de Cuba.* 3 vols. Havana: Massana, 1859–61.

Brownlee, W. C. *Letters in the Roman Catholic Controversy.* New York: J. Whitmans, 1834.

Calcagno, Franciso. *Diccionario Biográfico.* New York, 1878.

Casal, José M. *Discursos del Padre Varela, Precedidos de una Sucinta Relación de lo que Pasó en los Ultimos Momentos de su Vida y en su Entierro.* Matanzas: Imprenta Gobierno, 1860.

Ceremonies at the Laying of the Corner Stone of a Chapel in the Roman Catholic Cemetery . . . to the Memory of the Very Reverend Félix Varela. . . . Charleston: Councell & Phynney, 1853.

Del Ducca, Sister Gemma Marie, S.C. *A Political Portrait: Félix Varela y Morales, 1788–1853.* Unpublished Ph.D. dissertation. Universtiy of New Mexico, 1966.

Fernández de Castro, José A., ed. *Medio Siglo de Historia Colonial de Cuba. Cartas a José A. Saco Ordenadas y Comentadas . . .* Havana: Veleso, 1923.

Foik, Paul, *Pioneer Catholic Journalism.* New York: U.S. Catholic Historical Society, 1930.

Hernández Travieso, Antonio. *El Padre Varela: Biografía del Forjador de la Conciencia Cubana.* Havana: Montero, 1942.

————. *Varela y la Reforma Filosófica en Cuba.* Havana: Montero, 1942.

Kenneally, Finbar. *United States Documents in the Propaganda Fide Archives.* Washington, D. C., 1965.

Lazo, Raimundo. *El Padre Varela y las Cartas a Elpidio: Epílogo . . .* Havana: Editorial Universidad, 1945.

McCadden, Joseph and Helen. *Father Varela, Torch Bearer from Cuba.* New York: United States Catholic Historical Society, 1969.

Martínez-Ramos, Alberto. *Father Félix Varela: Cuban Catholic Apologist in the United States, 1823–1853.* Unpublished Master of Arts thesis. Coral Gables: University of Miami, 1979.

Menéndez y Pelayo, Marcelino. *Historia de los Heterodoxos Españoles.* Vol. 3. Madrid: Aldus, 1881.

Mestre y Domínguez, José Manuel. *De la Filosofía en la Habana*. Havana: Antilla, 1862.

Morales, José A. *Progressive Spanish Reader*. New York: Appleton, 1856.

Morales Coello, Julio *et al. Los Restos del Padre Varela en la Universidad de La Habana*. Havana: Editorial Universidad, 1955.

O'Callaghan, Jeremiah. *The Creation and Offspring of the Protestant Church* . . . Burlington, 1837.

Peraza Sarausa, Fermín. *Personalidades Cubanas*. Havana: Ediciones Anuario Bibliográfico Cubano, 1957–65.

The Religious Controversy between the Reverend Dr. W. C. Brownlee and the Reverend Drs. John Power, Thos. C. Levins, and Félix Varela. Philadelphia: Boyle and Benedict, 1833.

Rexach, Rosario. *El Pensamiento de Félix Varela y la Formación de la Conciencia Cubana*. Havana: Ed. Lyceum, 1950.

Rodríguez, José Ignacio. *Vida de Don José de la Luz y Caballero*. New York: El Mundo Nuevo, 1874.

_____. *Vida del Presbítero Don Félix Varela*. Havana: O Novo Mundo, 1878.

Roig de Leuchsenring, Emilio. *Ideario Cubano Félix Varela, Precursor de la Revolución Libertadora Cubana*. Havana: Oficina Historiador, 1953.

Saínz, Nicasio. *Tres Vidas Paralelas (Arango y Parreño, Félix Varela y José A. Saco): Origen de la Nacionalidad Cubana*. Miami: Editorial Universal, 1973.

Sociedad Cubana de Filosofía (Exilio). *Homenaje a Félix Varela*. Miami: Ediciones Universal, 1979.

Valuable Theological Library: Catalogue of the Large and Valuable Collection. . .Being the Library of the late Rev. Father Varela . . . New York: Bangs Brother & Co., 1880.

Valverdi y Maruri, Antonio. *La Muerte del Padre Varela: Documentos Inéditos Coleccionados y Comentados*. Havana: Siglo XX, 1924.

Vitier, Medardo. *Las Ideas y la Filosofía en Cuba*. Havana: Editorial de Ciencias Sociales, 1970.

Articles

Agramonte, Roberto, "El Padre Varela." *Universidad de la Habana, June–July 1937, 64–87.*

Amigo Jansen, Gustavo, S.J. "La Posición Filosófica del Padre Félix Varela." *Boletín de las Provincias Eclesiásticas de Cuba,* April 1953, 21--25.

Angulo y Perez, Andrés. "El Padre Varela. Sus Obras. La Producción Vareliana. Bibliograffía." *Anuario de la Facultad de Ciencias Sociales y Derecho Público, 1954, 21–35.*

Bachiller y Morales, Antonio. "Bibliografía: Obras Filosóficas del Pbro. Félix Varela." *El Estímulo,* July 1, 1862.

————. "Error Político de Don Félix Varela: Los Contemporaneos y la Posteridad." *Revista Cubana,* October 1885, 289–94.

Blakeslee, William Francis, C.S.P. "Félix Varela: 1788–1853." *American Catholic Historical Society of Philadelphia Records,* 1927, 15–46.

Boza Masvidal, Eduardo. "El Padre Félix Varela." *Cuba Diáspora,* 1976, 15–16.

Cabrera, Raimundo. "Nuestro Homenaje a Varela." *Revista Bimestre Cubana,* November–December 1911, 473–97.

Costales, M. "Lecciones de Filosofía." *El Faro,* January 1, 1842.

"Cuba: El Padre Varela en el 125 Aniversario de su Muerte (1788–1853)." *Osservatore Romano,* September 24, 1978.

Cuevas Zequeira, Sergio. "El Padre Varela; Contribución a la Historia de la Filosofía en Cuba." *Revista de la Facultac de Letras y Ciencias,* May 1906, 217–20.

Chacón y Calvo, José M. "El Padre Varela Como Apologista Católico." *Revista Cubana,* January–December 1944, 211–13.

————"El Padre Varela y su Apostolado." *Cuadernos de Divulgación Cultural de la Unesco,* 1953, 2–40.

————"Homenaje a Varela." *Revista Cubana,* January–February 1936, 191–92.

————"Varela y la Universidad." *Revista Cubana,* January 1935, 169–73.

Del Valle, Raúl. "El Padre Félix Varela, Sacerdote, Maestro y Patriota." *Comité Católico Cubano Newsletter,* November 30, 1977.

_____"Prólogo" to *Torch Bearer from Cuba,* by Joseph and Helen McCadden. New York: United States Catholic Historical society, 1969, vii–x.

"El Padre Varela." *El Noticioso de New York,* November 17, 1854.

"En Memoria de Félix Varela." *Revista Bimestre Cubana,* November–December 1911, 473–97.

Garcini Guerra, H. J. "Evolución del Pensamiento Político de Félix Varela." *Anuario Facultad de Ciencias Sociales y Derecho Público,* 1954, 37–59.

Gay Calbó, Enrique. "El Ideario Político de Varela." *Revista Cubana,* January–February 1936, 23–47.

Gay Calbó. "El Padre Varela en las Cortes Españolas de 1822 y 1823." *Universidad de la Habana,* August–September, 109–29.

González del Valle, Francisco. "Varela, Mas que Humano." *Cuadernos del Historiador de la Habana,* 1945, 9–27.

_____"Rectificación de Dos Fechas: Las de Nacimiento y Muerte del Padre Varela." *Revista Bimestre Cubana,* January–June 1942, 69–72.

Gran y Guilledo, Manuel F. "Varela y la Ciencia." *Cuadernos del Historiador de la Habana,* 1945, 149–70.

Guardia, Joseph Miguel. "Filosofos Españoles de Cuba: Félix Varela y José de la Luz." *Revista Cubana,* 1892, 233–47, 412–27, 493–505.

_____"Philosophes Espagnols de Cuba: Felix Varela-José de la Luz." *Revue Philosophique de la France et de l'Etranger,* January–June 1892, 50–66, 162–83.

Gurudi, Alejandro Angulo. "Dos entrevistas con el Pbro. D. Félix Varela." *El Fígaro,* 1904.

Hernández Corujo, Enrique. "Actuación Política y Parlamentaria del Padre Varela en las Cortes Españolas y en el Destierro." *Anuario Facultad Ciencias sociales y Derecho Público,* 1954, 61–87.

Hernández Travieso, Antonio. "Expediente de Estudios Universitarios del Presbítero Félix Varela." *Revista Bimestre Cubana*, January–June 1942, 388–401.

_____"Posición Filosófica de Varela." *Cuadernos del Historiador de la Habana*, 1945, 43–67.

Jorrín, Miguel. "Valoración Filosófica de Varela." *Vida y Pensamiento*, 1945, 29–42.

Lazo, Raimundo. "Epílogo," in Varela, *Cartas a Elpidio*. Havana: Ed. de la Universidad, 1945.

Luz y Caballero, José de la. "Sobre las Cartas a Elpidio." *Diario de la Habana*, December 29, 1835.

McCadden, Joseph. "The New York-to-Cuba-Axis of Father Varela." *The Americas*, April 1964, 376–92.

Martínez Dalmau, Eduardo. "La Ortodoxia Filosófica y Política del Pensamiento Patriótico del Pbro. Félix Varela." *Vida y Pensamiento*, 1945, 247–72.

_____"La Posición Democrática e Independentista del Pbro. Félix Varela." *Historia y Cubanidad*. Havana: Estudios Históricos e Internacionales, 1943, 247–72.

_____"Prólogo." Rodríguez, *Vida del Presbítero Don Félix Varela*. 2nd ed. Havana: Arellano, 1944, ii–xxv.

Merrick, D. A. S.J. "The Cuban Apostle of New York." *Messenger*, 1898, 613–26.

Montoro, Rafael. "El Padre Félix Varela." *Revista Bimestre Cubana*, November–December 1911, 485–97.

"150th Anniversary for Transfiguration Church in Chinatown." *Catholic News*, December 15, 1977.

Ortíz, Fernando. "Félix Varela, Amigo del País." *Revista Bimestre Cubana*, November–December 1911, 478–84.

Pérez Cabrera, J. M. "Varela, Félix." *New Catholic Encyclopedia*. 1st ed. Vol 14.

Portell Vilá, Herminio. "Sobre el Ideario Político del Padre Varela." *Revista Cubana*, February–March 1835, 243–65.

Portuondo, José Antonio. "Significación Literaria de Varela." *Cuadernos del Historiador de la Habana*, 1945, 69–91.

Rodríguez, José I. "Father Félix Varela, Vicar General of New York from 1837 to 1853." *American Catholic Quarterly Review*, 1883, 463–76.

Roig de Leuchsenring, Emilio. "Varela en 'El Habanero' Precursor de la Revolución Cubana." *Cuadernos del Historiador de la Habana,* 1945, 217–45.

Román, Agustín Aleido. "Padre Félix Varela y Morales," *El Habanero* by Varela. Miami: Ideal, 1974, iv–ix.

_____"Pilgrimage in Memory of Father Félix Varela." *Ermita de la Caridad,* February 25, 1978.

Salvador Bueno. "Félix Varela en Nuestra Historia." *Revista de la Biblioteca Nacional,* January–March 1954, 19–45.

Santana, Joaquín G. "Prologo" to *Escritos Políticos de Félix Varela.* Havana: Ed. Ciencias Sociales, 1977, v-xx.

Varona y Pera, Enrique José. "La Capilla del P. Varela." *Revista Cubana,* 1888, 380–84.

"The Very Reverend Félix Varela, D.D." *New York Freeman's Journal,* March 19, 1853.

Vitier, Medardo. "Prólogo" to *Miscelanea Filosófica* by Félix Varela. Havana: Ed. de la Universidad, 1944, vi–xxiii.

Zequeira, Sergio C. "El Padre Varela; Contribución a la Historia de la Filosofía en Cuba." *Revista de la Facultad Letras y Ciencias,* 1906, 217–20.

General Background

Books

Agramonte, Roberto. *José Agustín Caballero y los Orígénes de la Conciencia Cubana.* Havana: Montero, 1952.

Allo, Lorenzo. *Domestic Slavery in Its Relation with Wealth.* Translated by D. de Goicuria. New York: Tinson, 1855.

Bayley, James Roosevelt. *A Brief Sketch of the History of the Catholic Church on the Island of New-York.* New York: Dunigan, 1853.

Billington, Ray Allen, *The Protestant Crusade, 1800–1860.* New York: Macmillan, 1938.

Bourne, William Oland. *History of the Public School Society of the City of New York.* New York: Putnam, 1873.

Browne, Henri J. *The Catholic Church and the Knights of Labor.* Washington: Catholic University of America Press, 1949.

_____*The Parish of Saint Michael, 1857–1957.* New York: Church of Saint Michael, 1957.

Brownlee, W.C. *Popery an Enemy to Civil and Religious Liberty and Dangerous to Our Republic.* New York: Browne and Wisner, 1836.

Cheung, Mark. *Transfiguration Church: A Church of Immigrants, 1827–1977.* New York: Park, 1977.

Del Valle, Raúl. *El Cardenal Arteaga: Resplandores de la Púrpura Cubana.* Havana: Ramallo, 1954.

Dolan, Jay P. *Catholic Revivalism: the American Experience.* Notre Dame: University Press, 1978.

_____*The Immigrant Church.* Baltimore: John Hopkins University Press, 1975.

Drevniak, Aldus A. *José Díaz Espada: Un Obispo Ilustrado en America, 1802–1832.* Unpublished S.T.D. dissertation. Pontifical Gregorian University, 1963.

Dubois, John. *Pastoral Address to the Congregation of St. Patrick's Cathedral.* New York: Mitchel Printer, 1836.

Ellis, John T. *American Catholicism.* 2nd ed. Chicago: University of Chicago Press, 1969.

_____*Documents of American Catholic History.* 2 vols. Chicago: 1967.

Figueroa y Miranda, Miguel. *Religión y Política en la Cuba del Siglo XIX: El Obispo Espada Visto a la Luz de los Archivos Romanos, 1802–1832.* Miami: Ediciones Universal, 1975.

Finotti, Joseph M. *Bibliographia Catholica Americana.* New York: Catholic Publ. House, 1872.

Gannon, Michael V. *The Cross in the Sand: The Early Catholic Church in Florida, 1513–1870.* Gainesville: University of Florida Press, 1965.

García Pons, C. *El Obispo Espada y su Influencia en la Cultura Cubana.* Havana: Ministerio de Educación, 1951.

Guilday, Peter. *History of the Councils of Baltimore, 1791–1884.* New York: Macmillan, 1932.

_____*The National Pastorals of the American Hierarchy, 1792–1919.* Westminister: Newman, 1954.

Handy, Robert T. *A History of the Churches in the United States and Canada.* Oxford: Clarendon Press, 1976.

Hassard, John R. G. *Life of the Most Reverend John Hughes, D. D. First Archbishop of New York*. New York: Appleton, 1866.

Hernandez Travieso, Antonio. *La Personalidad de José Ignacio Rodríguez*. Havana: Cultural, 1946.

Hocedez, Edgar. *Histoire de la Theologie au XIX Siécle*. Paris: Desclee de Brouwer, 1948.

Litalien, Rolandus. *Spiritualité Sacerdotale d'apres Monsignor L–Z. Moreau, 1824–1901*. Montreal: Fides, 1970.

Martí, José Julian. *Obras Completas*. 73 vols. Havana: Editorial Trópico, 1936 *et sequens*.

Martínez Dalmau, Eduardo. *La Política Colonial y Extranjera de los Reyes Españoles de la Casa de Austria y de Borbón y la Toma de la Habana por los Ingleses*. Havana: Muñiz, 1943.

Mazzuchelli, Samuel. *Memoirs*. Translated by Sister B. Kennedy. Chicago: Priory Press, 1966.

Nolan, Hugh J. *Pastoral Letters of the American Hierarchy, 1792–1970*. Huntington: Our Sunday Visitor, 1971.

Olarra Garmendia, José. *El Archivo de la Embajada de España Cerca de la Santa Sede*. Madrid: Ministerios Asuntos Exteriores, 1973.

O'Meara, Thomas F, *et al.* gen. ed. *St. Thomas Aquinas Summa Theologiae*. 40 vols. New York: McGraw-Hill, 1968.

Pise, Charles. *Minutes of Correspondence between the Rt. Reverend John Dubois, Roman Catholic Bishop of New York and the Trustees of St. Joseph's Church* . . . New York: John M'Loughling, 1837.

Rodríguez, José I. *Estudio Histórico sobre el Origen, Desenvolvimiento y Manifestaciones Prácticas de la Idea de la Anexión de Cuba a los Estados Unidos de América*. Havana: Propaganda Literaria, 1900.

Shea, John Dawson Gilmary. *The Catholic Churches of New York City, with Sketches of their History and Lives of the Present Pastors*. New York: Goulding, 1878.

————*History of the Catholic Church in the United States* . . . *1521–1866*. 4 vols. New York: Akkron, McBride, 1886–92.

Smith, John Talbot. *The Catholic Church in New York.* 2 vols. Boston: Hall & Locke, 1905.

Villoslada, Ricardo G., gen. ed. *Historia de la Iglesia en España,* 5 vols. Madrid: Biblioteca Autores Cristianos, 1979.

Vitier, Medardo. *Las Ideas de la Filosofía en Cuba.* Havana: Editorial de Ciencias Sociales, 1970.

Willging, Eugene P., and Hatzfeld, Herta. *Catholic Serials of the Nineteenth Century in the United States: A Descriptive Bibliography and Union List.* Washington, D. C.: Catholic Universtiy of America Press, 1968.

Articles

"The Archdiocese of New York a Century Ago: A Memoir of Archbishop Hughes, 1838–1858."*Historical Records and studies of Historical Society of New York* 40 (1952): 129–90.

Aubert, R. "Le Pontificat de Pie IX, 1846–1878." *Histoire de l'Eglise Depuis les Origines Jusqu'a Nos Jours.* Edited by Augustin Fliche and Victor Martin. Paris: Bloud & Gay, 1952.

Carey, Patrick. "The Laity's Views of the Trustee Movement, 1785–1860." *Catholic Historical Review* 54 (January, 1978).

Catholic Telegraph. Padre Félix Varela, D.D., October 3, 1878.

Clemence, S. R. *José I. Rodríguez Papers.* Report to the Library of Congress, 1939. Washington, D.C.: Library of Congress, Manuscript Division, 1939.

Consentini, J. W. "Fenelon, Francois de Salignac de la Mothe." New Catholic Encyclopedia. Vol. 5.

Currier, Charles W. "The Church in Cuba." *The Conservative Review,* March 1900, 190–209.

De Bertier de Sauvigny, G. "La Restauration." *Nouvelle Histoire de l'Eglise.* Edited by L. J. Rogier *et al.* Paris: Editions du Seuil, 1966.

Edwards, O. D. "American Nativism." *New Catholic Encyclopedia.* Vol. 10.

Foik, Paul J. "Pioneer Efforts in Catholic Journalism in the

United States, 1809–1840." *The Catholic Historical Review* 1 (October, 1915): 258–70.

Hartzel, T. V. "Gallitzin, D." *New Catholic Encyclopedia.* Vol. 6.

McCadden, Joseph. "Bishop Hughes Versus the Public School Society of New York." *Catholic Historical Review* 50 (July 1964): 188–207.

McNamara, Robert F. "Trusteeism in the Atlantic States, 1785–1863." *Catholic Historical Review,* 30 (July, 1944): 135–54.

"Manifiesto del Clero Cubano Nativo." British Museum, Latin-American Rare Books Collection.

Mendoza Sadaba, Andrés. "Cuba y su Revolución." *Informes Pro Mundi Vita* 8 (1977): 1–37.

Perrin, J. M. "Works of Mercy." *New Catholic Encyclopedia.* Vol. 9.

Picard, Robert, "Feijóo y Montenegro." *Dictionnaire de Spiritualité.* Vol. 5.

Scaduto, M. "Works of Charity." *New Catholic Encyclopedia.* Vol. 4.

Tinsley, L. "Bossuet, Jacques Bénigne." *New Catholic Encyclopedia.* Vol. 2.

Verret, C. "Sacred Music (U.S.)." *New Catholic Encyclopedia.* Vol. 10.

BIOGRAPHICAL OUTLINE

1788

On November 20, Félix Varela is born in Havana, Cuba.

1791

Varela's parents die in Cuba.

His grandfather, Bartolomé Morales, is sent to St. Augustine, Florida. He takes with him young Félix.

1802

His grandmother, Rita Josefa Morales, dies in St. Augustine, Florida.

Félix is sent to Havana by his grandfather.

1804

Félix attends *San Carlos* Seminary and the University of Havana.

1806

Varela takes comprehensive exams.

1807

He receives Tonsure, Minor Orders and Subdiaconate.

1808

Varela attains the degree of Bachelor of Theology.
He teaches Latin classes at *San Carlos* Seminary.
He writes a play, "El Desafío."

1810

Varela is ordained a deacon.

1811

He helps to create the Philharmonic Society of Havana. On December 21, he is ordained a priest of the Havana Diocese.

1812

Varela begins to teach Philosophy at *San Carlos* Seminary. Archibishop Pedro Varela y Jiménez asks him to publish his lectures: *Institutiones Philosophiae Ecclecticae ad Usum Studiosae Juventutis.*

He preaches the Mass of the Holy Spirit at one of Havana's parishes.

1813

He begins to teach in the vernacular.

1814

Varela publishes *Resumen de las Doctrinas Metafísicas y Morales.*

1816

He publishes *Elencos para Exámenes de Filosofía* and *Apuntes Filosóficos para el Espíritu Humano.*

1817

On January 24, he is accepted in the Royal Patriotic Society and he delivers an important speech entitled "Demonstrar la Influencia de la Idiología en la Sociedad y Medios de Rectificar este Ramo".

1818

On March 10, he delivers "Elogio a Don J. P. Valiente y Bravo."

On December 12, he delivers "Elogio a Fernando VII".

1819

He publishes *Miscelánea Filosófica* and *Lecciones de Filosofía.*

He preaches a funeral oration for Charles IV.

Bishop Espada asks him to teach a course in Constitutional Law.

1821

He publishes *Observaciones sobre la Monarquía Española*.

He publishes a second edition of *Miscelánea Filosófica*.

On April 28, Varela leaves for Spain in the ship *Purísima Concepción*.

In July, he visits Cadiz, Seville and Madrid.

1822

In October, the Spanish *Cortes* begins in Madrid.

Varela presents a project entitled "Colonial Autonomous Government."

1823

Varela reports for the Commission of Ultramar and presents "The Abolition of Slavery."

He casts his vote to depose Ferdinand VII.

He escapes to Gibraltar with Gener and Santos.

On December 15, he arrives in New York City on the ship *Draper C. Thorndike*.

1824

Varela publishes a second edition of *Lecciones de Filosofía*.

He begins *El Habanero* newspaper in Philadelphia.

1825

On February 5, Bishop Connally of New York dies.

In March, an assassin is sent from Cuba to kill Varela.

On June 27, a royal order of Ferdinand VII is issued against Varela.

In August, Varela is invited by the President of Mexico to emigrate there.

The credentials arrive from the Chancery of Havana.

John Power is appointed Vicar General of New York.

1826

On June 18, W. C. Brownlee is installed as Pastor of the Protestant Reformed Dutch Church.

On October 29, John Dubois is consecrated as the third Bishop of New York.

In October, Varela translates Jefferson's *Manual of Parliamentary Procedure* and begins his ministry as assistant in the Church of St. Peter, New York City.

He publishes a collection of the poems of Manuel de Zequeira y Arango.

1827

On March 3, Varela buys Christ Church from the Episcopalians.

On July 15, Christ Church is dedicated. Varela begins his ministry as pastor.

1829

On September 20, Dubois leaves for Europe. He appoints John Power and Félix Varela as Vicars General.

On September 30, Varela assists at the First Provincial Council of Baltimore.

1830

On January 2, the newspaper entitled the *Protestant* begins. Varela publishes the *Protestant Abridger and Annotator*.

1831

On November 20, Bishop Dubois returns to New York.

Controversies between Varela and Brownlee take place in New York.

1832

On April 25, together with Power and Pise, Varela participates in a public debate at Broadway Hall.

He publishes a fourth edition of *Lecciones de Filosofía*.

The Spanish government gives amnesty to all who participated in the *Cortes* of 1823.

An outbreak of cholera occurs in New York City.

1833

On February 2, W. C. Brownlee challanges Varela to a written debate. Varela begins a public correspondence with W. C. Brownlee on Catholic doctrine.

Later in February, W.C. Brownlee organizes the New York Protestant Association.

On October 5, *The New York Weekly Register* and *The Catholic Diary* begin in New York.

1834

On August 11, there is an anti-Catholic burning of the Ursuline Convent in Charlestown, Mass.

1835

Varela publishes *Letters to Elpidio,* volume 1, in New York.

1836

On February 14, Varela becomes pastor of Transfiguration Church.

On April 12, Varela states that his health is very strong.

In September, St. James Church is dedicated. Andrew Byrne is appointed its pastor and the Congregation of Christ Church therefore becomes two new parishes.

Varela publishes *Letters to Elpidio,* volume 2, in Madrid.

1837

In April, Varela becomes procurator of the diocese of New York at the 3rd Provincial Council of Baltimore.

Dubois seeks a Coadjutor-Bishop.

A depression causes much poverty among the population.

1838

On January 7, John Hughes is consecrated Coadjutor-Bishop of the Diocese of New York.

The School controversy concerning anti-Catholilc bias becomes an issue in New York.

Varela publishes the *Letters to Elpidio,* volume 2, in New York.

1839

In the month of September, Varela begins the *Catholic Register* and finds himself in deep financial difficulty.

Hughes leaves for Europe.

1840

On February 9, Varela begins the New York Catholic Temperance Association.

On July 18, Bishop Hughes returns to New York from Europe.

1841

In April, Varela begins the *Catholic Expositor and Literary Magazine* with C. Pise.

The *Catholic Register* is absorbed into the *Freeman's Journal*.

Varela is awarded the degree of doctor of Sacred Theology by St. Mary's Seminary in Baltimore and publishes a fifth edition of *Lecciones de Filosofía*.

1842

On January 1, Fr. Muppietti begins his services at Transfiguration.

In the month of October, Varela writes to some missionary societies in Rome and Vienna asking for aid.

On December 20, Biship Dubois dies. Bishop J. Hughes replaces him.

The great public school controversy continues.

1843

On September 23, paralysis afflicts W. C. Brownlee.

On October 23, the New York Sheriff's office advertises the sale of Transfiguration Church.

1844

In April, Varela is elected President of the Board of Trustees of Transfiguration Church with its accompanying financial burden.

In the month of May, two churches are burned in Philadelphia.

Riots occur in Philadelphia against Catholic schools.

Constantine Pise leaves for Europe.

Varela's health begins to fail. He visits St. Augustine, Florida.

1845

From 1845 to 1847, the "Great Potato Famine" hits Ireland.

The debt of Transfiguration Church is reduced from the initial $60,00 to $36,222.

A great fire takes place in New York City.

1846

On March 20, Alexander Muppietti dies.

Together with Bishop Hughes and Bishop McCloskey, Varela attends the 6th Provincial Council of Baltimore.

Félix Varela is sent for a second visit to Florida for health reasons.

Father McClellan becomes the temporary Administrator of the parish.

1847

Félix Varela's signature appears in parish records only for the month of June.

1848

The annexation of Cuba to the United States becomes an important issue for journalists.

In this year, Varela's signature is absent from parish records.

1849

On April 14, John Power dies.

In the month of October, Varela is occupied by fundraising for Transfiguration Church.

On November 23, the last recorded signature of Félix Varela in Transfiguration Church is for the baptism of Marie R. Guiteras.

On November 24, Transfiguration is in danger of being sold at public auction.

Father Theobald Mathew, temperance crusader, comes to New York.

The cholera strikes New York, over twenty percent of Transfiguration parish perishes.

1850

Varela turns Transfiguration Church over to Archbishop Hughes.

Another depression strikes New York City.

1851

Varela visits Savannah, Georgia.

1852

On December 25, Lorenzo Allo is shocked at Varela's miserable situation.

Father Aubril gives hospitality to Varela in the parish of St. Augustine, Florida.

1853

Varela makes a profession of faith in Christ's Eucharistic Presence.

On February 23, belatedly, Mr. and Mrs. Casal leave Havana by ship to give Varela a sum of money and persuade him to return to Havana.

On February 25, Varela dies in St. Augustine, Florida.

On February 26, Father Stephen Sheridan writes to Archbishop Hughes concerning Varela's last days in St. Augustine.

On March 3, the Casals arrive in St. Augustine, Florida.

On March 22, cornerstone ceremonies take place for the chapel to be built in honor of Félix Varela.

On May 14, Archbishop Hughes dedicates the new church for Transfiguration parish and the financial crisis of the parish ends.

1855

On April 13, the remains of Father Varela are transferred

to a new tomb within a chapel built for this purpose in the Cemetery of St. Augustine.

1876

On June 10, Bishop Verot of St. Augustine is buried in Father Varela's tomb.

1878

Rodríguez publishes the first full-length biography of Father Varela.

1880

Father Varela's library is auctioned in New York.

1892

In July, José Martí visits Varela's tomb and calls Varela "the Cuban saint."

1911

On November 6, Bishop William J. Kenney of St. Augustine allows Varela's remains to be taken to Cuba.

1912

The University of Havana pays homage to the mortal remains of Félix Varela.

INDEX

Other Volumes in This Series

Walter Rauschenbusch: Selected Writings
William Ellery Channing: Selected Writings
Devotion to the Holy Spirit in American Catholicism
Horace Bushnell: Sermons
Alaskan Missionary Spirituality
Elizabeth Seton: Selected Writings
Eastern Spirituality in America
Charles Hodge: The Way of Life
Henry Alline: Selected Writings
William Porcher DuBose: Selected Writings
American Jesuit Spirituality
Phoebe Palmer: Selected Writings
Early American Meditative Poetry:
    Anne Bradstreet and Edward Taylor
Josiah Royce: Selected Writings